D1433761

Stevedores and Dockers

By the same author

A SHORT HISTORY OF THE T.U.C. (1968)
with B. C. Roberts

Stevedores and Dockers

A STUDY OF TRADE UNIONISM IN THE PORT OF LONDON, 1870–1914

John Lovell

*Lecturer in Economic and Social History
in the University of Kent at Canterbury*

Dunnigan '75

MACMILLAN

First published 1969 by
MACMILLAN AND CO LTD
Little Essex Street London W C 2
and also at Bombay Calcutta and Madras
Macmillan South Africa (Publishers) Pty Ltd Johannesburg
The Macmillan Company of Australia Pty Ltd Melbourne
The Macmillan Company of Canada Ltd Toronto
Gill and Macmillan Ltd Dublin

Printed in Great Britain by
HAZELL WATSON AND VINEY LTD
Aylesbury, Bucks

To my Parents

Contents

List of Plates

ACKNOWLEDGMENTS

The publishers wish to thank the following who have kindly given their permission to reproduce the illustrations: Plate 7 (top), 8: London Electrotype Agency; 4 (top): Mansell Collection; 1 (top), 2, 3 (bottom), 5 (top and bottom): Port of London Authority; 1 (bottom), 3 (top), 4 (bottom), 6 (top and bottom), 7 (bottom): Radio Times Hulton Picture Library.

Preface

This book is not intended as a straightforward history of labour organisation in the Port of London. Any such history would necessarily touch upon all the various aspects of union activity, including political activity. In so doing, however, it would discuss issues, problems and events that were not peculiar to the waterfront, but were rather the property of the British trade union movement as a whole. Such a work would be bound to tread a path already fairly well known to students of labour history. In this study it was thought preferable to focus attention upon the special characteristics of the waterfront and to explore the way in which these characteristics have influenced the unions operating in this sector. It is well known that the technological and other basic characteristics of a particular industry go a considerable way towards explaining the special features of trade unionism in that industry. Yet labour historians have not perhaps always paid sufficient attention to this very basic fact. It is hoped that this study, however imperfectly, has put waterside unionism firmly into the context of the industry in which it operated.

Every port has its peculiarities, and this is a study of waterside unionism in London during a specific period. The title chosen for the book proclaims its concern with the unique features of Britain's major port. Although some very general observations are made in the Conclusion, it is as well to state specifically that this is a local study which makes no claim to be a survey of unionism throughout the entire port industry. However, in so far as most great ports in Britain and abroad shared certain fundamental characteristics, it is to be expected that certain features of London waterside unionism will be present in a greater or lesser degree in other ports also. Comparisons with other ports are therefore made fairly frequently, and in so far as the study reaches out to place the London port unions in a wider context, it does so in terms of this wider *industrial* context.

The plan of the book is fairly straightforward. The first two chapters set the background for the remaining five. Chapter 1 is a purely descriptive account of the development of the port of London, with some general remarks about the technology of the industry. Chapter 2 discusses the general nature of the waterside labour force and its subdivision into various occupational group-ings. The remaining five chapters follow a basically chronological pattern, and deal with the main themes running through waterside unionism in London from the 1870s to 1914. By the latter year the formative period of London waterside unionism was over, and in the Conclusion some general remarks are made about more recent developments on the waterfront. It must, however, in the last resort be left to tne reader to judge how much light the pre-1914 period throws upon the modern problems of the industry.

Finally, I must emphasise that this book would not have been possible in anything like its present form had I not been given access to the records of the National Amalgamated Stevedores and Dockers Union. I would therefore like to express my gratitude to the officers and executive council of this union. It remains to add that this study is based upon my London Ph.D. thesis, submitted in 1966.

J. L.

1 The Port

THE Port as it stood in 1850 had not changed in essentials since the end of the Napoleonic Wars. Trade, it is true, had greatly increased in this period, and the tonnage entered in the foreign trade had in fact more than doubled.[1] There had, however, been no major changes in the facilities provided for the reception of this trade since 1828, and thus congestion in the river remained a feature of the port.[2] Sail continued to predominate as the motive power for shipping, while mechanical handling of cargoes was virtually unknown. Although railways had reached the riverside at Blackwall, Greenwich and North Woolwich, they had not yet affected the working of the port.[3] In short, the port of London in 1850 had not entered upon the modern age.

The docks in existence in London at the mid-century had been created mainly between the years 1802 and 1811.[4] The development of docks had come later in London than in Liverpool or Hull, and this was mainly due to geographical factors.[5] The eighteenth century had, however, seen such a vast growth in London's trade that it became necessary to relieve the pressure on the river, which had become intolerably congested.[6] This congestion was intensified by the fact that the landing of foreign goods was restricted to a very limited number of Legal Quays. But congestion was not the only defect of the port in the 1790s, for the pilfering of goods from ships and lighters had reached enormous proportions, and particularly affected the West India trade.[7] Thus it was that the construction of an enclosed dock to accommodate the West India trade was authorised by Parliament in 1799.[8] This dock was opened in 1802, and it was quickly followed by the London Dock, opened in 1805. The East India Dock was opened in 1806, and the Commercial Road was built to link it with the City warehouses.

All the above docks were built on the north bank, but developments took place at the same period on the south side. In the years following 1801 no less than four companies were concerned in exploiting the area of marsh between Deptford and Rotherhithe.

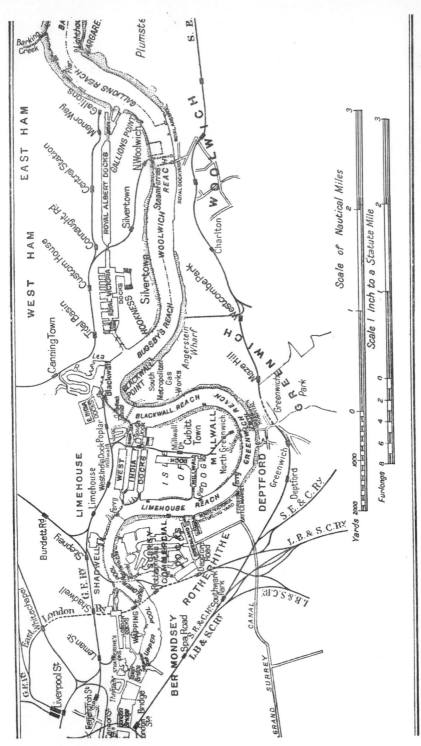

The London waterfront. A map showing the Thames and its dock systems as they appeared in the first quarter of the twentieth century.

The Surrey Canal Company was formed in 1801, the Commercial Dock Company in 1807, the Baltic Dock Company in 1809, and finally the East Country Dock came into existence in 1811. By the latter year the port had taken the essential shape it was to retain until mid-century, although there were two further developments before 1850. The Regent's Canal reached the Thames in 1820, and a small dock was subsequently built to serve it. More important was the opening of the St Katherine's Dock in 1828. This dock adjoined the London Company's Dock on the north bank, and was situated the farthest upstream of all the systems. Access to all these docks was guaranteed to lighters from the river by the 'free-water' clause. This clause exempted from charges all lighters using dock waters for the purpose of receiving goods from or delivering goods to ships.[9] At the beginning this provision was of little consequence, but by the middle of the century it had become the cause of much trouble.

At the mid-century these dock systems were in the control of five separate companies; the East and West India, London, St Katherine's, Grand Surrey and Commercial dock companies. (The Regent's Canal Dock was separately owned, and does not really rank as one of the major London systems.) Some consolidation had taken place since the docks were opened, for on the south side both the Baltic and East Country docks had been taken over by the Commercial Company, and on the other bank the East and West India companies had joined forces in 1838. Nevertheless there remained a number of competing private dock managements, a circumstance largely peculiar to the port of London. The docks at Liverpool had developed in a very different manner.[10] In the eighteenth century they had been controlled by the municipality, who finally relinquished control in 1857 to the Mersey Docks and Harbour Board. Competing private companies thus played no part in the development of the resources of the port. The experience of most other British ports was similar to that of Liverpool, with either the municipality or a public authority co-ordinating development. In London such a body was lacking until 1908, and this fact gives the port's history a distinctive character.

The dock systems of London were vast establishments by comparison with most other industrial enterprises in the first half of the century, but their work was subject to the violent fluctuations characteristic of the age of sail. Changes of wind and season resulted in alternating spells of idleness and intense activity, and the numbers employed at the docks thus varied very greatly. In 1849 the London Dock was worked by from one to three thousand labourers, while at the East and West India systems the numbers ranged from just over a thousand to four thousand.[11] These two companies stood out from the others in this period as being the greatest both in terms of the tonnage of shipping handled and of the value of the goods dealt with on the quays. They were both situated on the north bank, and indeed it was upon this bank that the vast bulk of the trade in the docks was concentrated. Here a large variety of valuable cargoes were handled, such as tobacco, sugar, wine and spices; here also were situated the great Bonded Warehouses of the port. The docks on the south side, on the other hand, had been deliberately intended for the reception of timber, and from the beginning specialised in this field.[12]

During the early years of their life the dock companies had been fairly prosperous concerns, but this prosperity of the companies on the northern bank was a precarious one, for it depended upon a set of circumstances which did not long survive.[13] These companies had been endowed with monopoly privileges for a period of twenty-one years. This gave them exclusive rights in the handling of certain cargoes. Furthermore, between 1800 and 1832, the Legal Quays and Bonded Warehouses of the port were largely restricted to the premises of the dock companies. These privileges were, however, quickly terminated by Parliament, and the companies on the north bank were thus left exposed to the effects of competition.[14] The Surrey companies had never enjoyed the extensive privileges of the other docks, but they were able to gain a firm hold on the timber trade of the port, and were therefore less affected than the other companies by the competitive atmosphere of the port at mid-century.[15]

Attention has been focused so far upon the dock systems of the port. The river wharves, however, continued to receive the larger share of the port's shipping. In 1835 the docks received 946,102 tons as against 3,694,130 for the port as a whole.[16] The foreign-trade tonnage for that year was 929,148, and virtually the whole of this was handled by the docks, but almost all the coastwise traffic was received by the riverside wharves. The river was to maintain this supremacy over the docks in the coastwise trade throughout the nineteenth century. The practice of overside delivery from the docks into barges destined for the wharves was to further enhance the importance of the river *vis-à-vis* the docks, but in 1835 this practice had not developed to any great extent.[17] By 1850, however, overside delivery was becoming important, and this development was to have the most far-reaching consequences for the functioning of the port.

Although by the middle of the nineteenth century the port of London had not greatly felt the impact of technical changes, it had developed certain characteristics which were to remain throughout the century. The most distinctive feature of the port was the lack of any single co-ordinating authority, with jurisdiction over both the river and the docks. In 1850 the docks were under the control of five competing companies, and the same multiplicity of authorities was found in the administration of the river. The Admiralty, the Trinity House and the Corporation of the City all had conflicting jurisdictions over the Thames and the interests of navigation suffered as a result.[18] It was not until the institution of the Conservancy in 1857 that there was anything like a unified control of the river,[19] and the port had to wait until 1908 for an authority which brought both docks and river under one central body. The result was a wasteful exploitation of the resources of the port. Already by 1850 the harbour had acquired its rambling character, which was to be further accentuated as the century progressed.

2

The vast growth of the capital ensured the continued expansion of the port of London in the second half of the nineteenth century. This expansion, after being very rapid at first, tended to slow down towards the end of the century. It was, however, continuous throughout the period.

Despite the growth in the trade of the port the period was marked by a drastic decline in the fortunes of the dock companies. This decline was accompanied, and partly caused, by the rise of the wharves to a new position of prominence in the structure of the port. The increasing failure of the dock companies to derive any substantial benefit from the expanding trade of the port can be appreciated from the following figures.[20] Despite an increase of 66 per cent in the tonnage in the foreign and colonial trade entering the docks of the London and East and West India companies between 1889 and 1901, the gross revenue derived from those docks only increased by about 18 per cent.[21] It is necessary to survey briefly the reasons for this strange anomaly.

The financial stability of the dock enterprises depended not so much on the tonnage received as on the amount of goods warehoused.[22] Unfortunately for them the latter half of the century saw not only a general falling off in warehousing business, but also

Table 1. TOTAL NET TONNAGE OF SHIPPING ENTERED AND CLEARED WITH CARGO (FOREIGN TRADE ONLY) AT THE PORT OF LONDON[23]

1869		6,102,686
1859		4,372,367
	Increase upon 1859:	1,730,319 or 39%
1879		8,781,669
1869		6,102,686
	Increase upon 1869:	2,678,983 or 43%
1889		12,071,671
1879		8,781,669
	Increase upon 1879:	3,290,002 or 37%
1899		15,286,643
1889		12,071,671
	Increase upon 1889:	3,214,972 or 26%

the vigorous challenge of the wharves for what storage business remained.[24] The relative decline in warehousing throughout the port was due to a complex of commercial and technical changes. The most important factor was the increasing tendency for goods imported into the country to be taken into immediate consumption. This change was chiefly due to the influence of the steamship, the telegraph and the railways.[25] In the days of sail, trade was much more seasonal than it was to become later, and goods were often shipped in large fleets. It was therefore necessary to carry large stocks in the warehouses. Improved techniques changed all this, for steamers ran regularly, and goods could be supplied according to demand instead of being brought over in vast quantities for storage. The telegraph enabled the merchant to wire for goods to be shipped when the price was right, and the railways permitted speedy assembling and distribution of cargoes. In short, the increasingly finely gauged way trade came to be conducted to some extent obviated the need for storage. The effect of these changes on the warehousing business of the dock companies can be seen from the following figures. Between 1880 and 1900 the amount of goods landed on charges (i.e. *not* delivered overside to wharves) by the London and East and West India companies increased by 100,000 tons, but the stock in warehouses fell by 140,000 tons.[26] This general decline in warehousing was rendered far more serious for the dock companies by the diversion of much of the storage business that remained to the wharves. Furthermore the wharves competed not merely in the storage of goods, but in the landing of foreign-commerce cargoes as a whole, whether they were destined for housing or immediate consumption.

In the earlier years of the century the riverside establishments concerned themselves almost entirely with coastwise shipping, and foreign commerce was exclusively the preserve of the docks. The Customs Consolidation Act of 1853 finally ended this situation by permitting the extension of the Legal Quays and Bonded Warehouses outside the limits of the docks, thus enabling many wharves to handle dutiable goods.[27] Between 1854 and 1857 fourteen additional wharves were granted privileges of one kind or another.[28] By 1866 the constant extension of landing and warehousing rights to fresh riverside establishments necessitated the preparation by the Customs of a revised list of wharves, warehouses and their privileges.[29] In that year there were 116 wharves enjoying widely varying landing and housing rights, and the process of extension of these privileges to fresh premises was still going on in 1870.[30] The wharves were aided still further by the coming of free trade, which reduced customs restrictions to a minimum.

The wharves were not, of course, able to receive large ocean-going shipping themselves; this continued to go to the docks. Increasingly, however, it was the wharves rather than the docks which received the cargoes from abroad, which were transported from the docks to the wharves by means of lighters. They were only enabled to compete with the docks in this manner because of the 'free-water' clause of the Dock Acts, which exempted lighters and their cargoes from dock dues. This gave the wharves a decided advantage over the docks, for if the cargo of a ship was discharged onto the dock, quay dues were paid, whereas if a cargo was unloaded overside into barges there was no charge. Furthermore the wharves enjoyed the advantage of proximity to the City markets, shared only by the London and St Katherine's docks. Thus it came about that the wharves were able to wrest from the docks the handling and warehousing of the bulk of foreign-trade cargoes. Their success in this field can be gathered from the fact that by 1898 for every 4 tons of cargo entering the docks of London (except Millwall and Surrey docks) 3 tons were discharged overside for delivery to the wharves.[31] The same was true with regard to the forwarding of goods to the docks, and it was estimated at the turn of the century that 80 per cent of the cargo loaded into ships at the above docks was brought alongside in lighters.[32]

The rise of the wharves resulted in a ruinous competition in the warehousing business of the port, and also undermined the whole financial structure of the dock companies. The large-scale extension of warehousing and landing privileges to the wharves had come mainly in the 1860s and 1870s, at a time when trade was expanding more quickly than at any other time during the century. At this period, furthermore, those factors which were to cause a decline in warehousing had not had time to really make themselves felt. It thus seemed rational at the time to extend accommodation. However, the general falling off in warehousing and the diminishing rate of increase of trade in the last quarter of the century meant that the port became over-warehoused. In this situation a ruinous competition developed which affected adversely both the wharves and docks.[33] Rates came tumbling down, and by the end of 1886 there were few wharves which were making much of a profit. In this situation shipowners and merchants were able to play the wharves and docks off against each other, until the 1889 strike finally awakened them to their identity of interest. An agreement was reached between the leading docks and wharves, but in the event it failed to remedy the situation.[34]

It was the dock companies who were the hardest hit by this competition, for not only did they lose much of their warehousing business, but the practice of overside delivery deprived them also of dues on goods entering and leaving the docks. As early as 1855 they had tried to remedy this situation by attempting to get Parliament to abolish the 'free-water' clause, and they were driven to try again in 1899.[35] The only outcome of this effort was the setting up of a Royal Commission to investigate the condition of the port, and from then on the days of the dock companies were numbered.

It is now necessary to examine the role the wharves had come to play in the functioning of the port of London by the end of the nineteenth century. In addition to their dramatic entry into the ocean trades by means of overside delivery, the wharves continued as always to handle directly a large amount of shipping in the coastal and continental trades.

Table 2. DISTRIBUTION OF SHIPPING ENTERING LONDON IN 1899[36]

	Foreign Trade	Coastwise	Total
Docks	6,319,653	1,000,000	7,319,653
River, i.e. wharves, moorings, etc.	2,622,446	4,920,784	7,543,220

It will be seen from these figures that the river continued to receive directly the vast bulk of the coastwise trade, and in fact handled a slightly larger share than the docks of the total tonnage of the port. It was, however, the practice of overside delivery to the wharves which revolutionised the working of the port. London became a lighter port—that is, a port which depends on lighters for the forwarding and delivery of goods, and this has remained its most characteristic feature until the present age.[37]

The wharves which handled this traffic fell into several categories.[38] In the upper reaches of the river, in Wapping, Southwark, Bermondsey and in the City itself, were situated wharves and warehouses dealing in products of a non-bulk variety—tea, coffee, cocoa, sugar, spices, wool and so on. A second group consisted of those wharves, usually lower downstream, which specialised in the handling of bulky materials, such as timber, stone or corn. Particularly noticeable in this category were the granaries that lined the south bank of the Thames at Rotherhithe. These two groups had certain features in common. They were primarily engaged in the storage and preparation for the market of certain specialised products. Most of these products were imported in long-distance vessels, and so were lightered to the wharves from the docks. In addition to these two groups there were the shipping wharves, situated chiefly in Wapping and Bermondsey. These concerns received short-sea vessels directly, and each wharf was usually connected with the trade of a particular steamship company. Some establishments, such as the Carron and Hermitage wharves, dealt with the Scottish trade; others, such as Stanton's, with trade to a particular English port, and others again dealt with lines running to near continental ports, such as Antwerp. The life-blood of these shipping wharves was the transhipment business. Cargoes of wool, jute, coffee and other goods unloaded at the docks, were lightered to the shipping wharves for distribution to Scottish, Irish, provincial and near continental centres. There was also, of course, a considerable flow in the opposite direction. Some large wharves in Wapping and Bermondsey were composite establishments, for while they had departments engaged in the storage of tea, coffee and other 'colonial' goods, they ran shipping departments as well. Notable among these composite establishments were Hay's wharf and Mark Brown's wharf, both in the Tooley Street area.

The pattern outlined above was already emerging clearly in the 1860s and 1870s.[39] Subsequent years, however, were to bring into greater prominence a final category of riverside wharf. This was the private wharf, associated with some industrial establishment. The private wharves were scattered over a far wider area than the other categories, and they spread not only along the banks of the Thames, but along those of the Lea as well. There were wharves to serve gasworks, flour mills, cement works and so on. Many of these wharves received their raw materials and dispatched their products by lighter, but those situated downstream often handled cargo ships directly. By the early twentieth century the most notable of these downstream establishments were the wharves serving the cement and paper industries. Situated as they were in regions of deep water, at Northfleet, Greenhithe, Purfleet and other centres, these wharves were well placed for the reception of shipping.

The role of the wharves in the port was thus a widely ramified one. By the beginning of the new century there were 320 of them lining the river,[40] employing collectively 41 per cent of the labour force of the port.[41]

The rivalry between the docks and the river was a characteristic feature of the port in the second half of the century, but equally intense was the competition that developed between the dock companies themselves. It was the opening of a new dock by a separate company in 1855, which really intensified competition. This new dock was the Victoria, and both in its design and its immediate effects it inaugurated a new era in the port.[42] It was built farther downstream than any of the other docks and was provided with the largest entrance lock in the port; these factors making it the most suitable for the reception of the larger ships that were appearing. The Victoria was also the first dock in the port to be provided from the outset with direct links with the railway network. Finally, it was the first dock to make use of hydraulic machinery.[43]

The success of the new dock was assured both by its modern design and by the very low dues at first charged to shipping. By 1860 it handled a larger tonnage than any of the other docks, and severely threatened their position.[44] The opening of another new dock some years later—the Millwall—was a further blow to the established systems. The Millwall Dock, opened in 1868, resembled the Victoria both in its modern construction and in the policy of low rates pursued by its managers.[45] It was thus likewise able to attract a large quantity of business to itself, especially in the grain trade. The Victoria Company was, however, quickly taken over by another company, while Millwall retained its independence until the creation of the Port of London Authority in 1908.

The emergence of modern docks charging low rates inevitably affected adversely the older systems.[46] This was the case with the docks of the London and St Katherine's companies, and by 1863 the dividends of both companies had seriously declined. Thus in 1864 an amalgamation was carried through between the London, St Katherine's, and Victoria companies, thereby not only ending the rivalry between the older companies, but also giving them control of the most modern dock in the port. The year 1864 saw a consolidation of interests on the south bank also, for here the Surrey Canal and Commercial Dock companies joined to form the Surrey Commercial Dock Company. The East and West India docks had amalgamated back in 1838, but they had done little since to modernise their systems. Consequently they suffered heavily from losses of trade to the Victoria and Millwall docks. In order to retrieve their position they opened the South West India Dock in 1870, but little foresight was shown in the planning of this dock, for its entrance lock was inferior to both the Victoria and

Millwall systems. The dock was popular during the 1870s, but, in face of the ever-increasing size of shipping, the inferior entrance was to prove a fatal defect. For the dock enterprises of the port as a whole the third quarter of the nineteenth century was a transitional period. Ships were getting bigger, improved docks were becoming necessary, competition was becoming more intense; yet this was but a foretaste of the pressures which were to overwhelm the East and West India and London companies during the last quarter of the century.

The two decades following the opening of the South West India Dock saw the transition from sail to steam as the chief motive power of the ship.[47] Up until around 1870 the total tonnage of sailing vessels for the whole kingdom had been rising, but after that date it steadily declined for the rest of the century.[48] By 1890 the tonnage of steamships had overtaken that of sail, although in 1901 there were still over 10,000 British sailing-ships. The supplanting of sail by steam was indeed a very lengthy process, due mainly to the delay in the development of a steam engine that was economical over long distances. This transition to steam power was of course accompanied by a large increase in the size of ships.[49] The early steamers had been relatively small and in the 1860s and 1870s were not usually much above 2000 tons. It was only really from 1880 onward that vessels of some size began to appear in the port in any numbers, for although there had been a steady increase in size before that date, the really dramatic change occurred in the last two decades of the century. Thus in 1870 there was but one steamer registered in Britain of over 3000 tons, in 1890 there were fifty-one. The change was even more pronounced between 1890 and 1900; in the former year only two steamers over 5000 tons, ten years later—fifty.

These changes in the size and motive power of ocean-going shipping affected the working of the port in two main ways. In the first place they created a need for docks deep enough to accommodate the modern steamer of vastly increased size. Secondly, the greatly increased value of these ships made it imperative that they should be turned round with the greatest possible speed. It is, however, the impact of the large steamer on the dock systems of the port that is the concern of this section.

The 1880s in both London and Liverpool saw the creation of great new docks.[50] In London, however, the provision of the additional accommodation required was the occasion for a battle for survival between the two chief dock enterprises—the London and East and West India companies.[51] Before 1880 only the Mill-wall and Victoria docks could claim to be modern systems, but the state of the river, especially in Woolwich Reach, limited even their capacity to receive the largest ships.[52] The London Company, in view of this defect affecting its Victoria Dock, decided to carry out the long-projected scheme for extending the latter dock eastward to Gallion's Reach. This would give the dock an entrance in relatively deep water. The extension was opened in 1880 as the Albert Dock, and it was at the time of its opening capable of receiving the largest ships afloat.[53] The construction of this dock, however, set off a chain of events which had far-reaching consequences.

The opening of the Albert Dock by its chief rival forced the East and West India Company to take drastic action in order to retain some share of the larger shipping entering the port. The neglect of the river by the Conservancy made pointless any attempt to thoroughly modernise the existing docks of the company and so the only course open was to construct a new dock farther downstream. The site chosen was Tilbury, where the water was so deep that the dock would be independent of the state of the channel, and thus able to receive the largest vessels. In 1886 the new dock was opened. This Tilbury venture brought nothing but misfortune to the East and West India Company, and the London Company too was to share its rival's troubles. The problem was that trade was increasing only slowly at this time, and 1886 was a particularly bad year. There was thus no demand for the additional dock space created by the opening of Tilbury, and the port therefore became over-docked as it had become over-warehoused. The result was the collapse of rates all round.[54] By 1888 the East and West India Company was in receivers' hands and the position of the London Company was not much better. The misfortunes of the two companies inevitably drew them together, and a joint committee for the management of the docks of the two concerns was formed. The final step of amalgamation was taken in 1901, but it occurred under the shadow of a royal commission which was to recommend the control of the docks by a public authority.[55] Finally, in 1908, the Port of London Authority took over the management of all the enclosed docks in the port, the Surrey and Millwall as well as the systems of the London and India Company.

The competition from the wharves had undermined the financial structure of the companies, but it was the necessity of competing with each other for the accommodation of the large steamer which dealt the final blow to the two large companies.[56] The Surrey docks were less affected by the trends in ship construction than the other companies, for the timber trade in which they specialised was an exceptional case. Ships used in this trade remained small, and therefore the pressure for deeper docks was less intense.[57] Furthermore the south-side docks benefited from the great expansion in the grain and timber trades in this period,[58] for they specialised almost entirely in the reception of these products. In 1902 the Surrey Commercial Dock Company was stated to be the most prosperous dock concern in the port.[59] The distinctive position of these docks was to some extent shared by the Millwall Dock, for this system also came to specialise in grain and timber, and there grew up a working understanding between the two companies as to the rates charged to the public.[60] The Surrey and Millwall docks were thus so distinctive that they almost constituted a port within a port.

The construction of new docks to meet the increased size of ships has been considered above in the context of its effect on the fortunes of the dock companies. It remains to examine the more important consequences which sprang from the manner in which the docks were developed in this period. The neglect of the river channel had meant that the port could be adapted to receive modern shipping only by building new docks farther downstream. This resulted in the stagnation of the older docks, and thus between 1871 and 1899 none of the upstream docks of the two large companies received any substantial increase of business. It was the lower docks which absorbed most of the increases in the trade of the port, and the chief centres of activity tended to move farther and farther downstream.[61] The Victoria Dock was the first of the modern downstream docks and as such prospered in its early days, particularly at the expense of the India systems.[62] Its expansion was, however, ended by the opening of the Albert Dock in 1880.[63] This modern dock was so large and convenient that it dominated the foreign commerce of the port for almost two decades; in 1899 it was receiving a greater tonnage than the

London, St Katherine's, West India, East India and South West India docks put together.[64] The opening years of the twentieth century, however, saw a vast expansion in the shipping received by Tilbury, and by 1904 this dock had replaced the Albert as the premier dock of the port.[65] Thus transfers of business to Tilbury actually caused a decrease in the tonnage handled by the Albert between 1899 and 1904.[66] The Report of the Committee on Unskilled Labour (1908) summed up these developments as follows: 'While the tonnage [received by the port] as a whole is increasing, the increase is taking place almost entirely in respect of the large vessels for which only the Tilbury and to a smaller extent the Albert dock have sufficient room.'[67]

Thus during the last quarter of the century the vast bulk of ocean shipping in the port came to be handled by the three down-stream docks, none of which had been in existence in 1850. Table 3 brings out the contrast between the old and the new areas of the port in the year 1899, and again in 1904.[68] It will be noticed that between the two years the combined tonnage of the old systems continued to fall, while that of the downstream docks greatly increased.

Table 3. SHIPPING TONNAGE ENTERING THE OLD AND NEW DOCK SYSTEMS [69]

		1899	1904
Old Docks	London Docks	447,988	403,930
	St Katherine's	200,731	174,932
	West India	292,084	270,958
	East India	275,315	276,429
	South West India	132,373	144,425
	TOTAL	1,348,491	1,270,674
New Docks	Victoria	637,492	969,344
	Albert	1,455,924	1,174,892
	Tilbury	839,482	1,754,668
	TOTAL	2,932,898	3,898,904

The old-established areas of the port suffered heavily from these developments. They were forced to rely on sailing-ships or small steamers in the coastal or near continental trades.[70] With the important exception of the Surrey Docks, it may be said that the

old-established docks of the port entered upon a decline in the
1880s, which was to be halted only by the great dredging and dock-
improvements scheme carried out by the Port Authority in the
inter-war years.[71]

The prosperity or decline of any dock system has to be seen in
the context of the area in which the docks stand. The prosperous
parts of the port became situated outside the boundaries of the
metropolis, the Albert and Victoria being sited in the rapidly
expanding industrial district of West Ham, while the Tilbury
Dock was located right out in the countryside—26 miles downstream from London Bridge.[72] Thus trade expanded in these
comparatively sparsely populated areas, while it declined in the
congested riverside districts of the metropolis. The position of the
upstream districts was rendered worse by the steady decline of
other riverside industries during the second half of the century.
Industries ancillary to dock work, such as sack-making, cooperage
and the hand manufacture of ropes had virtually ceased to exist by
the end of this period.[73] More important was the rapid decline of
the Thamesside shipbuilding industry, which was transferred to
Clydeside in the 1860s.[74] Although thriving wharves and warehouses grew up in the old waterfront districts they were no
replacement for the lost industries.[75]

The coming of the large steamer, and the wasteful way the port
was adapted to meet its requirements, were factors which had
dispersed the activities of the port over an unnecessarily large
area. In doing this, they had seriously depressed those districts
which had for long depended on the docks for their livelihood. In
1908 the Port of London Authority was faced with the task of
modernising the older dock systems and thus preventing any
further wasteful proliferation of docking facilities. Only thus
could some balance be restored to the activities of the port.

The impact of the steamer has been considered so far chiefly in
relation to the evolution of the dock systems of the port. The
manner in which the docks were developed under this pressure
was something which was peculiar to London, but the steamships
also brought changes in methods of working which were universal
in their application. The high cost of the steamer made it imperative that it was used to the maximum.[76] This was so from the
beginning, but the need for a quick turn-round in port became
more pressing as steamers began to sail on longer and more

complicated routes,[77] for whereas the triumph of steam in the short-sea trades had been achieved fairly easily, the ousting of sail from the long-distance routes was a lengthy process and entailed a ceaseless striving for the reduction of operating costs. Time spent in port had to be kept at a minimum, and thus the rapid handling of cargoes became an absolute necessity. Mechanisation was one way of achieving the necessary speed-up in dock operations.

The only cranes employed in London in the early part of the century were manually operated, as were the winches, and the first hydraulic crane in the docks appeared in 1855, at the Victoria Dock.[78] The emergence of the hydraulic quay crane at mid-century is closely associated with developments in the coal trade. The first steam-screw collier had appeared in 1852, and this had led to a demand for a faster discharge, this in turn resulting in the increasing employment of hydraulic machinery.[79] Coal, as a bulk cargo, lent itself to mechanical handling,[80] and so by the mid-1880s the majority of colliers in London were discharged by machinery.[81] By this time the hydraulic quay crane was being used in the docks for general cargo work, and by the turn of the century there were said to be 576 of them in operation in London.[82] The other main mechanical advance of the period was the harnessing of steam to drive ships' winches. As with the quay crane, the steam winch was employed at the middle of the century in the unloading of the screw collier.[83] As steamers increasingly came into use in other trades, so they brought the steam winch with them, and thus by the early 1870s the power-driven winch was beginning to have a considerable impact on methods of work.[84]

The power-driven ship's winch was in fact the most characteristic mechanical appliance of the industry during this period. Modern vessels were increasingly supplied with machinery of such scope as to enable them to dispense entirely with quay cranes in loading or discharging.[85] In Liverpool shipowners relied heavily on ships' gear and quay cranes appear to have been little used.[86] The case of New York was even more striking, for here shipping came to rely almost completely on a combination of winches on the ship and on the pier.[87] In London there were plenty of cranes in the docks by 1900, but they were apparently not fully utilised.[88] This neglect of the quay crane in favour of the ship's own appliances seems to have been partly due to the fact that it was cheaper for the shipowner to employ his own gear. If he used the quayside

installations he had to pay charges for crane hire.[89] Another
reason was that the manœuvrability of the quay crane was
strictly limited throughout most of the period, because of the lack
of the luffing motion.[90] The Port Authority did much to improve
the quayside appliances of the port in the years before the First
World War,[91] but the fact remains that throughout the period it
was the ship's winches which played the major role.

Despite the advances outlined above, it must be said that before
1914 operations in the dock industry were generally carried out in
a comparatively primitive fashion. 'With the exception of lifting or
hoisting from the ship's hold to the deck, which is usually effected
either by the ship's winches, steam gadgets or cranes, cargoes are
discharged and landed almost entirely by manual labour.'[92]

This statement referred to Bristol in 1905, but it was true to a
greater or lesser degree of most ports at the time. The Annual
Report of the Chief Inspector for Factories in 1899 contains a
revealing survey, illustrating the rudimentary devices upon which
the industry continued to depend for cargo handling.[93] It was
really only in the grain trade that advanced mechanical methods
were widely used. Grain is a bulk commodity, like coal or timber,
and thus lends itself to mechanical treatment more than general
cargo. By the early 1890s the chief grain docks—the Millwall and
Surrey—were employing elevators on a considerable scale.[94] And
yet even here the use of the elevator was by no means universal
before 1914. Often elevators were only provided at certain berths
adjoining granaries, and if these were occupied cargoes continued
to be 'bushelled' into sacks as of old.[95] Apart from grain, the coal
trade was perhaps the most affected by mechanisation, but here
reliance was mainly on cranes rather than elevators.

The coming of the steamship had created a need for a quick
turn-round, but it was not primarily on mechanisation that shipowners came to rely for dispatch. This can be appreciated from a
comparison between the ports of Hamburg and New York.[96]
Hamburg was before 1914 the best-equipped port in the world;
its machinery was the finest the dock industry had to offer. New
York was perhaps the worst equipped mechanically of all the great
ports at this time. Despite these facts shipowners considered
Hamburg to be inferior to New York for dispatch. This surprising
circumstance was largely due to the greater pressure at which
labour was worked in the latter port. The fact was that in most

ports shipowners relied for a quick turn-round chiefly upon a pliable labour force, worked for long hours and at high speed. Labour was plentiful and shipowners generally made little attempt to economise in the number employed.[97] It was no unusual thing in 1900 for two, and sometimes more, gangs to be working in a single hatch in order to secure greater dispatch.[98] As long as labour was plentiful there was little incentive to mechanise on a large scale, as an experienced commentator on the industry pointed out in 1912.[99]

The conquest by steam of the long-distance shipping-routes after 1870 affected every port by speeding up the tempo of dock work. In London, however, the effects went further and revolutionised the whole structure of the port. For the reasons already outlined, the port was allowed to sprawl over an unnecessarily large area, one-half of which expanded while the other stagnated. Thus instead of the old port being modernised to meet the changed circumstances, a new port was created, and in 1914 the two existed side by side. The rambling character of the dock systems, noticeable in 1850, had therefore been immensely accentuated by the coming of the large steamer in the second half of the century. The rise of the wharves had further complicated the structure of the port. In a sense these numerous concerns merely duplicated the functions of the dock companies; they landed, stored, worked up, delivered or transhipped the cargoes of the harbour. Their existence spread the activities of the port over a much wider area than was usual or desirable. Today we have cause to regret, with Sir Joseph Broodbank, that Parliament had entrusted the destiny of our finest harbour to 'opposing bodies pledged from the first to use the port as an arena for fighting merely for their own hand'.[100]

2 The Labour Force

THE growth of the port of London, as we saw in the previous chapter, was entirely without plan. In fact until the creation of the P.L.A. in 1908 the port did not even exist as a formal institution. It was merely an unregulated meeting-place for a vast number of diverse interests—shipowners, wharfingers, lighterage concerns, merchants, dock companies. After 1908 there was some regulation, but the meeting-place remained as crowded and as full of diversity as before. In this situation it would indeed have been surprising if the port's labour force had formed a homogeneous body. In fact, of course, port workers were as lacking in cohesion as the industrial complex that gave them employment. They were subdivided into numerous occupational groupings, and in the early days these groupings were no more bound together by a sense of common interest than were the port employers.

In seeking to analyse the nature of the waterside labour force, and especially its subdivision into so many sections, attention must of course be paid to the character of the work itself, its skills, variety and physical demands. These, however, tell only part of the story. As important as the work itself was the manner in which it was conducted. The confusion of relatively small and diverse employers operating on the waterfront was perhaps the decisive factor moulding the structure of the labour force. It is therefore to the system of employment that we shall first turn our attention.

Port employment has, by and large, meant casual employment.[1] The prevalence of the latter system derived from the great fluctuations in the volume of work performed by port employers.[2] The latter might keep a small permanent staff, equal to the minimum requirements of their business, but for the rest they relied on labour engaged by the hour or day. Reliance upon casual labour was inevitable while businesses remained small and specialised. In bigger concerns, however, there was not this inevitability, for these concerns embraced a number of different departments of trade, and fluctuations in these various departments did not always correspond. Labour could thus be transferred from a department where business was slack into one where it was brisk, and in this manner could be retained in permanent employment.[3] The biggest concerns in the port of London were the dock companies, and at various times in their history they experimented with permanent labour, especially in the period after 1891.[4] Most concerns in the port were not, however, very large employers of waterside labour, and even where they embraced several departments of trade, as at the larger wharves, each department tended to function as an independent unit so far as the employment of labour was concerned.[5] The bulk of the port's labour force thus remained casually employed. The system of small employers and casual labour had far-reaching consequences in London, as in other great ports. The most profound consequence was the chronic under-employment of the waterside labour force.

At this stage it is necessary that we should be quite clear about the meaning of the term 'waterside labour force'. Although casually employed, this labour force was in fact a regular body. It was composed of men who regularly looked for work at the waterside, and who rarely sought, and even more rarely obtained, work anywhere else.[6] Furthermore the majority of these men were, as we shall see, specialists in some one sphere of port work. It is necessary to make this point, because in the nineteenth century waterside work was regarded by the public less as a genuine industrial occupation than as a residual employment for the refuse and unemployed of society at large.[7] Port workers were represented as a motley horde of unfortunates, without roots in the port industry or anywhere else, and the work acquired a stigma it has retained to the present day.[8] The source of the confusion was quite simple. Outside of the class of regular port workers there existed a broad fringe of complete casuals. The services of this class were required by the industry to meet the very widest fluctuations in business, but it did not constitute part of the regular labour force. It was composed of two distinct elements. On the one hand were the unemployed from other trades, and on the other were the men demoralised by irregular work in the port or some other industry. This latter group subsisted chiefly upon the earnings of their families, and upon charity. In common parlance they were referred to as 'loafers'. Booth's survey classified them as a 'leisure class'.[9]

The port worker justifiably resented his identification in the public mind with the fringe element of waterside society.[10] Yet the identification was understandable, for the dividing-line between the regular and the outsider was an extremely shadowy one. In the less skilled grades of port employment the regulars themselves were largely recruited from the unemployed of other trades,[11] for in this sphere few fathers encouraged their sons to follow them in the work. Furthermore it was not always easy to distinguish the regular from the loafer, for many port workers received so little work that they drifted gradually into the class of unemployables.[12] The boundary between the regulars and the unfortunate fringe was thus blurred, and the public made no distinction.

In all great ports the regular waterside labour force was the victim of acute under-employment.[13] Regular workers were, as a general rule, restricted to the employment offered by one small centre, operating in one sector of the port. The centre was often a separate business concern, but sometimes it was a department of a dock company or a large wharf. Except in unusually prosperous times, these centres only required a full complement of regulars for certain limited periods; for the rest they could make do with a skeleton staff. In the days of sail, periods of idleness for regular workers tended to be lengthy, due to seasonal causes, and due also to the fact that adverse winds could halt the movement of shipping for weeks on end. The steamship modified influences of season and weather, and tended to spread trade more evenly throughout the year.[14] Thus even in a fairly dull year, such as 1891, a regular man working on a steamship line would not expect to be idle for more than seven to nine days at a time.[15] Although the steamers reduced the length of spells of idleness, they scarcely improved the level of employment taking the year as a whole. Thus, again in 1891, regulars at the Victoria and Albert docks did not average more than four days a week taking the year through.[16] Most London men would have been much worse off than this, for the Albert and Victoria docks were by far the busiest in the port at this time.[17]

In view of the restricted opportunities for employment at any one centre, the question arises why port workers could not move to other centres when work was not available at their usual place of employment. They were, after all, casuals, and therefore not formally bound to any one employer. Some mobility there was, of

The age of sail: two of the early nineteenth-century docks, West India (above) and *St Katherine's (below). Note the extensive warehousing facilities.*

The age of steam: The Royal Albert Dock, opened in 1880 to cater for the large steamships

course, but not much. One reason for this was that the men were simply ignorant as to their chances of employment at other centres, for information as to when or where work was available only circulated informally on a local basis.[18] The regular was loath to leave a centre where he was known, and therefore sure of work sooner or later, in order to hunt for employment in sectors where he was a stranger. By such a course of action he risked missing his chance at his usual centre, for he could never be sure when the employer would require his services, due to the irregular hours at which ships arrived. The average port worker preferred the certainty of even a very small amount of work to absolute uncertainty, and so he generally remained immobile. It was said of the London wharf workers that they 'usually follow up one wharf or one ship, and do not go to another wharf unless there is a certainty of a job'.[19] This attitude was broadly true of port workers as a whole.

The immobility of the men received powerful encouragement from the employers. Each employer wanted to be self-sufficient as regards his labour requirements. He wanted men to be waiting for his work, so that in a rush of business there would be no delays. It was not only a matter of numbers, but of quality also, for employers wanted to be sure of having men experienced in their branch of business. The following comments, made by a London wharfinger in 1908, may be taken as typifying the attitude of employers generally.

> You want to make it worth the while of reliable and satisfactory men who understand your work to come and wait outside your place. When one of the holds are finished early, all the strangers are the first to be paid off. We have little interest in them. We do not care very much whether they come again or not.[20]

One way of keeping the 'reliable and satisfactory' men together when trade was dull was to share the work out amongst them. 'In many instances employers deliberately spread the work out amongst the greatest number in order that they may keep as many men about as possible.'[21] This was written of Liverpool in 1912, but the practice was widespread in London.[22] Its obvious effect was to retain at each centre many more men than could receive adequate employment.

The immobility of the port worker was the crucial factor in his under-employment, for it spread the work of the port over a far greater number of regular workers than was really necessary.[23] Only in quite exceptionally busy times was the total labour force fully employed, for at other periods there were always some sectors where men were out of work. In 1892, when trade had slackened off after the boom of 1889, it was estimated that on an average throughout the year 7000 men were standing idle on the London waterfront, out of a total regular labour force of 22,000.[24]

The survival of this wasteful system for so long was only rendered possible by the unrestricted movement of workers into the dock labour market, for any restrictions on the inflow of labour would have compelled port employers to pool their labour resources in order to meet increases of business. The trade unions attempted at various times to impose restrictions, as we shall see in subsequent chapters, but they were rarely successful, and so employers were permitted to expand their labour reserves at will. The labour surplus thus mounted as trade increased and employment centres proliferated. The bigger the port the more serious the problem became,[25] and in the early years of the twentieth century the dock labour markets of London and Liverpool were the subject of numerous public and private inquiries.[26] The port of Liverpool was the more thoroughly investigated of the two, and the picture that emerged here was indeed appalling. In 1912, a good year for trade, there were 27,000 men dependent on the Liverpool docks for subsistence. At least 7000 of these constituted a surplus over and above 'the requirements of the port at its busiest possible season'.[27] The position cannot have been any better in London, and may well have been worse. Over-supply of labour was indeed the fundamental characteristic of waterside employment, and more than anything else it moulded the attitudes of the port worker and shaped the policies of the organisations that came to represent him.

The disorganised manner in which the port industry met its labour requirements produced not only a labour surplus, but other enduring characteristics as well. Prominent among these was a rigid division of occupations, and any analysis of the occupational groupings of the waterfront would be entirely superficial unless placed in the context of the casual system.

The port worker was a specialist *par excellence*. In 1914 an observer of port labour wrote of the docker: 'He can, and will, handle *one* class of goods for *one* firm; occasionally he will handle the same class of goods for another firm, but very seldom will he try to handle a different class of goods . . .'[28] Specialisation was in fact endless at the waterside. There were men expert in the un-loading of chemicals, or orange boxes, or casks of tobacco, or frozen meat, and so on.[29] This specialisation was primarily the result of immobility. As another observer wrote in 1912: 'artificial and imaginary specialisation is the product of the labour system, which compels a man to restrict himself to one place of call'.[30] The situation certainly suited the numerous employers, each of whom could rely upon his own nucleus of specialised workers. It came also to suit the dockers themselves. Specialisation came near to giving the casual port worker some degree of security and status. His facility in a particular branch of work was valued by employers in that sphere, and constituted therefore some sort of guarantee of employment.[31] Furthermore port workers develop-ed a somewhat exaggerated pride in their specialised skills. They worked in an industry commonly regarded, as we have seen, as the dustbin of society. Specialised skills enabled them to retain their self-respect. Any slight differential in skill or experience tended to be stressed by the waterside worker, who desperately needed to feel that he was something other than a 'dock rat'. The various occupational groups were in fact so assertive of their identity that waterside society developed in the nineteenth century something of the stratification of a caste system.[32]

Specialisation had its positive and negative aspects. Springing, as it did, from immobility, it tended to further reinforce that immobility and therefore aggravated the problem of oversupply. In 1912, in Liverpool, an imaginative attempt was made to reduce the labour surplus by placing the regular men on a register and making them mobile over the various employment centres.[33] The scheme failed, due partly to the employers' lack of co-operation, but due also to the hostility of the men. Indiscriminate employ-ment over a wide range of tasks was offensive to the port worker's pride, and this in part explains his resistance. There was also another factor involved. Under-employment produced among port workers a strongly monopolistic tendency. Particular groups regarded their employment in a certain sphere rather as a vested interest. Thus in Liverpool, in 1912, men would not be moved to other centres because they felt that they were trespassing on the preserve of another group. The men's attachment to immobility and specialisation had a further negative significance. It was at one with their attachment to casual employment and rejection of permanency, traits of which we shall have more to say later.[34] With all the hardship that it brought, casual employment nevertheless gave to port workers a certain freedom. The more prosperous dockers led a far more independent life than workers in most industries, and they had little taste for regular weekly employment. The following comment of a London docker was characteristic: 'if you are made permanent you are made a white slave of directly; you are transferable from here to there and everywhere'.[35] The port worker counted his specialisation as one of the freedoms of casual employment. He was not obliged to perform any task, just as he was not obliged to work every day of the week. In bad times when work was very scarce this freedom was a doubtful blessing; in good times it really did bring an independence of which few industrial workers could boast.[36]

Specialisation undoubtedly operated as a drag upon any attempt to reorganise the dock labour market, but it had, nonetheless, its positive side. The most wretched port workers were those for whom specialisation was impossible. In big employing concerns, and in extremely unskilled spheres of work, men were found with no pride of calling and no vestige of security of employment. These traits applied to the lower stratum of regular workers, and to the broad fringe element described above. These were the really hopeless cases on the waterfront, and in London and in all great ports there were very many of them. On the other hand, where specialisation existed, self-respect tended to exist also, and it was from this class that the most competent workmen, and the most loyal trade unionists, were drawn.

In the above paragraphs an attempt has been made to examine the general impact of the system of employment upon the character of the port's labour force. It is now necessary that we should examine the various occupational groupings that went to the making of that labour force. In this examination an attempt will be made to discover how far these groupings were based on real differences in the nature of the work performed, and how far they were merely the artificial creation of the port's employment structure.

2

The most fundamental distinction in dock work was between the worker on the ship and the worker on the shore. This division between ship and shore workers was universal in the industry, and whether the port was London, Hamburg, New York or Manchester the same distinction was always found.[37] In the period prior to 1914 the spheres of work tended to be quite separate, and the extent to which men were interchangeable between ship and shore work was extremely limited. The two groups were often taken on for work quite separately,[38] even when they were working for the same employer. This distinction may have owed something to the pre-dock era, when ships were worked in midstream and when therefore the separation between the two groups was a very real one. The basic reason was, however, the fact that work on board ship was believed to require a superior type of worker tò that needed on the quay. Thus shipworkers sometimes enjoyed wage differentials over shore workers, and always commanded a high status among dock workers.

The status of shipwork as a skilled occupation was derived in part from certain operations, requiring considerable expertise, which had to be carried out on board a vessel. In the first place it must be remembered that in the age of sail, and for long afterwards, all the gear required for loading or discharging was situated on the ship itself. It was a long time before the quay crane became the predominant mode of working a ship, and in the meantime operations depended upon a complex of ropes and hoisting tackle, driven at first by hand, and later by steam, winches. The 'rigging' of this gear required a knowledge almost equal to that of a sailor,[39] and in fact throughout the nineteenth century there tended to be a considerable interchange between sailors and shipworkers.[40] The introduction of power-driven winches in the 1870s in no way altered the expertise required for the erection of the ship's gear, and in 1912 at the Albert Dock the 'gearers' were still at work erecting ropes and tackle on board a great steamship.[41] The utter lack of standardisation in the methods of dock work, and its continued reliance upon a host of improvised devices, perpetuated the skills attached to this branch of shipwork.[42] It must, however, be emphasised that these skills were not usually required of ship-workers as a whole, but only of a small proportion of men who tended to specialise in the work.[43]

The erection of the ship's gear, of course, preceded the actual work of loading or discharging. In these operations the unit of work was the hatchway, and the men were divided therefore into a number of gangs; usually one gang to each hatch.[44] Each gang was sub-divided into hold men and deck men, and sometimes also included a few men on shore or in barges. When the ship was taking in cargo, certain men working in the hold needed to possess very considerable skill, for the work of stowing goods required the very greatest care.[45] This was especially the case in the age of sail, for the stability of the small ships depended on the efficiency with which the cargo was packed. The advent of the large steamer lessened the importance of this factor, but did not drastically diminish the skills of the packer. The safety of the cargo itself continued to depend on its careful stowing, and the heavy cost of running a steamer made it essential that the maximum use was made of its carrying capacity. No similar expertise was required in the hold during discharging operations, and consequently discharging work has traditionally enjoyed much less prestige than loading. A higher rate was in fact sometimes paid for export work.[46] The special skills attached to the work of stowing cargo became, however, increasingly small in relation to the work as a whole. On the sailing-ship the number of men working below deck had been small, for the holds were not large. Furthermore the hand-driven winches required the presence of a number of men on deck. At this time there was a marked distinction between the skilled workers in the hold and the men doing the rougher labour at the winches on deck.[47] The steam winches and enlarged holds of the steamship changed this; more men were needed down in the hold and fewer on deck. Hold work as a whole ceased to be an especially skilled operation. The men who actually packed the goods had indeed to be highly skilled, but the bulk of the gang were engaged in bringing the goods from the hatchway to the place where it was being stowed.[48] Stowing operations thus came to depend upon a team of men, rather than upon a few specialist hold workers.

The packing of cargo and the rigging of gear were special skills which fell within the sphere of shipwork, and generally speaking it can be said that their relative importance tended to diminish under the impact of technological change. Despite this, however, the need for competent workers on board ship became more and not less pressing as the nineteenth century progressed. This was due to the increasing speed at which operations were carried out. Shipwork became more arduous, and, above all, more dangerous. The men working in the hold were required to work faster in order to keep up with the winches, and they received fewer periods of respite.[49] Employers in the 1880s continually stressed the fact that they needed strong men for the work and could not make do with inferior labour.[50] Stamina was the more necessary, in that the need for a quick 'turn-round' often subjected shipmen to long periods of continuous labour; often exceeding twenty-four hours.[51]

The presence of power-driven winches on the ship's deck also introduced certain comparatively new elements into shipwork. There is evidence to show that it made shipworkers a more homogeneous body by eliminating the crudest branch of the work—the manning of the hand winches.[52] It placed, moreover, a great responsibility in the hands of those men who remained on deck; the winch driver, and 'gangwayman' or 'hatchman', who directed the movements of the ship's gear.[53] The greater speed at which cargo was transferred between ship and shore required greater vigilance on the part of those at the seat of operations— the deck. The deckmen thus acquired a considerable status, and usually extra payments,[54] for upon their care depended the lives of the men in the hold. The employers in London did not always recognise the responsibility attaching to work on deck, and this was sometimes the occasion for bitter complaints by dockers. Old men and boys were used for the work, either for reasons of economy, or in order to release the stronger men for work in the hold.[55] Such practices were not general, however, for if employers did not always consider the lives of their employees they usually considered the safety of the cargo.

The demarcation-line between ship and shore work varied endlessly between different ports, and also with the operations being carried out. Generally, however, there were some ship-workers who were positioned on shore or in lighters. When the ship was taking in cargo, it was the job of these men to secure the goods for hoisting onto the ship. When the ship was discharging, these men sometimes received the 'sets' of goods being swung from ship to shore or lighter; the 'slinging' in this case being done by men in the hold.

It was perhaps the risk attaching to shipwork which above all perpetuated its isolation from quay labour.[56] The men on the ship were compelled by machinery to work at speed, in cramped and precarious positions, for long hours. There was a constant risk of cargo coming loose from the 'sets' and falling onto the men in the hatchway below; there was an equal risk of men falling down unprotected hatches or overboard. The risks of the work thus placed a premium on strength, competence and responsibility. Men were required to perform comparatively simple operations, but they were required to perform them quickly and without error. A mistake in the slinging of a set could mean the loss of life. A shipworker was thus obliged to rely absolutely on the proficiency of his workmates, and it was this atmosphere of mutual reliance which more than anything else bound shipmen together as a distinct group.[57] The circumstances of dock work were such that whereas it was possible to make do with inefficient workers on the quay, it was impossible to do so on the ship. Inexperienced shipmen put both the cargo and men's lives in jeopardy.

The shore work of any port falls naturally into two distinct spheres; quay labour and warehousing labour. The quay labourers were directly involved in the work of receiving or dispatching goods to or from cargo vessels; the warehouse worker was concerned with the handling and preparation for sale of goods in the warehouse. This latter work was often done outside the actual dock systems, and warehouse workers were therefore somewhat isolated from the general body of port workers.[58] Thus it is the field of quay work that is our immediate concern.

In broad terms the work of the quay labourer in the import trade consisted of the removal of goods from the ship's side to either an adjacent warehouse, or more often to a transit shed and thence to a vehicle of delivery.[59] The vehicle would then dispatch the goods either to an outside warehouse or direct to consumers. The second half of the nineteenth century saw virtually no change in the manual basis of the work, for the operations of the machinery introduced on the ship or quay were usually confined to the swinging of goods from ship to shore. Once on shore, the goods continued, as in Mayhew's day, to be 'trucked' into the sheds or warehouses by means of hand trucks. The trucking of goods on the quay was the most unskilled operation in dock work. Thus W. Langdon, writing in 1912, commented that absolutely unskilled labour in the docks 'is confined almost entirely to trucking, and some parts of the discharging and warehousing business. This is the work which is sought for by the lowest casual.'[60] It was not merely that the work was unskilled, it was also the least arduous sector of dock work, and thus boys were occasionally employed at it.[61] Perhaps the general attitude of employers towards this sphere of work was summed up by a Master Stevedore in his evidence to the Sweating Commission: 'We could not employ the inferior labour' he said, 'they are only fit for trucking.'[62]

Trucking was the staple of quaywork, although other operations scarcely more demanding were also present. In discharging operations the unit of quaywork, as with shipwork, was the ship's hatch. Thus the men were divided into gangs, each one receiving the goods coming from a particular hatchway. Some men were stationed at the ship's side to receive the goods, another group trucked them into the sheds and a third group piled the goods inside. Sometimes the work of delivery of goods to vans or barges went on simultaneously with the discharge of the vessel, and further men were therefore required to truck the cargo to its respective vehicle (in London usually a lighter). Of these operations, only the work of piling goods could be described as demanding.

The coming of the steamer, steam winch and quay crane did not of course leave quay work untouched, though they did not destroy its manual nature. The pace of the work inevitably tended to become faster for the goods came over the ship's side at a faster pace and therefore required quicker removal. In this connection, however, it is important to remember that the delivery of goods was an operation that did not always take place simultaneously with the discharging of the ship. As cargoes became bigger and more complex they came to require an elaborate process of sorting before they could be delivered. Taken as a whole, therefore, work on the quay was a more continuous process than shipwork, and one conducted at a slower pace. Cargo was turned out of a ship as rapidly as possible, in order that the vessel could be turned round with the maximum dispatch. Her cargo had, however, to be sorted to marks in the transit sheds, and might not be finally delivered until long after the ship had departed from the quayside. Congestion and inadequate sorting facilities usually further prolonged the process of delivery, especially in London.[63] Quaywork thus tended to be spread more evenly throughout the year than shipwork,[64] but it lacked generally what has been called the 'swing and rhythm' of work on board the vessel.[65] Broadly speaking, it was safer, lighter, less skilled and less intense. It might have been expected that the increased complexity of general cargoes, and the process of sorting which this entailed, would have demanded a more efficient type of labourer. In fact, however, the process of sorting was normally directed by foremen and did not draw on any expertise from the ordinary docker. The same thing applied to other precise operations, such as weighing.

In London, quay labour was not of course confined to the docks, for a large number of labourers were engaged at the riverside wharves in receiving cargoes either from small vessels or from lighters. The wharf labourers engaged in the unloading and trucking of goods from lighters were perhaps the least accomplished of all port workers. The reception of goods from lighters was an operation which involved none of the pressures or complexities which to some extent mitigated the purely unskilled nature of quay work in the docks. It is significant that in New York, a port which like London depended on lighterage, this work was performed by the notorious class of 'shenangoes'; the most demoralised and poverty-stricken element in the waterside population.[66]

The general survey of quaywork given above has been confined to labour in the import department, much the most important in London. The export branch of quay labour was on the surface merely the same operation as the import, only reversed. In fact, however, there was a considerable distinction. Long-distance vessels normally called at a number of ports, and consignments had therefore to be taken on board in a specific order, according to their various destinations. The correct stowing of a vessel therefore depended to a considerable extent on shore workers in the export department, for it was these men who marked the various articles for shipment and brought them in their proper order to the ship's side.[67] So close were the links between ship and shore operations in export work that in Liverpool the shipworkers did most of the quaywork in this sphere, carrying out the whole process of loading from the bringing of the cargo to the ship's side to the packing of it in the hold.[68] In London the two branches remained separate, but the export quayworkers constituted a distinct group among shore workers, and they partook of much of the status of shipmen. In the India docks, in fact, they acquired the nickname of 'gentlemen dockers'.[69] This separation between the export and import

divisions of quaywork was of course normally confined to ocean
shipping and little affected the short-sea trades.

3

The fundamental groupings of the port industry will by now have
emerged in their broad outlines. It is now time to sketch in the
more important details, especially those that were peculiar to
London. In the first place it must again be stressed that in the
port industry occupational groupings were as much related to
employment structure as they were to the nature of the work
performed. While the groupings noticed above were almost
universally applicable to the industry, they were subject to modifications from port to port due to variations in the character of the
employing concern. The predominant feature of London's
employment structure was the status of the dock companies as
employers of labour. This circumstance had a very considerable
influence on the character of the port's labour force and produced
one quite unique feature. Shipwork in the export trade was in
London performed by a separate class of men; instead of loading
and discharging being done by the same men, there existed two
groups of shipworkers.[70] This unique circumstance was the
result of employment structure.

The large-scale employment of labour by the managers of dock
enterprises has not been a common feature of the port industry. It
has no parallel in Liverpool or New York, for instance, where labour
has always been employed either by contractors acting on behalf of
shipowners and merchants, or by these latter directly.[71] In London,
however, from the beginning the work of discharging and warehousing at the London, St Katherine's, East and West India (and later
the Victoria, Albert and Tilbury) docks was under the control of the
companies.[72] At the Surrey and Millwall docks the managements
were not averse to letting some work out to contractors, but both
retained control of employment in their grain departments.[73] These
two companies apart, however, it can be said that in the docks of
London, up until the 1890s, only the work of loading vessels remained outside the control of the companies. Such work involved too
much responsibility,[74] and so from the beginning it was done by contractors, called 'master stevedores', who acted for the shipowners;
these employed their own labour. This unusual structure is chiefly
notable for the division it created among shipworkers, noted above.

The distinction was originally between those shipworkers in the employ of the companies, and those outside the latters' ambit.[75] The former were lumped together with quay workers under the generic title of 'dock labourers'. The latter group acquired at an early date the title of 'stevedores'. The sphere of employment of the stevedores can best be defined as that part of shipwork which was *not* under the control of the dock companies. In the docks managed by the London and East and West India companies this meant that the work of the stevedores was confined to the loading of vessels, for discharging operations in these systems remained the monopoly of the companies until 1891. The restriction of stevedores to the work of loading in the most important docks of the port has been responsible for the fact that the occupation has often been mistakenly defined as the work of stowing vessels.[76] This is understandable, for, due to the fact that the dock companies would not undertake loading work, the stevedores necessarily monopolised shipwork in the export trade, and thus came to be primarily identified, both in their own eyes and that of observers, with the work of stowing vessels.[77]

There can be no doubt that it was the stevedores' monopoly of export shipwork which enabled them to secure a status far above that of the ordinary shipworker. As was seen above, employers were often prepared to pay higher rates for loading work, and the stevedores' monopoly in this field enabled them to secure a substantial differential over the ordinary shipworker, who was confined to the less skilled branches of the work.[78] Yet it would be wrong to regard the stevedores purely and simply as a class of shipmen specialising in loading operations. In those docks where the companies did not monopolise the work of discharging— namely, the Millwall and Surrey systems—stevedores did un- loading work (though sometimes for reduced rates).[79] There existed a class of stevedores in Liverpool, but this group had little in common with the London men. In Liverpool the stevedores were a small class of highly skilled specialists who confined their activities to the packing of cargo in the ship's hold.[80] Such a class had existed in London until the 1870s and had enjoyed differentials in wage and status over the ordinary stevedore. These men had, however, lost their separate identity and become merged into the general body of stevedores.[81]

The London and India companies' monopoly of discharging had

thus drawn an artificial demarcation-line across the shipwork of the port. In every other port, export and import work was done by shipworkers indiscriminately. In London, export shipwork was divorced from the import department. This not only spread the work over a greater number of men than was necessary, it had the further effect of exaggerating the status of one group and depressing that of the other. This demarcation-line was viable only so long as the dock companies retained their control of discharging work. Shipowners did not gladly submit to the monopoly of the companies. They objected to paying for the discharge of their vessels, and pointed to the example of Liverpool where the shipowners were permitted to do their own discharging. As long as discharging operations yielded the companies a profit they ignored the protests of shipowners. It was only the 1889 strike and the subsequent mass unionism on the waterfront that induced the companies to hand over discharging work to the shipping-lines. They retained control of warehousing operations, and such discharging as was closely linked with their warehousing business, but in fact this meant that they virtually confined themselves to the upstream docks. The Victoria, Albert and Tilbury docks were left to the devices of the shipowners.[82]

Thus from the 1890s onward shipowners and their master stevedores performed unloading work as well as loading; who should do this work, stevedores or dockers?[83] The stevedores did unloading work at the Millwall and Surrey docks, and they claimed in 1890 the right to shipwork throughout all the docks.[84] In their view the dockers were not bona fide shipworkers and should be restricted to quay and warehouse work. The dockers, on the other hand, accustomed to discharging vessels at the London and East and West India companies' docks, claimed the right to discharge at the Millwall Docks also.[85] What was more, there seemed now to be no reason why they should not also load vessels. Export and import shipwork was done by the same men in other ports, why not in London? The position of the stevedores was basically a false one, and in the long run they were unable to retain their unique position.[86] In the short term, however, they were successful in defending and even extending their sphere of employment. The reasons for this success lie in the main outside the scope of this chapter, but certain points are relevant to this section. The composite group of shipworkers known as stevedores had hardened over the years into a distinct craft; a craft with its own traditions, loyalties and standards of workmanship. Thus employers after 1891 continued to pay high wages for the services of this accomplished group of port workers. This emergence of the stevedores as a distinct waterside craft was intimately associated with the fact that their original employers were essentially specialists in their field. For master stevedores shipwork was their *raison d'être*. They employed only shipworkers and they performed no other class of work. For those shipmen in the employ of dock companies the situation was different. It was not merely that workers in the employ of small contractors enjoyed a stronger bargaining power than those employed by large enterprises. Equally important was the fact that feelings of occupational identity tended to be smothered by large employment concerns. Inside these organisations shipwork constituted only a very small part of the total amount of work done: there was no specialisation, no traditions and no loyalties. In the conditions of the nineteenth-century casual dock labour market such enterprises were essentially anonymous and arbitrary. The cohesion of the stevedores as an occupational group was thus bound up with the small and specialised nature of the employing concerns in their sphere of employment.

The discussion of shipwork has so far been confined to the dock systems of the port, for it was here that the ocean shipping was received. Short-sea vessels, however, were received mainly at the riverside wharves or in the river itself. Shipwork in this sector was performed by a class of men distinct from both the 'stevedores' and 'dockers'. This division between the ocean and short-sea trades was common to all ports.[87] The latter class were considered to be inferior to the former in skills, and were usually paid at a lower rate. Apparently much less care was required in the stowing of vessels for short voyages than for long ones, and this would seem to have been the chief reason for the inferior status of short-sea shipmen.[88] By the end of the nineteenth century, however, the distinction appears to have become somewhat artificial, in London at any rate. Work in the short-sea trades had become to all intents and purposes as arduous and dangerous as in the ocean trades, and the hours worked were as long, if not longer.[89] The preservation of the old division probably had much to do with the different locations of the two branches of shipwork. Wage differentials were in fact based on these separate locations, work in the docks being paid for at a higher rate than work in the river or at the wharves. This differential existed, however, only between the stevedores and the short-sea workers, for the shipmen in the employ of the dock companies were paid at a lower rate than both the other groups. The demarcation-line between the stevedores and short-sea shipmen had, by the 1880s, become a rather shadowy one, for the latter class sometimes worked in the docks at the stevedores' rate of pay, while stevedores occasionally worked in the river at shipmen's rates.[90]

Short-sea shipworkers in London were not a homogeneous group and their status varied greatly according to their particular employment concern. The most coherent group amongst them, and the one which approximated closest to the stevedores in status, had the title of 'steamship workers'.[91] These men, like the stevedores, were employed by contractors, and their cohesion was obviously not unconnected with this circumstance. Other river shipworkers worked for shipping-lines such as the General Steam Navigation Company, and others still were attached to a particular wharf.[92] This latter group was normally the least privileged of the short-sea shipmen, and their status and rates of pay often approximated to those of the dock companies' shipworkers. This was not surprising, for the position of the two groups was somewhat similar. In neither field was the employer specialist, for they both controlled ship, shore and warehousing work. Thus at the wharves, no less than the docks, the occupational identity of shipworkers was stunted by a composite employing concern.

Prior to 1891 the shipwork of the port of London was performed by three main groups: dock company employees, stevedores, and short-sea shipworkers. Within the last group the steamship workers formed an enclave of cohesion. The changes of 1891 had the effect of greatly upgrading the first group, formerly the lowest in the hierarchy of shipworkers. The changes in the employment structure of the port after 1891 were also to affect shore no less than ship work. The status and remuneration of quay labourers, like shipworkers, was bound up with the character of their employing concern. Thus quay workers in London were regarded as being of a much lower calibre than their counterparts in Liverpool.[93] The basic reason for this difference in status appears to lie in the different employment structure of the two ports prior to 1891. Quaymen were, in Liverpool, employed by contractors called 'master porters', or by shipowners directly. Master porters were specialists in their sphere of work, just as master stevedores were specialists in shipwork. Furthermore master porters would not only confine themselves to quaywork generally, they would carry out this work on behalf of a limited number of merchants, in whose work they were thoroughly well versed. Employees of these small masters were thus permanently identified with some specific sector of dock work, and they became highly proficient workers in their own field of employment. In London prior to 1891 the situation was quite different. All operations within the London and East and West India companies' docks, with the exception of loading, came under the control of the dock companies; no matter whether it was ship, quay or warehouse work. In this situation what usually happened was that the best labour that could be obtained was put on the ship, and the residue was employed at trucking and piling on the quay.[94]

The dock companies in London were not themselves directly interested in the efficiency with which dock operations were carried out. Unlike contractors, they performed the work as of right and were not worried by competitors in the same field. Moreover, it was not their ships or goods that were being dealt with. Although they were under pressure from shipowners and merchants (who wanted respectively a quick turn-round for their vessels and rapid delivery of their goods) the companies had no direct personal interest in the work being done. Thus they were more ready to rely upon low-grade labour than shipowners, merchants or contractors would have been.[95] There was a plethora of such labour in London and it could be readily utilised in the undemanding sphere of quaywork. The companies were the more prepared to utilise cheap labour in view of their depressed condition in the second half of the century.[96]

Quay labour in the great north-bank docks of London was in the days of dock company employment inferior in status, calibre and conditions to that utilised in Liverpool.[97] Furthermore the control of employment by the dock companies meant that quay labourers were unable to specialise in the handling of any particular product, or identify themselves with the work of any particular line of ships. Feelings of occupational identity and professional pride were thus stunted, for the quay worker was employed indiscriminately on any line of vessels or type of produce. The change-over of 1891 transformed the position of the docker in the downstream docks of London. The monopoly of the London and East and West India companies in the import departments of their docks had had a disastrous effect upon the status of both shipmen and quaymen in this sphere, and the ending of this monopoly revolutionised the port's occupational status structure. The 1889 strike had established a minimum rate of 6d per hour for day work and 8d per hour for overtime.[98] Immediately the dock companies' monopoly was ended, however, wages rose again in those sectors now controlled by shipowners and contractors. By 1891 7d per hour day work and 1s overtime was being largely paid by shipowners in the Albert and Victoria docks. In certain cases, as in the discharge of frozen meat, dockers actually received the stevedores' rate of 8d per hour. In addition to the flat rate the new employers paid a large number of extra payments for work involving special dangers, unpleasantness or skills. Meal times were also paid for. These advantages did not accrue to those dockers in the upstream regions of the port where employment continued to be controlled by the companies. Here the rate of pay remained at the basic level of 6d and 8d, with no payment for dinner hours.[99]

The transformation of the status of the docker in the ocean trades was the direct result of the ending of the companies' monopoly. Shipowners and contractors had an immediate interest in the efficiency with which the work was performed, and they competed with each other for the services of the most proficient dock workers. They thus raised wages and conditions in order to attract to their service the pick of the waterside labour force.[100] In return for these conditions the men were expected to work harder and faster than before,[101] and there can be little doubt that after 1891 employment under shipowners and contractors was far more exacting than under the dock companies.

The lesson of 1891 was an important one and needs to be stressed. It was that in the dock industry the status of any one group was something that was essentially relative to the position of other groups. Thus the privileged position of the stevedores in London has to be seen against the background of the stunted occupational identity of ship and shore workers in the employ of the London and East and West India companies. Any scaling up in the general efficiency and cohesion of port workers as a whole was thus bound to affect the status of the more privileged group. The change-over of 1891 therefore led to ever more insistent demands by the dockers for equality of status with the stevedores.

4

Warehousing work in London and in most other ports was a field of employment somewhat distinct from the rest of waterside work. This was largely due to the fact that warehouses were often situated at a distance from the docks. Thus in London the bulk of the warehouses were either located in the City itself, or its immediate vicinity, and goods were either carted or lightered to them from the docks. Those warehouses that were actually situated within the docks were also concentrated upstream: at the London, St Katherine's and India systems. Here also goods were often lightered up from the downstream docks rather than being received direct from cargo vessels. Even where warehousing and shipping operations were carried on in close proximity to each other, as at some riverside wharves, the two departments were run independently of each other.[102] Warehouse workers were thus distinct from other port workers for topographical reasons. Until 1891 the London storage workers were also distinctive for another reason. Unlike the dockers at the great north-bank docks, they were permanently associated with the handling of a particular product.

Warehouses specialised generally in the housing and preparation for sale of a particular product or category of products, and the workers at these centres became habituated to the handling of one class of goods.[103] Their identification with a specific trade was further reinforced when a trade was concentrated in a well defined area. Such was the case in London, where the majority of tea and wool warehouses were situated in the City, grouped together under the title of 'uptown warehouses'. Similarly, there existed in Wapping a distinct group of warehouses known as 'colonial'. These dealt with sugar, coffee, cocoa and other tropical products. On the south bank much storage space was given over to the grain trade, and these granaries formed another distinctive group. The sense of occupational identity found among warehouse workers applied to those in the employment of the dock companies no less than to those working for outside proprietors, for in both spheres warehouses were specialist.

Warehouse work generally could not be described as a skilled operation.[104] When the work was of a demanding nature, it was essentially physical strength that was required rather than any expertise. The tea and wool trades were cases in point. The tea trade remained throughout the latter half of the nineteenth century largely seasonal in character, even though the steamer had reduced the length of the slack season. The wool trade, however, ceased to be genuinely seasonal, but activities tended to revolve around certain customary dates when the sales were held. Activity in these two spheres thus tended to be concentrated at certain periods of the year, and at these times work was carried out at very considerable pressure. During such periods of intense activity men were able to command high wages, either by working heavy overtime or through piece-work rates. In slack times they were condemned to long periods of idleness and sank deeper and deeper into debt.[105] For such men their specialisation was both the curse of their lives and its sole redeeming feature. Thus, while it condemned them to terrible irregularity of employment, it nevertheless gave them a status which lifted them out of the 'dustbin' of ordinary dock employment.[106] Thus the 'Wools' and 'Teas' of London regarded the ordinary casual docker as a very inferior being. When work was slack in their particular sphere they would search for employment in other sectors of warehousing, but they disdained to scramble at the dock gates for work. As one of Booth's investigators was told in 1891, they 'pride themselves on not being as "dockers" are'.[107]

There were other spheres of warehouse work less seasonal but not less arduous than tea or wool work, and here again there existed distinct occupational groups. The men engaged in housing frozen meat at the downstream docks were such a group, and they were able to command high wages at piece-work prices. It was rare for these men to touch any other goods besides refrigerated meat. Much labour in the sphere of warehousing was, however, not of a very arduous nature, nor was it carried out under any intense pressure. Such work was usually concerned with the preparation of goods for the market. Thus at the colonial wharves of Wapping much labour was expended in the 'working up' of products such as cocoa and coffee. The evidence is that the degree of expertise required for such labour was not high.

In London the superior status of storage to quay workers was only to a very small extent due to differentials in skills. Some experts there obviously were, but these must have been small in relation to the total numbers employed. The status of the warehouse worker, like that of the stevedore, was essentially relative to the degradation of ordinary port employment. The specialisation so characteristic of the warehouse worker was for long checked in the spheres of quay and ship labour by the employment system of the port. After 1891 this situation changed, and specialisation became a feature of port employment as a whole.[108]

5

In the above paragraphs the waterside labour force has been broken down into three broad groups—ship, quay and warehouse workers. Within these categories, it has been shown how employment structure influenced the formation of coherent occupational groups, and how it either encouraged or checked the tendency towards specialisation. Specialisation was based either upon the performance of a particular function, such as export shipwork, or upon the handling of a particular product, such as the housing of tea as opposed to grain. It was in the latter field that specialisation appeared most clearly to be the result of employment structure, rather than of any special features inherent in the work itself. Nevertheless different products did differ in the demands they made upon the labour that handled them, and it is necessary that this factor should be taken into account.

In the days before mechanical handling the heaviest branch of port labour was that concerned with bulk goods—namely, coal, corn, timber and, in Liverpool, salt. The handling of these respective products was often, though not always, performed by separate groups of labourers. Workers in these trades were generally paid by the piece and were in receipt of higher wages than the average waterside worker. Before the introduction of the elevator, the discharge of grain in bulk was perhaps the most demanding sphere of dock work.[109] The discharging was done in London by gangs of seven men, and the composition of the gang was virtually always the same, for the men were an *élite*. The grain had to be 'bushelled' into sacks in the hold of the vessel, weighed, and then swung ashore. The work was not only arduous, but also extremely injurious to the men's health, due to the grain dust in the hold. While his strength remained, however, the bulk-grain worker was rewarded by high wages and status. Where it was possible for him to do so he confined himself entirely to grain work. In the Surrey and Millwall docks, which largely specialised in the reception of grain cargoes, there existed gangs of shipmen who confined themselves entirely to the discharge of grain boats. In the Surrey Docks these men were referred to as 'overside corn porters', to distinguish them from the equally specialised, but less privileged, quay corn porters at this system. In the downstream docks, where bulk grain often arrived as a part cargo together with general goods, the corn gangs were unable to devote themselves entirely to the trade. They thus formed the pick of the shipworkers in the discharge of general cargo, though they disliked doing the lesser-paid work in this sphere.[110]

The workers who specialised in the manual discharge of grain vessels had to face a steady contraction in their sphere of employment in the last quarter of the nineteenth and early part of the twentieth centuries. Bulk grain lent itself to mechanical handling far more than general cargoes, and from the 1880s onward the grain elevator made inroads into the work of the corn gangs.[111] It was not merely a question of a displacement of men, but also of the destruction of a craft. When an elevator was used the only men required on the ship were trimmers, and their work was regarded as 'unskilled'.[112] Thus in the Surrey Docks the overside corn porters completely dissociated themselves from machine work, which was performed by a separate group of men; to perform other than manual discharging work was in their eyes to lose 'caste'.[113]

The shore corn porters[114] were as specialised a group as the overside men, but as shore workers their status and remuneration was inferior to the shipworkers. Shore grain workers as a distinct occupational grouping were confined to the south bank of the river, and their cohesion owed much to the localisation of the trade in this area. Their work, though more demanding than normal quaywork, was much less arduous than grain shipwork, and they would not have remained so distinctive a group without this localisation. Until the last quarter of the nineteenth century the landing and warehousing of grain had been largely confined to the south side of the river. Grain vessels were unloaded at the Surrey Docks, and the corn was either stored there in the companies' granaries, or was transported by lighter to the numerous granaries that were built along the river bank in Rotherhithe and Bermondsey. Thus the handling of corn was bound to become a specialism for men residing in the neighbourhood, for it was, together with timber, almost the only product received there on any scale.[115]

Timber work, even more than corn, was an intensely localised sector of employment, though this statement applies to the softwood rather than the hardwood trade. The former trade was centred almost entirely upon the Surrey Docks. The intensely specialised nature of work in the softwood sector was not, however, merely a product of localisation. On the contrary the work formed one of the most genuinely skilled branches of waterside labour. Reversing the pattern normally found in the industry, in the timber department it was the shore workers who surpassed the shipmen in skill. The shipworkers who discharged the timber vessels had formed a distinct group in Mayhew's day, and were known then as 'lumpers'.[116] The specialisation of south-side shipworkers in the timber trade was somewhat inevitable, for the only other work available was in corn. There was little interchange between the grain and timber departments, for at first both trades were dependent upon the Baltic season, so that their slack and busy periods tended to coincide. In any case, grain shipwork became concentrated in the hands of the overside corn porters in the employ of the Surrey Commercial Dock Company, while the lumpers worked for contractors. The work of the lumpers was very arduous and required considerable experience, but it was the shore workers who were the highly skilled men in this sphere. Once the timber had been discharged and piled upon the quay by the lumpers, all the work subsequently done on the shore was performed by a group of men called 'deal porters'.[117] Of all shore workers in London these men were the most skilled and the highest paid. They removed the deals from the quayside to the piling grounds, where they were sorted and piled awaiting final delivery. These operations were done entirely by hand and required great strength and dexterity. The work of merely carrying the deals was arduous enough, but the process of piling them high into stacks was highly dangerous and would have been impossible for unskilled labourers. The continued dependence of the soft-wood trade upon the Baltic season, however, rendered the timber workers subject to long spells of idleness. As with the 'Wools' and 'Teas' their specialisation was thus far from being an unmixed blessing.

Coal, together with timber and corn, formed the chief items of heavy merchandise received by the port of London. The work of unloading colliers in London was originally carried out by a process called 'whipping', and up until the mid-century the coal boats were all discharged in midstream in the pools by a group of specialist workers known as 'coal-whippers'.[118] The coal-whippers much resembled the overside corn porters of the Surrey docks, for they were an extremely close-knit group and were concentrated in a compact neighbourhood—in this case Wapping and Shadwell. The cohesion of the coal-whippers as a group was, however, undermined long before that of the corn gangs. Hydraulic machinery gradually replaced the manual whipping process, and the work, instead of being concentrated in the pools, was scattered over numerous docks and wharves. By the mid-1880s this process had advanced far and coal-whipping as a distinct occupation was fast disappearing. By this period, however, the steamship was being introduced at an ever increasing pace, and it appears that some of the redundant whippers turned to the work of loading these vessels with coal as fuel.[119] In the 1890s the work of bunkering steamers was still largely a manual process, in which hand winches continued to be used,[120] and so the whippers must have found their new work not too far removed from the old. They carried all their sense of occupational identity into their new work, and as 'coalies' they continued therefore as a specialised group of shipworkers. Like the corn porters, their sphere of employment was, however, gradually encroached upon by mechanical innovations, for the work of bunkering vessels was increasingly carried out by machinery. In 1912, however, the old hand methods of the winch coalies were still not entirely obsolete.[121]

Under the impact of mechanical changes in the coal trade the coal-whippers had thus been transformed into 'winchmen', and as such they had come to undertake shipwork other than discharging. The actual unloading of colliers passed into the hands of a different class of men. It appears that coal-whippers, no less than overside corn porters, were dissociated from the new methods of mechanical discharge. The unloading of coal vessels had been gradually transferred from the pools to a number of 'stations' in the docks or river.[122] These stations made use of hydraulic machinery, but, in the absence of the grab crane, the work of the tank fillers in the hold of the vessel differed little from that of coal

shipmen in an earlier period. The men continued to work in
regular gangs at piece-work rates, and to earn high wages. The
work also remained extremely arduous and unhealthy, and, as in
other spheres of shipwork, operations were carried out at speed.
The tank fillers, however, never developed into such a well
defined occupational grouping as the coal-whippers had been.
Unlike this latter group, they were scattered over a number of
docks and wharves, and because coal ships were discharged more
and more at quays and wharves, instead of in midstream, the coal
shipmen developed closer links with other branches of coal
workers. These links were not only with shore workers in the
seaborne trade, but also with workers in the inland coal trade. They
came in fact to regard themselves as coal workers rather than as
port workers, and ceased therefore to be an essentially riverside
grouping.

The specialisation of the coal, timber and grain handlers was
not an artificial one. It was found to a greater or lesser degree in
most ports, and was based primarily upon the heavy labour
entailed in dealing with these goods. In London, however, the
separate identity of corn and deal porters was clearly reinforced by
the early concentration of these trades in a particular sector of the
port. Complete specialisation was possible and indeed inevitable
on the Surrey side, for the corn and timber trades were isolated
from the other commercial activities of the port. The corn gangs
which grew up in the newer areas of the port never exhibited the
cohesion of the overside corn porters, because, for one thing, they
were unable to confine themselves entirely to the grain trade. The
cohesion of the occupational groupings on the south side also
owed much to tradition. These groups had roots which stretched
right back to the beginning of the dock era and perhaps beyond.
This long record of continuous specialisation gave to the groupings
of grain and timber workers in London a rigidity that was quite
exceptional in the port industry.

Specialisation in the handling of items of heavy merchandise
was, however, only one form of product specialisation. After 1891
port workers generally attached themselves to the work of a
particular shipping-line, and became experts in the trade with
which it was primarily concerned—meat or fruit, for example.
Specialisations such as these were, however, so numerous that
they rarely resulted in the creation of distinctive occupational

groups. In these cases product specialisation resulted essentially from the system of employment and the attitudes such a system engendered among port workers. Only in the case of bulk goods did product specialisation genuinely result from the nature of the work performed.

6

The labour force of a great port was, as we have seen, an immensely complex body. The diversity of products handled and of functions performed, together with the large number and variety of employers, was bound to make this the case. The casual system had reinforced these tendencies by restricting workers to particular localities and types of work. This lack of cohesion among the body of port workers was strengthened in the early days by the manner in which they were recruited.

Waterside labour was, in many of its departments, an extremely arduous occupation. The inferior physical condition of the Londoner in the eighteenth and nineteenth centuries only fitted him for the less exacting branches of the work,[123] such as trucking on the quay. In most of the heavier manual occupations of the metropolis it had long been the practice of employers to rely on English rural immigrant labour,[124] but this was not the case on the waterfront. Countrymen avoided the waterside,[125] largely owing to the stigma attaching to the work. It was thus the Irish who took over the more arduous branches of waterside work. Already in the middle of the eighteenth century it was reported that two-thirds of the men engaged in unloading coal boats were Irish.[126] By the middle of the nineteenth century an observer could remark that 'in London the loading and unloading of ships, and the principal hard work all down the river, was done by Irishmen'.[127] The vigorous Irish labourer was especially welcome to employers in occupations of a taxing nature, such as coal, corn and timber work, and in shipwork generally. While the numbers of Irish tended to decline in the less demanding work after the falling off of immigration (from 1851 onward),[128] in the better paid work their dominance was permanent. The work was passed down from father to son, and the second generation of Irish inherited the pick of the work along the waterfront.[129]

In the long run the Irish element brought stability and cohesion to wide areas of waterside employment. In particular, the tradition of son following father in the work did much to raise the calibre of the labour force. At the outset, however, the consequences of the Irish immigration were disastrous.[130] The gross ignorance and poverty of the immigrant placed him at the mercy of his employers, and the workers in the coal, timber and ballast trades were for long enmeshed in a vicious truck system.[131] Furthermore the Irish were intensely clannish. They crowded into distinct localities, such as Wapping and St Georges, and lived and worked in self-contained communities, quite apart from other workers in neighbouring districts and trades.[132] In short, they accentuated the tendency for the waterside labour force to become fragmented into little isolated groups, between whom there was little contact or co-operation.

Isolated from each other, waterside groupings were even more cut off from other industrial workers, and no doubt the Irish immigration contributed also to this effect. Dock work, like mining, is an essentially localised occupation, and demands that its labour force should reside in close proximity to the place of work.[133] In London, the port's labour force was packed into the congested urban areas that developed along the river banks; on the north bank Wapping, Stepney, Poplar and West Ham: on the south side Bermondsey, Rotherhithe, Deptford.[134] The Irish, with their close-knit family groups, and allegiance to the Roman Catholic Church, gave to these areas much of their distinctiveness. Unfortunately, however, the most distinctive mark of all waterside districts was poverty.[135] Poverty that resulted from the most distinctive feature of the dock labour market—oversupply.

3 The Earliest Unions, 1870–89

THE characteristics of the port's labour force, noted in the previous chapter, did not make for an easy growth of trade unionism. The localised character of the port industry might be thought to be a factor favouring organisation, as in the case of coal mining, but localisation does not in itself produce stable and cohesive communities conducive to union growth. A large sector of port employment, quay work mainly, was open to constant infiltration from outside, from the unemployed of other trades, so that the waterside population existed in a state of constant flux. It was furthermore, as we have seen, a population that had been inflated by the casual system to a size far beyond the real requirements of the port. Only in quite exceptional circumstances did labour shortages occur, so that normally employers had little difficulty in replacing troublesome employees. Nevertheless there are references to strikes on the London waterfront extending back at least as far as the eighteenth century.[1] In the age of sail the work of the port was sometimes held up by long spells of adverse winds, and, in the feverish activity that followed, workers could exploit the situation by indulging in sudden stoppages. Times of trading prosperity, as in the early 1850s, also provided port workers with an opportunity to improve their position by industrial action.[2] This record of sporadic industrial activity was, however, unaccompanied by any evidence of trade union organisation, until 1871 at any rate. Undoubtedly rudimentary clubs of port workers must have existed in the metropolis before this date, especially among shipworkers of various kinds, but there was nothing resembling a formal trade union with sophisticated rules and objectives. In the years 1871–2, however, a change took place. The early 1870s were exceptionally prosperous years for the British economy, and, as in the 1850s, they were marked by successful strike action on the London waterfront. This time,

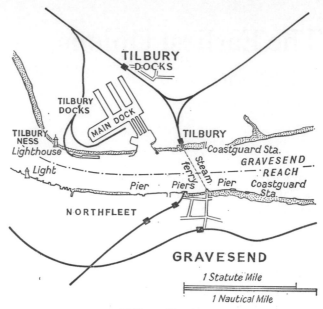

Tilbury Docks.

however, the strike was accompanied by the formation and development of trade unions on a large scale. A breakthrough had been made into the sphere of modern trade union activity.

The movement had its origins in July 1871.[3] Colonel du Plat Taylor had recently been appointed Secretary of the East and West India Dock Company, and his efforts to restore the declining fortunes of that company led to economies in the labour field. In July an alteration was made in the system of payment which meant in effect a reduction of wages from 20s to 15s a week. The dockers appear to have been slow to react to this development, but ultimately one of their number, a Mr Caulfield, organised a meeting at some schoolrooms in the East End. The rector of Bethnal Green, the Reverend Hansard, was asked to preside at the meeting. The tone of this gathering was extremely interesting, and was no doubt largely set by Hansard. The speeches that were made, both by the rector and by dockers, were to the effect that the labourers were too weak to organise. Unions were for the labour aristocrats, all that labourers could do was to throw themselves on the mercy of public opinion. Any attempt at strike action would merely result in the strikers being replaced by other workers. Here we can see at work the conventional wisdom of the mid-Victorian labour movement, the notion that unionism was a device relevant only to skilled artisans.[4] These views found further expression in the editorial columns of the *Eastern Post*, a paper that devoted considerable space to labour activity in the East End. Referring to the dockers' meeting, it commented:

> The men are comparatively helpless in the matter. They are so poor that a strike or even a combination with a view to joint action is not to be thought of. They can only appeal to the companies to reconsider the whole question, and ask the public to sustain that appeal.[5]

Within a month, however, the *Eastern Post* had another meeting to report. The dockers were again gathered at the Bethnal Green schoolrooms, but this time Patrick Hennessey was in the chair. Hennessey's influence was of a kind altogether different from that of Hansard. An Irish trade unionist and tailor by trade, Hennessey was also a prominent member of the Land and Labour League, and as such his attitude towards 'unskilled' labour diverged sharply from the traditional standpoint.[6] The meeting reported in the *Eastern Post* on 26 November 1871 was for the purpose of establishing a trade union among the dock labourers to resist the reduction of wages, and at the meeting a society was duly formed and Caulfield (the originator of the agitation) elected as its Secretary.[7] A further meeting took place the following month, at which Hennessey again presided.[8] Also present on this occasion was Charles Keen, Secretary of the English Federal Council of the International Working Men's Association, and, like Hennessey, active in the Land and Labour League. Both men were firm believers in the possibility and desirability of organising the 'unskilled', and Keen had considerable experience in the field of labour organisation.[9] At the December meeting an effort was made to get the new society properly established; entrance fees and subscriptions were fixed, draft rules submitted, and provision made for the establishment of branches in various parts of London and in the provinces. The union also received a title; The Labour Protection League.

The Labour Protection League did not get off to a flying start. As George Shipton, a member of the aristocratic trade union establishment who had taken an interest in the formation of the

league, was to remark, 'hitches were inherent in the first formation of most trade societies'.[10] The hitch in question seems to
have sprung from Mr Caulfield's method of celebrating his
appointment as Secretary—namely, by decamping with the union's
funds. The decision of Hennessey and Keen to encourage dockers
to run the new society themselves from the very start had thus
had unfortunate consequences. Caulfield's defection came close to
killing the new-born league. The fact that it did not die appears to
have been largely due to the appearance on the scene of a Mr T.
Venner, an employee of a City tea merchant, who probably gave
financial help at the critical moment. Together with Hennessey
and Keen, Venner bears the main credit for the successful launching of the union. In January 1872 adherents of the league met
once more at the Bethnal Green schoolrooms to repair the damage
that had been done. Shipton took the chair this time, but
Hennessey and Keen were much in evidence again. The appointment of Caulfield as Secretary was cancelled, and, on the recom-
mendation of Venner, a Mr Ellwood was elected to succeed him.
Unfortunately this choice was to prove scarcely more fortunate
than that of Caulfield. Venner himself was chosen as Treasurer.[11]

The Labour Protection League had been founded as a result of
the unrest among the dockers at the East and West India Company's docks. It had been this unrest which had drawn Hennessey,
Keen and Venner into activity on behalf of port workers. They
had ousted Hansard, the first outsider to be involved, and set up a
trade union in order to redress the dockers' grievances. The
league made little progress, however, in enrolling dock labourers
among its membership. In this respect the Caulfield episode had
hardly helped, but ordinary dockers were in any case difficult to
organise; they were poverty stricken, without any corporate tradition, and very much at the mercy of the dock company when it
came to employment opportunities. It seems very likely that much
of the support for the league in its earliest days came not so much
from dockers strictly so-called, as from workers at the tea and
other warehouses in the City and inner East End. Even here,
however, the league's following was certainly very limited. It was
in the event the stevedores who were really the first to take
advantage of the framework which Hennessey had provided for
formal trade union activity.

It would not be strictly true to speak of the stevedores as being organised by the Labour Protection League, for it is virtually certain that the stevedores in Poplar had formed an organisation on their own account, even before the league was launched.[12] By January 1872 this society had affiliated to the league as Branch No. 3.[13] The formation of the league did, however, greatly stimulate further activity on the part of the stevedores. During the spring of 1872 union membership in this occupational group mounted rapidly. At one meeting 250 stevedores were reported as enrolling in a body. The rules of the league fixed the membership of branches at 500, and so in April, the stevedores' membership having surpassed this level, a second branch was opened in Poplar, becoming No. 4 of the league.[14] In view of this great activity the league held a public meeting in Poplar towards the end of March.[15] Ellwood took the chair, and Hennessey, Keen and Venner were the principal speakers. It was, however, notice-able that the stevedores took a prominent part in the proceedings and one of their number, a Mr Haley, was subsequently to play a prominent part in the league's leadership.[16] At the end of April the total membership of the Labour Protection League was about 1200, and it is probable that the majority of members were stevedores.[17] The organisation of this group continued into the summer. By the beginning of June, 1400 stevedores had enrolled, and Branch No. 3 had split into two sections, so as to be able to contain the flood of recruits.[18] When organisation was complete, in August 1872, there were five stevedore branches (six if the two sections of No. 3 are counted) with a total membership of about 3000.[19]

The rapid growth of the stevedores' organisation at last triggered off developments in other sectors of the port. Trade was good and, with the arrival of summer, much of the surplus labour on the waterfront was drawn off into other industries.[20] The port workers' bargaining power was at its peak. The first men to follow the example of the stevedores were the wharf workers, especially the shipmen. During the course of May branches were rapidly formed in Wapping, Southwark, Horsleydown and Green-wich.[21] The first and most powerful of the new branches was No. 5 at Horsleydown, composed mainly of employees of the General Steam Navigation Company. By the end of June this branch numbered 750.[22] Organisation also developed among the corn porters on the south side and at Millwall, both those working in the riverside granaries and at the docks. Spreading outward from the most coherent and strategically placed occupational groups, the league went on to embrace almost the entire waterside labour force. The pace of organisation was terrific. At the end of April, as we have seen, the total membership of the league was 1200. At the beginning of July it was reported as being 12,000.[23] In October it was 30,000.[24] By this time there were fifty-four branches. Not all of the 30,000 members were port workers. Hennessey, Venner and Keen thought of the league in terms of a general labour organisation. It was stated in the summer of 1872 that while the union consisted in the main of port workers, it was intended to embrace other groups; builders' and engineers' labourers being specifically mentioned.[25] Some workers in the latter category were enrolled at Millwall, and the league also enrolled numbers of dustmen, slopmen and scavengers in the East End.[26] In Deptford an attempt was made to enrol coal porters and carmen, but these groups were mainly recruited by organisations independent of the league, as were certain categories of warehousemen.[27] The Labour Protection League remained basically a port workers' organisation, but it contained pockets of men in other trades who lived and worked in the waterside districts. This was a pattern that was to be followed by the unions set up in 1889. Geographically it seems that the main strength of the league was concentrated on the south side. Many years later an old member estimated that 18,000 of the total membership of 30,000 were on the south bank.[28] Whether or not this figure is accurate, events seventeen years later were to demonstrate how deep were the roots of the league on the Surrey side.

The expansion of organisation was accompanied by a large-scale movement for improved wages and conditions. There was little co-ordination from the centre. Instead each branch, or group of branches, acted when it felt the time was ripe. Considerable success was achieved in this manner. The stevedores' movement will receive separate consideration.[29] So far as the general mass of waterside workers was concerned, it was the men at the wharves who set the pace, especially those on the south side. The movement got under way at the beginning of June 1872.[30] One by one the wharves and short-sea shipping companies were struck and concessions were invariably obtained. The men wanted an increase in the hourly day rate and extra payment for overtime. Day rates

The quayside: two pictures of the quay at the Albert Dock. Note the hand trucks.

Dockers: waiting to be called-on for work (above), *and on strike*

were pushed up from 3*d* or 4*d* to 5*d* or sometimes 6*d*, but occasionally employers jibbed at an extra penny for overtime work. In general the men showed a desire to extract the maximum possible advantage, whereas Venner and Keen, who constantly made an appearance at trouble spots, advised 'moderation in demands and demeanour'.[31] As in the great movement of 1889, the leadership wished to win permanent recognition for the union, and was anxious lest extravagant demands by the men should lead to the complete alienation of the wharfingers. Towards the end of June a conference was organised between the Labour Protection League and various wharfingers (organised in the Wharfingers' Association). At the meeting the wharfingers complained of the policy of selective action, whereby the wharves had been struck one by one, instead of demands being presented to them in a body. They also felt aggrieved because no action had been taken as yet against the dock companies, who were of course their competitors. Unless demands were pressed in this sphere they felt unable to make further concessions. So far as the first point was concerned, the fact was that it was to the men's advantage to attack the wharves singly. As Venner, the men's spokesman, admitted, 'there was a time or season when each wharf or warehouse could be more successfully treated with. The men themselves knew the seasons of each particular business and action was probably taken on these grounds. It would be useless to strike just when wharfingers or warehousemen invited'.[32] A wharf handling perishable goods was of course particularly vulnerable to attack at its busy season.[33] As for the dock companies, the league had not as yet acted there because it did not feel strong enough. Venner implied as much when he told the wharfingers 'that strikes this side of the water [the south side] were necessary to try the strength of the society before the large docks were interfered with'.[34] It was one thing bringing pressure to bear upon a small specialised concern at its most vulnerable time. It was quite another to attack the large dock companies on the north bank; companies which were, by the standards of the time, very large enterprises indeed, with correspondingly great powers of resistance. The upshot of the conference with the Wharfingers' Association was an agreement to suspend strike activity for one week, after which further talks were to take place. Talks were indeed resumed, but they quickly broke down and the leadership acquiesced in the strike activity that followed.[35]

This renewed activity did not, however, last long. Virtually all the wharves conceded the 5*d* day rate, with 6*d* per hour overtime. This was the minimum, and some shipmen, such as the employees of the General Steam Navigation Company, obtained higher rates.[36]

The leadership of the league knew that sooner or later it would have to tackle the docks. The wharfingers would be loath to accept the new wage rates for long unless the dock companies could be brought up to the same standard. In any case, the league was pledged to improve conditions at the docks, and had indeed been founded with this object. Organisation was, however, still weak at the docks in the early summer of 1872, and no doubt the union's leaders were wary of taking any action until the position improved. Perhaps also they hoped that the companies would concede an increase without a struggle. In the event the men forced their hand. On 25 June the dockers at the West India Dock struck for an advance from 4*d* to 6*d* per hour, and the stoppage quickly spread to the other docks of that company.[37] In response to the men's request, the league organised a meeting at Stepney Green and Ellwood came down to speak. He reproved the dockers for acting without prior consultation, but, now that the battle was joined, he advised them all to organise themselves into branches of the union.[38] The company at first refused concessions, and made an attempt to obtain alternative labour, but in the boom conditions prevailing in the summer of 1872 it met with limited success.[39] The strike spread to the other dock companies. The Millwall company had expected trouble earlier in the year and had accordingly increased its permanent staff (this was a device that was to be used to the full against the unions in the years ahead). It had tried to persuade the other companies to take similar precautions, but to no effect. Now it was involved along with the rest, for the strikers at the India docks persuaded the Millwall men to leave work.[40] The London and St Katherine's docks were also brought more or less to a standstill.[41] After a few days of disruption the companies offered the men a penny per hour increase and extra payment for overtime, bringing their rate up to the 5*d* and 6*d* level conceded by the wharfingers. Although this was less than the men had originally demanded, they returned to work on this basis.[42] Trade being extremely buoyant, the increased costs were passed on by the companies to port users.[43] Shortly afterwards the companies also began to safeguard themselves against further strikes by gradually increasing their permanent staffs, as the Millwall management had advised. This policy was, however, later put into reverse when the companies were beset with financial difficulties in the 1880s.[44]

By early July 1872, the vast majority of London port workers had obtained wage increases and the membership of the league was growing by leaps and bounds. It was at this juncture, with enthusiasm at its height, that the men's leadership staged a massive demonstration of strength in the East End. The description in the local Press is worth quoting at length, if only to serve as a reminder that mass unionism on the London waterfront began in 1872, not in 1889—the year of the great dock strike.

On Thursday evening, the League and its well-wishers assembled to the number of upwards of 20,000, with bands and flags in the neighbourhood of the Town Hall, Shoreditch. The different sections marched thither in good order from along the river side, from Stratford and other eastern outlying districts, and from Southwark and Horsleydown. These branches assembled at the Old Rose Inn, Russell Street, Horsleydown, and marched from there with band and banners, under the superintendence of Mr. Dunmoody and the committee. The utmost order prevailed. The whole end of Old Street from the Town Hall right round into Shoreditch was densely filled, and as many as could find room in the Town Hall entered it, and formed a meeting, presided over by the Reverend Hansard. The rest, headed by bands, proceeded into Hoxton Market where an open air meeting was held.[45]

It was almost exactly a year since du Plat Taylor had introduced his labour economies into the India docks and so paved the way for the foundation of the league. The origins and development of this union must, however, be seen in a context wider than that of the London waterfront. Stimulated in part by the great Nine Hours Movement of engineers on Tyneside in 1871, masses of labourers in many parts of the country and in many occupations flocked to join unions in the early 1870s. Railwaymen, seamen, carmen, agricultural labourers, gas workers, as well as port workers were involved. In Derby, in February 1872, a union for general labourers was formed with the title Labour Protection Association; clearly the Labour Protection League in London was no isolated phenomenon.[46] No doubt scenes such as that described above were re-enacted many times and in many places during the course of the hectic summer of 1872.

The resolutions passed at the mass meeting in Shoreditch Town Hall looked forward to further improvements in the conditions of the mass of London port workers. In particular, a 6d minimum rate and the abolition of contract work at the docks and ware-houses were demanded. (Both these demands, unfulfilled in the 1870s, were to be taken up again in 1889, though not by the league.) While the Shoreditch meeting was on the whole an impressive display of the league's strength, it did not pass off entirely harmo-niously. All was not well with the leadership of the union, and Charles Keen took the opportunity of the meeting to bring the problem into the open. The immediate problem was trivial enough, comic even. Not long before, the Prince of Wales had visited the East End to open the Bethnal Green Branch of the South Kensington Museum. An address had been presented to the prince on this occasion by the Reverend Hansard, ostensibly acting on behalf of the league. Keen now told the meeting that he was going to reveal the background to this affair, which, he suggested, would make the members' hair stand on end. Not surprisingly, Keen's pronouncement caused a sensation. The full story followed hard upon the meeting.[47] In the first place it appeared that Hansard had presented the address without troubl-ing to obtain the sanction even of a single branch of the league. Secondly, Ellwood, who had supported Hansard in this matter, had obtained tickets for the committee of No. 1 branch to attend the opening ceremony. As this meant losing time at work the committee compensated themselves out of the branch funds. Furthermore they entertained themselves to dinner, also at the expense of the branch. As a trustee of Branch No. 1, the original nucleus of the league, Keen was well aware of what was going on and he had no scruples about revealing it publicly.

The affair described above was trivial enough in itself, but it raised certain questions concerning the constitution and policy of the league. In the first place, Keen's anxiety to bring the incident into the open was in all probability due not only to indignation over the improper use of the funds, but also to a desire to rid the league of the conservative and traditionalist element in its leader-ship. Hansard's address was to him 'Toadyism and Twaddle', and it was intolerable that it should be allowed to pass as representative of league opinion.[48] But there was also a constitutional question involved. Hansard, Ellwood, and their clique enjoyed a status in the league out of all proportion to their official position. It is not clear whether Hansard had any position in the union at all. Ellwood was officially Secretary of Branch No. 1. The trouble was that the league had grown into a large organisation without any proper provision being made for representative government. It is true that as soon as a number of branches had been formed an executive council was established, consisting of delegates from each branch. Such a council was formed at the end of April.[49] It met at the Three Compasses, Mile End, as this was the meeting-place of No. 1 Branch, which had transferred its headquarters from the schoolrooms in Bethnal Green. Once established, the council certainly met regularly, and in the middle of June delegates were reported as attending 'from the City, Greenwich, Horsleydown, Limehouse, Poplar, Southwark, Tooley Street and Wapping'.[50] The council in its turn sent delegates to the London Trades Council.[51] The central body did not, however, possess any officers of its own. Instead Ellwood, as Secretary of the original branch, acted as the union's principal official. Together with the rest of the Branch No. 1 Committee, he constituted in effect the league's leadership. Venner, the Branch's Treasurer, chaired the council meetings. He had played the greatest role in the early organising activity and was already by the summer of 1872 being referred to as 'the founder of the league'.[52] It was noticeable, however, that Keen made no attempt to cast aspersions on Venner's integrity when he launched his attack on the Branch No. 1 Committee, even though the latter was in a vulnerable position by virtue of his office as branch treasurer. Subsequent investigations in fact cleared Venner of any responsibility for what had happened.[53]

The speech of Keen in Shoreditch Town Hall was certainly something of a shock to the union. Shortly after the Shoreditch gathering, the council met to consider the position. Venner was in the chair, and he explained that 'through the rapid increase of lodges and enrolment of members, the council had not been in thorough working order'.[54] An attempt now had to be made to establish proper constitutional machinery for the union, and he told the delegates that it was their duty to elect a President, Secretary, Treasurer and Trustees. In the election that followed

Venner himself was returned as President without opposition. His reputation in the league stood very high indeed; he had in fact been recently dismissed by his employer for his union activities.[55] The election for Secretary produced some excitement, as Keen and Ellwood were the two candidates. The latter was, however, able to muster only three votes, so that Keen, who had previously been Secretary of Branch No. 5 (probably the largest in the union), was able to enjoy what must have been a considerable personal triumph. As if to symbolise the change in the character of the league's leadership that had taken place, the executive council, having completed the elections, left the Three Compasses at Mile End and resumed its meeting at the Crown and Anvil, Swan Street, Minories. This establishment was then adopted as the future union headquarters. Ellwood and his clique were thus effectively ousted from their general position of influence in the league. Nonetheless they retained their hold on No. 1 Branch, much to the annoyance of Keen. In September the Secretary was reporting to the council 'that if the committee of No. 1 Branch continued to introduce politics into their branch, opposed to the working classes, the members of No. 1 Branch must be appealed to, in order to prevent their dividing the league. Such a course was playing into the hands of employers and open to the gravest suspicion.'[56] It is not clear precisely what game Ellwood was playing (whether or not, for instance, he was involved in Tory politics), but his views were certainly not those of the Land and Labour League or the International Working Men's Association.

The elections of July 1872 gave to the Labour Protection League a properly constituted central government. The question for the future was whether or not this government would be able to effectively control and co-ordinate the activities of the fifty or so branches. The centrifugal forces operating within the league were very strong indeed. Branches had been formed upon the basis of occupational grouping,[57] and among the more coherent and strategically placed groups a sense of sectional interest was highly developed. Some waterside occupations had in fact remained outside the league, the men electing instead to form their own independent societies. This was the case with the coal-whippers and lightermen, both of whom formed their own separate unions during the course of 1872.[58] Separatism was based primarily upon two factors. First, there was the question of job monopoly. Some of the branches of the league, No. 33, for instance, composed of overside corn porters, were made up of men who were organised by their employers in regular gangs which always had first preference in the work.[59] For such gangs the preservation of this system of local job control was the one thing that really counted. Solidarity with other riverside workers was very much a secondary consideration. In the second place, there was the sheer diversity of the waterside labour force, a point dealt with at some length in the last chapter. This diversity manifested itself in endless variations in conditions of employment; rates of pay, systems of payment, make-up of gangs, working customs, all these differed endlessly. In great ports like London or New York this complexity was to raise acute problems for unionism;[60] its immediate effect was to impede the development of a sense of common identity among port workers as a whole. Such a sense was certainly notably lacking in the early days of waterside unionism. The central government of the league must have found itself in a situation similar to that described by James Sexton, the well-known Liverpool dockers' leader.[61] In his autobiography he recounts how, when he took over the leadership of the Liverpool union in 1893, he found himself at the head of what was virtually a federation 'of almost innumerable small clubs and societies all hostile to each other'.[62]

Keen and Venner worked hard to combat the disintegrating forces within the league. Their task was the more difficult in view of the suspicion and distrust that developed in the union as a result of the exposure of Ellwood and his colleagues. The bulk of the funds of the league were held by the branches for their own use, but there had been some mutual assistance between the lodges in financial matters. Quarrels now developed over these transactions. Within individual branches suspicion was also aroused about the uses to which funds were being put by the branch committee. Venner travelled around addressing branch meetings. He warned the members against giving credence to rumours, any malpractices could be properly investigated and dealt with by men appointed for that purpose. The members, he urged, should in these and other matters make use of the executive council of the union, and not allow local disputes and misunderstandings to divide the league and undermine the fabric of unionism.[63] This was exactly the sort of campaign that Sexton was to conduct twenty years later in Liverpool.[64] In August 1872 the council took a big step forward towards increasing the effectiveness of the central government.[65] On the initiative of the south-side representatives, it was decided to appoint district delegates, who were to act on behalf of the executive in the localities. For this purpose the league was divided into three sectors: (1) the City, Stepney and Mile End, (2) Greenwich, Deptford, Woolwich and Southwark, (3) Poplar, Limehouse, Ratcliff, Wapping and Canning Town. Four delegates were allocated to each district, and were appointed from among the membership of the council. The delegates were given wide powers. They were to be responsible for opening new branches and attending their first meetings. They were empowered to visit established branches and deal with any grievances that existed. In industrial disputes they were given full authority to act short of actually calling a strike (a strike required the council's consent if it was to be supported by a union-wide levy). The delegate system promised to make central influence a reality in the union. It did not mean the ending of branch autonomy, which was deeply entrenched. Branches still controlled the bulk of the union's funds, and had the power to pass by-laws affecting their own particular sphere of employment.[66] It did mean, however, that branches were to be subject to inspection from the centre, in order to ensure that their conduct did not in any way undermine the position of the league as a whole. In September 1872 Keen told the council that he hoped all the branches would be visited that autumn, in order 'to complete a thorough organisation'.[67] Precisely how successful these measures were it is difficult to gauge, although it is likely that in the nature of things they fell short of the leadership's hopes. They sufficed, however, to maintain the league intact for a number of years ahead, and when the gradual weakening of the organisation got under way in the mid-1870s external rather than internal factors seem to have been responsible.

The early history of the Labour Protection League has been dealt with above in considerable detail. This is because the league has received little consideration in the past, attention being largely focused on the movement of 1889–90, a movement which is often supposed to mark the real beginning of trade unionism on the London waterfront.[68] It is true that much more is known about the later movement. For that reason we shall, when dealing with it, not attempt a comprehensive treatment, but concentrate instead in the main upon certain basic problems of waterside unionism which can be examined in some detail. The material is just not available to examine these problems in the early 1870s.[69] We simply do not know, for example, how much control the league was able to exercise over hiring procedures, whether it attempted to restrict entry, or at what point the edifice that had been built up began to crumble. Details such as these exist in abundance for the late 1880s and early 1890s, and the functioning of mass waterside unionism can be closely analysed. But, although we know much less about it, the Labour Protection League of 1872 was in almost every respect as significant an organisation as the Dockers' Union founded seventeen years later. If outsiders, such as Hennessey and Keen, played an important role in getting the league off the ground, the same was true of the Dockers' Union, which also drew on outside assistance. In this respect it is not too fanciful to see a parallel between the activities of the Land and Labour League in the 1870s and the Social Democratic Federation in the 1880s.[70] So far as the strength and durability of the two organisations is concerned, there is little to choose between them. Both bodies probably achieved a more or less complete organisation of the sectors in which they recruited, but in neither case was this position maintained for very long (about a year in the case of the Dockers' Union).[71] If anything the league was the more durable of the two, for the Dockers' Union was virtually extinct in London within a dozen years of its foundation, while the league achieved at least two secure footholds for unionism in the port—in the stevedores' and overside corn porters' sectors. In short, there is no good reason why the movement of the early 1870s should be regarded as merely ephemeral and 1889 taken instead to mark the real starting-point for union development in the port of London. The record clearly shows that mass unionism on the London waterfront began in 1872 and vestiges of that movement have survived to the present day.

The details of the league's history after 1872 need not concern us in this study. The precise sequence of events in any case is not entirely clear. In general terms, it may be said that the strength of the league was gradually worn away during the depression that set in during the second half of the 1870s. Most unions in Britain, especially those newly created, lost members heavily at this time, and some were indeed extinguished.[72] Higher levels of unemployment than those prevailing earlier in the decade gave hostile employers a whip hand over the unions. Furthermore the incomes of members fell and the payment of society subscriptions thus became a burden that many could not bear. There was also the fact that in the newly organised industries such as the docks, a union tradition was lacking, so that in adversity members felt no deeply rooted obligations to keep up their membership. It may also be the case that within the individual branches the committees were incapable of coping when things began to go wrong, again no doubt because there was so little experience of unionism within the industry. Frank Brien, a tea warehouse worker, later recalled:

> Unfortunately the men let the union fall through, or at any rate it fell through for the want of backers. They had no body of men to back them up, nobody to work and assist them in it, and nobody who knew the proper tactics and how to pursue them.[73]

It may well be doubted whether this was a basic reason for the league's decline, in view of the independence shown by some of the union's branches in the early 1870s, but it is a remark worth recording nonetheless.

The league did not succumb without a struggle. Already at the end of 1872 Keen had been casting about for ways of strengthening the union's power of resistance to employer counter-attacks. Like the leaders of the Dockers' Union in their turn, he attempted to bolster the strength of the society by federation with other in-dependent organisations. In December a conference was held between the Labour Protection League, the Carmen's Union, the Lightermen and Watermen, and the Railway Servants.[74] It was agreed to establish one joint executive for the four associations, which would then co-ordinate industrial action in the transit trade as a whole. The alliance was to be called 'The Amalga-mated Labour Union', though it was in reality a loose feder-ation. It was an ambitious scheme, but, as might be expected, there is no evidence that it ever functioned effectively, and in the early 1890s federation builders had to begin at the foundations. Basically the league had to depend upon its own strength for survival. The big test appears to have come in 1876.[75] In that year the Millwall Dock Company locked out the corn porters in its employ. The council of the league imposed levy after levy upon the membership in order to support the Millwall men, but the company imported agricultural labourers to replace them and the dispute had eventually to be closed; the labourers stayed on permanently in Millwall giving it something of a rural flavour for many years.[76] The lock-out was a severe setback for the league. It drained its finances and must have greatly sapped its morale also. By the end of the decade membership had in all probability sunk to under 2000, though this is a mere guess based upon the level during the following decade.

The early 1880s were potentially fairly favourable for union activity. After the downturn of the late 1870s, the trade cycle was once more on the upswing. However, although a stoppage for improved conditions occurred at the docks of the London Company, it was not accompanied by any revival of the mass unionism of ten years before.[77] The absence of such a revival profoundly affected the character of the league. It had by the early 1880s been reduced to six branches. Five of these were stevedores' branches on the north bank; the remaining one was of overside corn porters on the Surrey side. The league had thus become predominantly a stevedores' organisation, and so it remained throughout the 1880s. The stevedores had already formed a committee of their own to co-ordinate the policies of their five branches, and in 1881 they asked Keen to serve as corresponding secretary to this body.[78] Keen, who was presumably still the league's General Secretary, agreed, and he served in this capacity during the first half of the decade. The executive council of the union remained in existence, but it was naturally dominated by stevedores delegates and really served only to maintain the link between stevedores and corn porters. The delegates to the council did, however, try to preserve something of its past character. They took some interest in the possibility of extending union membership, and continued to exercise the functions of watching over branch expenditure and deciding cases of appeal within the union.[79] The fact was, however, that the majority of delegates saw themselves increasingly as members of a stevedores' union rather than a general organisation of port workers. In view of this situation, perhaps the best course of action would have been to convert the Labour Protection League into a federal body, linking stevedores and corn porters, and to turn the stevedores' committee formally into an executive of a separate stevedores' union (it functioned as such unofficially from at least 1880 onward). Instead, sometime towards the end of the 1880s, the council decided to change the title of the society from the Labour Protection League to the Amalgamated Stevedores Labour Protection League, thus claiming for the stevedores exclusively the inheritance to the traditions of 1872.[80] Not surprisingly this decision resulted in the secession of the overside corn porters' branch from the organisation. This was, however, not quite the end of the league as a general organisation of port workers. The overside corn porters' branch survived in isolation until the great movement of the summer of 1889. It then became the nucleus of a revived Labour Protection League on the south side of the river.[81] Of this we shall have more to say at a later stage.

2

The emergence of a distinct stevedores' union was the most important outcome of the movement of 1872 in London and it was to profoundly affect the future development of trade unionism in the port. The stevedores cannot really be compared with the overside corn porters, the only other occupational group within the league to maintain their organisation intact right through from 1872 to 1889. The overside corn porters' organisation consisted of but one branch. In the case of the stevedores five separate branches had been welded together into a unitary trade union. Furthermore, whereas the overside corn porters' organisation existed as an independent society only for a brief spell, at the end of the 1880s the stevedores were to remain separately organised from the 1880s down to the present time. Only one other group in the port has a record of independent organisation that parallels at all closely that of the stevedores—the lightermen. The lightermen were in some respects a group apart from the rest of London waterside workers, and for that reason they were excluded from our survey of the port's labour force in the previous chapter. This distinctiveness was clearly manifested in the early development of trade unionism on the waterfront, for the lightermen organised themselves apart from other port workers from the very beginning. Like the stevedores, they have remained separately organised down to the present day. Thus the unionism of stevedores and lightermen, established well before 1889, forms a vitally important and continuing theme running right through the story of organised labour in London. For this reason it is now proposed to examine some of the characteristics of these two societies, beginning with the Stevedores.

Stevedores differed from most other strategically placed port workers in that they were to some extent mobile.[82] The men, it is true, usually attached themselves to a particular employer, but the work of this employer was often not confined to any one sector of the port. A master stevedore would contract to load vessels for shipping-lines whose vessels might be berthed at a number of docks, or even in the river. In following up the work of their employers stevedores might be required to work sometimes at the Victoria Dock, sometimes at the East India Dock, and so on. In this respect stevedores differed from groups like the coal-whippers or overside corn porters, whose specialisation in a particular product confined them to a particular neighbourhood. The five stevedores' branches were thus *not* based upon five distinct sectors of employment; the unit of organisation was merely situated in the locality in which numbers of stevedores resided. The oldest branch was in Poplar, as was the union headquarters (at the Wade's Arms in Jeremiah Street). There was another branch in Poplar, and the other three were situated in Millwall, Canning Town and Stepney. Co-operation between the branches was thus not impeded by considerations of local job monopoly, nor was it impeded by variations in conditions of work from one branch to another. All alike were export shipworkers, and their sphere of employment extended to all the dock systems on the north bank.

The factor which marked the stevedores off as a distinct group was not locality, but the character of their employers. Some stevedores worked for shipping companies direct, but these were probably very much in a minority in the early days of organisation. The bulk of the men worked for small firms of master stevedores, and it was in these firms that unionism was able to establish lasting roots. In the first place this was because, as we saw in Chapter 2, small specialised concerns tended to foster a strong sense of occupational identity among the men. But there were other more concrete factors involved. Tom McCarthy,[83] Secretary of the Stevedores in the later 1880s, commented that the men preferred working for master stevedores because they were 'weaker men to deal with in a dispute'.[84] Stephen Sims, a subsequent secretary, elaborated the point. The master stevedores, he said, were engaged in competition with each other, and if one objected to pay the usual rate another would do so and take the work. He concluded that it was much easier to maintain rates amongst the small employers than against large companies.[85] The validity of these opinions was certainly borne out by the facts of the industrial situation in the 1870s and 1880s.

In 1870 stevedores received three to four shillings per day of twelve hours and four shillings per night. In 1872, under boom conditions and with 3000 stevedores organised, wages were raised to five shillings for the twelve hours and ninepence per hour overtime. This advance was followed up by the establishment of a nine-hour day. Wages continued to rise, and, although with the falling off in trade an unsuccessful attempt at a reduction was made in 1876, by the 1880s the stevedores had established a standard rate of six shillings per day of nine hours, and one shilling per hour overtime.[86] Not only had the stevedores' organisation possessed sufficient bargaining power to be able to greatly improve conditions of employment, it had also, in the main, been able to maintain these standards through periods of dull trade. It was significant that the only substantial reverses in the union's fortunes occurred at the hands, not of the master stevedores, but of the shipping companies. But of this point we shall have more to say later.

The success of organisation in the sphere of employment controlled by master stevedores was, however, not simply the result of effective industrial action. The small masters, for their part, were prepared to accept trade unionism in a way that large companies never were before 1914. For one thing, a fixed union rate of wages was perfectly acceptable to a large number of competing employers, provided that it was enforced upon all alike; it was even an advantage in that it set a limit on price competition. Moreover, the union could be of advantage in providing machinery for the orderly settlement of disputes. The society was also a factor in raising the efficiency of the labour force, for it encouraged high standards of workmanship in order to secure for its members a preference in employment. Perhaps the most important factor inducing the masters to accept the union was, however, simply their personal knowledge of their employees. In large undertakings there was little sympathy between employer and employee, but in the small stevedoring firms a close personal relationship existed, and in such a climate trade unionism took root and thrived.[87]

The master stevedores of the port did not therefore give ground in boom periods for merely tactical reasons. They were prepared to recognise the union on a permanent basis. Furthermore, lacking cohesion themselves,[88] they were ready to accept the elaborate code of working rules which the society formulated to govern work operations. It was this permanent recognition which gave stability to organisation among the stevedores.[89]

Full recognition carried with it one decisive advantage on the waterfront—a preference in employment for unionists. Among the handlers of heavy merchandise the existence of such a preference was not so important, for the men were in any case organised by their employers in regular gangs. In the Surrey Docks, for instance, the unloading of bulk grain was the monopoly of twenty or so regular gangs which were employed in rotation, and these gangs enjoyed the right of employment before any extra gangs were engaged.[90] In such a situation trade unionism was not fundamentally necessary as a means of restricting labour supply. Most port workers, however, including stevedores, were not employed in regular gangs of fixed composition. Instead, they applied for work daily at 'places of call' situated at the entrances to the various dock systems. At the places of call operated by the dock companies there were sometimes frightful scrambles for work,[91] but each master stevedore had his following of regular workers and these had always enjoyed an informal preference in the work.[92] There often arose occasions, however, when a master was particularly busy, and was obliged to go outside the pool of his regular employees. In this situation employers did not always discriminate between strangers and regulars who usually worked in other concerns. The trade was thus exposed to infiltration from outside. The union preference was designed to end this system.

The stevedores' branches evolved elaborate rules to govern the 'calling-on' of men for work, and this code was accepted by the masters. The union did not attempt to enforce a completely closed shop, for, due to the wide fluctuations of trade which created occasional shortages of regular workers, extra labourers had sometimes to be employed. What it insisted upon, however, was priority for unionists. It was thus a rule that no member was to work with a non-member if other members were unemployed at the place of call.[93] In order to enforce this rule the society insisted that the foremen who took on the men for work should be unionists, and it was arranged that an inspection of union cards should take place before the men went into work.[94] The times at which 'call-ons' were to take place, and the specific locations of the places of call were also carefully regulated, in order that unionists should have every opportunity of being present when men were needed.

Recognition of the union preference was the basis upon which the Stevedores' Union rested. It offered an incentive to regular stevedores to join the union and keep up their membership, for the organisation was able to offer to its members an assurance that, at any of the dock systems, they would stand a better chance of employment than outsiders. This incentive alone might not have sufficed to sustain continuous organisation among the stevedores, had it not been for certain features that went hand in hand with the union preference. Unions in casual trades lived a hand-to-mouth existence financially, due to the intermittent employment of their members, and it was only too easy for men to fall heavily into arrears with their dues, until in fact they ceased to be financial members at all. The inspection of cards at the place of call, however, was an instrument that could be used to maintain the level of financial membership, for union cards were issued quarterly and differed in colour from one quarter to the next. Delegates could thus detect at a glance a man who was heavily in arrears, and if necessary block him from employment. The inspection of cards was important for union stability in another context. Waterside workers were a turbulent race, and were not easily induced to accept the regulations the union imposed. The society of course developed a system of fines for breaches of rule, but such a system ran the risk of driving members out of organisation. There had to be some final sanction with which to enforce discipline, and in the Stevedores' Union, as in subsequent waterside organisations, this final sanction existed at the place of call. As long as a union preference existed it was possible, in the last resort, to block a recalcitrant member from employment. In the early primitive days of organisation such a sanction was vital for the achievement of internal cohesion. Influence over hiring procedures thus enabled the Stevedores' Union to attract, retain, and discipline a stable membership throughout the period from 1872 to 1914.

As we have seen above, the essential advantage of the union

preference was that it made possible the restriction of stevedoring work to those men who regularly followed up the trade. A further advantage of the preference was that it enabled the number of these regulars to be kept at a strictly fixed and limited figure, so that under-employment could be kept at a minimum. The union thus rigorously limited its intake of new members, and in 1888 Tom McCarthy, the Secretary, told the Sweating Commission that admissions were 'simply enough to cover the death rate'.[95] This, however, was at a period when trade had been consistently dull for some time, and when therefore the union naturally clamped on its entrance restrictions. In good years, however, the society generally re-opened its books, but even then much of the intake was composed of 'run-out' members, who had been unable to keep up their payments in the slack times. Thus the overall growth of the union was slow, as indeed was the growth of trade after the mid-1870s.[96] In the boom of the early 1870s around 3000 stevedores were organised;[97] in the boom of 1889–90 the figure was just over 4000,[98] but this includes two branches of lumpers, an occupational group not included in the stevedores' organisation of 1872.

The admission of new recruits to the Stevedores' Union was based essentially upon the hereditary principle, a fact perhaps not surprising when it is remembered that shipwork in London was dominated by the Irish communities.[99] The hereditary basis of recruitment can be seen clearly in the functioning of the entry controls, controls which by the early 1880s had emerged in a clearly defined form. Members were admitted as boys or as adults, but in both cases they had to be proposed and seconded by members of a branch. If the boy was a member's son he was initiated into the union by the branch without further ado, if not, like all adults, he had to go before the Stevedores' committee for acceptance. The stevedores, of course, never had a formal system of apprenticeship, but boys were admitted with the deliberate intention that they should learn the trade.[100] In fact, master stevedores occasionally sent their sons into the union with this object in mind.[101] Entry as a boy, however, with the opportunities this afforded for a thorough grounding in the work, was mainly restricted to members' sons, and in 1881 the Stevedores' committee actually passed a resolution that no-one under eighteen could be admitted except upon this hereditary principle.[102] Although this restriction was not maintained consistently, the weighting of the entrance charges ensured that the hereditary character of the trade would be preserved. Thus the entrance fee for the admission of members' sons as boys was only half a crown in the early 1890s, whereas youths generally were charged one pound.

The admission of adults to the union was always strictly controlled. In the 1890s the entrance fee for adults was two pounds, whether they came from stevedoring families or not. Restrictions did not end there. A new member had to be either working at shipwork prior to his being nominated, or he had to be a seaman.[103] The links between the seafaring and stevedoring trades were indeed very close and the General Secretary of the Stevedores estimated in 1895 that 50 per cent of union members had been to sea.[104] Some of these were sailors first and foremost, who had only settled down to shore work after years at sea, but most must have been stevedores by trade who had recourse to the sea for only a short period. What is important here, however, is the fact that the union demanded a thorough experience of shipwork from those who were admitted as adults. In this way it safeguarded its standards of workmanship, and thereby its relationship with the masters. In addition to the high entrance fee and experience that were demanded, the union periodically closed its books against all but members' sons as boys. The entrance mechanisms of the union were thus weighted heavily against the outsider. Ben Tillett, a Bristolian of whom we shall have more to say later, was refused admittance to the union when he moved to London, although at that time he was a seaman.[105]

Closed unions of the type evolved by the stevedores suffered from one inherent weakness. Their very stability brought in its train a certain inflexibility, and the Stevedores' Society found itself faced with considerable problems in adjusting to the changes that were taking place in the shipping industry.

In the first place, the union found that the creation of new docks downstream began to seriously hamper the effectiveness of its exclusive policies. The society of course aimed to keep the number of those engaged at export shipwork down to a level where all could obtain a reasonable amount of employment. Yet demand for labour varied daily as between the different docks, and conditions of surplus and shortage sometimes occurred at adjacent places of call. If there was to be only a limited number of stevedores, clearly there had to be a fair amount of mobility between the various places of call. The union recognised that its limited membership would not be perfectly adjusted as between the various centres, and allowed for this fact by insisting upon a preference rather than a monopoly of employment. However, as long as the ocean trades of the port were largely confined to the old dock systems in Poplar and Stepney where the bulk of the men resided, the places of call were sufficiently close to each other to allow for a reasonable amount of mobility. In this situation the society preference ensured that the bulk of the work was performed by union stevedores. The opening of the Albert Dock in 1880 and Tilbury in 1886, and the gradual transference of ocean shipping to these remoter centres, created a new situation. With the work spread over so wide an area, the mobility of the limited supply of unionists began to break down, and in the early 1880s the Stevedores' Committee became more and more alarmed at the proportion of work in the new centres that was going to non-unionists.

The society would have liked to obviate this difficulty by having employers take on men in the morning at the old places of call, and afterwards transferring them to the downstream docks. There were, however, few employers amenable enough to put up with this inconvenience, and most wanted to either take on the men at new places of call downstream or be able to give them instructions overnight, so that they could proceed direct by train to the new centres the following morning. The union had, reluctantly, to make concessions on these lines, and so far as the Albert Dock was concerned the problem did not appear insuperable. Tilbury was, however, a different matter, for it was so far removed from the old centres of activity. In 1889 a new branch was created at this dock, but the expansion of business at Tilbury was such that the deployment of unionists became hopelessly unbalanced. Various expedients were tried, and of these the following executive resolution of 1892 will serve as an example:

> That all members at Tilbury should refuse to work with non-society men while members were idle in London and to facilitate this the General Secretary be empowered on receipt of a telegram from foreman or employer to take down [by train] the necessary number of men required.[106]

Neither this expedient, nor later ones, sufficed to solve the problem. Given the drift of trade downstream, no device of the society was capable of preserving the work intact in the hands of the close-knit London Irish community of Poplar and Stepney. In the long run, the breakdown of mobility was to prove a powerful factor in forcing the stevedores to revise the whole basis of their organisation, as will be shown in later chapters. The full impact of Tilbury upon the society is, however, something which belongs to the new century.

There was another, more serious, sense in which the society found problems in adjusting to developments in the latter part of the century. The union had established itself at a time when ocean-going trade was still largely carried in the sailing-ship. In the last quarter of the century, however, foreign trade became increasingly dominated by the large steamship companies, some of whom did their own stevedoring work instead of employing contractors. These companies were to prove more independent in attitude than the master stevedores, and they were much less prepared to accept the jurisdiction of the society in matters of working rule. There were several reasons for this. This was the age when the steamship was at an experimental stage, and when the reduction of running costs was an absolute necessity. Employers were therefore distrustful of the organised power of their employees, and any restrictions or higher costs which this might impose upon them. By the 1890s, however, these factors counted for less, as the steamship had established its supremacy over sail. Yet the steamship owners retained a great hostility to unionism, and their autocratic character was perhaps only rivalled by that of the railway companies. The conflict was no longer mainly over economic considerations, but over power. The steamship companies were proud and independent undertakings, whose leaders were far removed in all respects from the men who loaded and unloaded their ships. Thus the West Ham survey of 1907 reported:

It has been stated to one of the writers by a director of an important shipping line that dock labour is 'such a bagetelle' in the business of managing a large shipping concern that the heads of firms are not inclined to consider the question from the men's point of view.[107]

The personal contact that characterised the relationship between master stevedores and their men was not found when large shipping companies were the employers; the latter were concerned only with preserving their perfect freedom of action.

The transition from sail to steam, and the changes in the character of employers which this brought about, acted against the men's organisation in most ports. It did so in Liverpool,[108] in Glasgow,[109] in New York particularly,[110] and also, of course, in London. Until the late 1870s probably all the major concerns performing export shipwork in the docks of London had recognised the stevedores' organisation and accorded its members a preference in employment. The five branches had formed in effect a small watertight labour market within the wider London port labour market. In the depression of 1879, however, the Peninsular and Oriental Line quarrelled with the society and brought in outsiders to replace the unionists.[111] In the succeeding years other steamship companies followed the example of the P. and O., including the British India Line,[112] which was by this time probably the largest single employer of stevedores in the port.[113] No doubt the break with union labour was the more easily achieved, in view of the difficulties of organisation in the downstream areas, where the larger shipping-lines berthed their vessels. Thus, following the pattern in other ports, the Stevedores' Union found itself increasingly powerless in those sectors of employment controlled by the large steamship lines. This development placed the society in an awkward position. No longer was the entire export shipwork of the port performed by concerns which recognised the society and abided by its rules.

The union could in theory have reacted to this situation in two ways. On the one hand, it could have temporarily abandoned the attempt to limit supply in the trade, and could have set out to recruit the outsiders that had been introduced to the work in the non-society firms. On the other hand, it could have rested content with a contraction in its sphere of influence, and could have continued to operate its exclusive policies within the boundaries of the society firms that remained. The union followed the latter course, for two reasons. First, members working for society firms feared that if outsiders were recruited at places where the union preference was no longer recognised, then there would be an influx to those places where it was acknowledged, thus intensifying competition for work. The second reason stemmed from the desire of the society to maintain intact the elaborate code of working rules that it had developed. If a portion of its membership worked in concerns where these rules were not observed, then it would be difficult to persuade society firms to conform with the union's standards. Wherever union stevedores worked there had to be one uniform standard governing operations. If one exception was made it was feared that the whole edifice would collapse. With these considerations in mind the society closed its ranks. Members were forbidden to work in non-society firms, and the 'strangers' working there were excluded from the union. This rigid policy, of course, brought hardship to the members who had once worked for the firms in question, but union leaders felt that, even if these men were lost to organisation, this was better than any modification of fundamental principles. The dilemma described above was to prove a recurrent one, as we shall see in later chapters.

The preference of the Stevedores for a contraction in their area of influence, rather than a modification of fundamental rules, was unfortunate when seen in the general context of port unionism. The executive council of the Labour Protection League tended in the early 1880s to be more aware of this general context than the Stevedores' committee. The delegates of that council showed themselves anxious that organisation should be extended to the stevedores who worked in the non-union firms. It was clear that most unionist stevedores were adamant against the enrolment of these men in the same organisation as themselves, and so in March 1881 the council suggested that the employees of the National Line should be formed into a branch 'independent of the league until it is ascertained how they get on'.[114] This new branch was in fact formed, and the men were given a separate colour union card in order that they could be excluded from the enclosed labour market of the society firms. The new branch appears, however, to have disintegrated after a short while. The executive council made another gesture towards strengthening unionism in the sphere of the shipping companies. It tried to persuade the Stevedores' committee to allow members to work in non-society firms, providing they were paid the society rates.[115] The gesture, however, was in vain. In 1887 the excluded stevedores at the non-union firms decided to form an organisation of their own, and the United Stevedores' Union emerged from their efforts. This separate organisation had two branches; and by the beginning of 1889 it had achieved a membership of 1000, which compared with the figure of 1500 for the Amalgamated Union.[116] The total number of stevedores working in the port at this time was probably about 5000.[117]

The rigidity of the Amalgamated Union seemed in the 1880s to be condemning it to an ever more obscure role in the life of the port. Yet the bulk of the members of the five branches did not appear greatly disturbed by this obscurity. Their stable relationship with the master stevedores had not been disrupted, and, in any case, they were men of essentially limited horizons. Despite the advanced state of trade unionism among stevedores as compared with other port workers, their organisation was still in the 1880s at a very rudimentary stage. The branches enjoyed a wide degree of autonomy, and the early Stevedores' Committee does not appear to have possessed any funds of its own. Prior to 1889 the society possessed no full-time officials, and when Tom McCarthy was Secretary after 1885 he remained at work as a stevedore, receiving 3s 4d a week for the time he devoted to society business.[118] The union often in fact appeared to be hovering on the verge of anarchy. It was difficult to develop orderly methods of conducting business at meetings, and such was the turbulent character of these proceedings that it was sometimes hard to get anyone to take the chair. Vendettas between branches were often vigorously prosecuted in the committee, and on such occasions 'very hot discussions' became the order of the day. Nevertheless, as we have seen, the society had maintained itself intact, and this was no mean achievement in the conditions of the nineteenth-century waterfront.

Cohesion had, however, been achieved on the basis of common interests that were essentially limited in scope. Apart from matters relating to working rule and limitation of entry, the five branches had a common interest that stemmed from the dangers of ship-work.[119] Already in the 1880s some branches had a fund which covered light accidents, and by the 1890s the whole society was levied for serious accidents. The union also showed a keen interest for many years in supporting the local Poplar hospital, and frequently organised benefits on its behalf. Inevitably the Stevedores, like all subsequent waterfront unions, found themselves quickly embroiled in the problem of compensation for accidents. The Employers' Liability Act of 1880 had opened up possibilities in this respect, although there remained too many loopholes through which employers could evade their responsibility. Thus in 1882 one member of the society was of the opinion that, 'it would be advisable to employ a solicitor for the Five Branches to take up cases for members such as accidents or trade disputes which at present the society cannot interfere with'.[120] It was, however, some years before the idea was translated into reality. The danger of their work was something the stevedores had also in common with the overside corn porters' branch, and, although on most other matters the two groups functioned entirely independently of one another, they were prepared to co-operate on the issue of employers' liability.[121]

In so far as the Stevedores' Union took an interest in the affairs of the wider labour movement, it was chiefly through this concern with accidents. When in 1891, after much delay, it was decided to send an official representative to give evidence to the Royal Commission on Labour, the commission was informed that the union 'wished to be heard principally with regard to the working of the Employers' Liability Act'.[122] Similarly, when the stevedores began to send delegates to the Trade Union Congress in the 1890s, their chief aim was 'to bring up the question of compensation for accidents on foreign ships'.[123] Generally, however, the stevedores showed little interest in the affairs of the outside world, and exhibited the utmost caution in their dealings with outside bodies. They were particularly distrustful of any publicity in the Press.

The Stevedores' Union, like most small unions of its type, was not merely a trade organisation but a social one as well. The annual excursion complete with band, banners and fireworks, was an important event, and its planning took up an inordinate amount of the union's time. Yet the social world in which society stevedores moved, like the industrial one, was severely limited. Lightermen, corn porters, these were social equals, but other groups of waterside workers might as well not have existed for all the contact there was with them.[124] In this isolation stevedores were not exceptional, it was the same with all waterside groupings, as we saw in Chapter 2.

The development of trade unionism amongst the lightermen

arose in part from factors quite distinct from those generally operating on the waterfront.[125] The history of the lightermen was inextricably bound up with that of the Thames Watermen. Watermen were men responsible for carrying passengers upon the river, and they had existed as a distinct grouping since time immemorial. The Watermen's Company, founded in 1556 to regulate the trade, was primarily aimed at restraining these workers from combining to obtain excessive fares, and the watermen are known to have had small societies as long ago as the fourteenth century.[126] Lightermen were an off-shoot from the class of watermen, and were responsible for navigating barges on the river. Due to the decline of passenger traffic on the Thames, and the increasing dependence of the port upon lighterage, the lightermen had by the mid-nineteenth century become much the more important of the two groups, and the number of watermen in fact dwindled to an insignificant level.[127] The lightermen, like the watermen, were subject to the jurisdiction of the Watermen's Company, and entrance to the occupation was restricted by means of an apprenticeship, and a system of licensing carried out under the auspices of that company. They formed very much of an *élite* among London port workers, and their privileged status was enhanced by the fact that a lighterman who had served his full apprenticeship became a freeman of the Watermen's Company. The lightermen were thus a unique group among the port workers of London, and they alone were able to restrict entry to the trade by means of a formal apprenticeship system.[128]

The appearance of unionism among the lightermen was the result of the intrusion of capitalism into the old guild structure of the Watermen's Company. Up until the mid-nineteenth century lighterage concerns were small and it was possible for journeymen to set up their own business, but thereafter the distinction between masters and men became marked. The division of interest between the two sides became abundantly clear when master lightermen attempted to break through the apprenticeship regulations which governed admission to the trade, and it was this which finally stirred the lightermen into action. The trouble was that the controlling body for the trade, the Watermen's Court, had become dominated by employers; and thus the journeymen were unable to ensure that apprenticeship regulations were enforced by the company. Thus in 1866 the Watermen and Lightermen's Protection Society was formed, whose principal object was to obtain legislation securing for the journeymen adequate representation on the Watermen's Court.[129] The 1866 society failed to achieve its primary object and broke up in 1871. In the boom of the early 1870s, however, there were many men who wished to see immediate action taken on wages and hours, and in 1871 and 1872 there were strikes on these issues. Out of this conflict there arose an enduring lightermen's union—the Amalgamated Society of Watermen and Lightermen—founded in June 1872. Although this union owed its origin to a wages movement, it was, like the society of 1866, to become much involved in the problem of securing representation upon the Watermen's Court.[130] The difficulty facing organisation in the lighterage trade was the circumstance that the union was a union within a union; for the trade was regulated by rules made, not by the men's organisation, but by the Watermen's Company. The fact that the constitution of the company could only be altered by Parliament had meant that from the beginning the lightermen were forced to spend much time and money in trying to secure the special legislation which alone would enable them to preserve their privileged status. The union also expended large sums in securing the enforcement of legislation already existing, and was constantly prosecuting unlicensed men for working on the river. These special circumstances governing the lighterage trade did not make for an identity of interest with other port workers, and the Lightermen's Union was kept fully preoccupied with its own peculiar problems.[131]

The lightermen were the most exclusive of all riverside workers, for in their case the normal pressures making for exclusiveness were reinforced by their unique history and conditions of employment. As freemen of the Watermen's Company they had a corporate tradition dating back to the sixteenth century, and the restricted entry to the trade made it very much of a close corporation. In the early 1890s it was estimated that 80 per cent of the apprentices were either the sons of lightermen or near relations.[132] The lightermen were isolated from other waterside workers, not only by their ancient traditions, but also by the character of their occupation. Their conditions of work impelled them to spend long hours on the river (often sixteen hours for a day's pay before 1889) and they were thus forced to keep largely to themselves.[133]

Outside of the close-knit community of freemen there existed the class of unlicensed barge workers.[134] These 'non-freemen' were not licensed to navigate craft on the tidal waters of the Thames, and their work consisted mainly in navigating barges in the docks and canals, and looking after them in the river as watchmen. Non-freemen were regarded by licensed men virtually as men of a different nationality,[135] and they were excluded from the Lightermen's Society. This exclusion was no doubt based not merely on social ostracism, but upon the desire of the freemen to protect their sphere of employment from the intrusion of unlicensed workers. The non-freemen made some effort to organise themselves in the 1870s, but it was not until 1889 that they established a proper union of their own. This society did not, however, endure, and until 1900 organisation in the lighterage trade was confined essentially to the privileged *élite* of licensed workers.

The early achievement of trade unionism by the lightermen, and their continuous organisation throughout the period from 1872 to 1914, was, as we have seen, in part the result of factors peculiar to the London lighterage trade. Yet in many respects their unionism was all of a piece with that of other port workers. The lighterman's clannishness, his preoccupation with limitation of entrance to the trade, his isolation from other port workers, these features were common to all waterside groupings, although perhaps not to the same exaggerated extent. Waterside unionism was essentially defensive and restrictive in character. This was so whatever the trade, the port, or even the country.[136] In a casual, overstocked labour market such a form of organisation followed inevitably from the insecurity of employment. The 'new unionists' of 1889 were to find that this was the framework within which they had to work. Expansive gospels of general unionism carried little weight on the waterfront.

4 The Great Strike, 1889

THE revival of mass waterside unionism in the summer of 1889 occurred in circumstances that were in some respects notably different from those that characterised the movement of 1872. Whereas the movement of the early seventies achieved little publicity, being unaccompanied by a port-wide strike (or indeed any prolonged stoppage), the opposite was true of 1889. The great dock strike that year attracted so much attention nationally that it became one of the most celebrated events in the annals of the British labour movement, and it was this strike which directly stimulated a revival of organisation throughout the port. Public interest in the 1889 strike stemmed from its somewhat sensational and dramatic quality. Small-scale stoppages of short duration were nothing rare on the waterfront, but this one embraced all port workers simultaneously, including the most despised and degraded quay labourers at the north-bank docks, and its length came to be measured by weeks rather than days. The fact that it occurred in the metropolis, and that the strike leaders daily conducted the men in great orderly processions which marched from dockland right into the heart of the City of London, served further to focus the attention of public opinion. The strike was seen almost as an allegory, with the part of Privilege being played by the City-based Dock Companies, and the part of Downtrodden Underdog by the wretched dockers inhabiting the slums of the East End. The role of Cardinal Manning, in at last bringing about a settlement, provided a final colourful touch.[1]

Although the great strike of 1889 appeared as a very remarkable phenomenon to contemporary public opinion, port employers had little reason to be surprised at this turn of events. Waterside workers had demonstrated seventeen years before that collective action was not beyond their power when the market for labour was tight, which it certainly was in the summer of 1889. A revolt on the waterfront was in fact overdue, for among the mass of workers conditions had scarcely improved since the early seventies, and in some respects had in fact deteriorated. During the 1880s the port passed through a serious crisis, as we saw in Chapter 1. Surplus capacity at the docks and warehouses reduced charges to rock bottom, and in 1888 the East and West India Dock Company went bankrupt. Other dock and wharf enterprises, while not reduced to bankruptcy, were placed in severe difficulties. Inevitably these developments had an unfortunate impact upon working conditions in the port. By the early summer of 1889, overside corn porters, tea workers, granary workers, and steamship workers had all suffered wage reductions.[2] Among ordinary dock and wharf workers conditions had also deteriorated, particularly in the case of the former group. Hourly wage rates had not been reduced, it is true, although the East and West India Dock Company had reverted to the pre-1872 rate of 4d in the case of purely casual labour employed at the newly opened Tilbury Dock.[3] But if hourly rates remained unchanged, other conditions did not. Neither of the two great companies on the north bank operated a straightforward system of time payment. In the case of the India company the men received, in addition to the 5d hourly rate, an extra payment at the end of the job calculated on a tonnage basis. It was a kind of piece-work system, the extra payment being known as 'plus'. The company did not, however, disclose to the men the tonnage scales on which the 'plus' was based, and during the late 1880s these scales were revised downward.[4] The men were not informed of the change that had been made, but they suspected very strongly that they were being cheated, and it was in fact a dispute over the payment of plus on a ship at the South West India Dock which sparked off the 1889 strike. The other great dock company, the London and St Katherine's, operated the so-called contract system of employment, whereby the work was let out to small contractors who were usually the preference labourers of the company. Contractors, of whom there were no fewer than 250 at the London Dock alone, were paid on a tonnage basis and they employed the casuals they required at a rate per hour. The system had been in operation in the 1870s, and was extremely unpopular with the majority of the men. Its abolition had been one of the points in the programme of the Labour Protection League. It encouraged contractors to maximise their profits by employing as few men as possible and working them as hard as possible. No doubt these features were accentuated in the 1880s, for the financial straits of the company may well have resulted in reductions in the tonnage prices paid to contractors, thus squeezing their profit margins and thereby intensifying the pressure on the casuals. Although dockers working under contractors had managed to obtain a rise from 5d to 6d per hour in 1880, this was little compensation for the disadvantages inherent in the system. This was especially the case in view of the corruption that existed in the 1880s. Labourers were often obliged to treat or bribe contractors before they could obtain employment. The London Dock was particularly notorious in this respect, and the local public house was here the recognised avenue to employment.[5]

The abuses of the plus and contract systems had become a potent cause of discontent among dockers by the late 1880s, as the evidence given before the Commission on Sweated Industries in 1888 amply demonstrates.[6] One other feature of dock employment was also of considerable importance at this time. Employment in London was literally by the hour, men being taken on and paid off at all times of the day, just as it suited the employer. In Liverpool the men, once taken on, were entitled to not less than half a day's employment. The same had been true in London forty years before. Now the casual nature of dock employment in the metropolis was absolute.[7] The men were not keen on permanency, but they did want taking-on times to be limited in number. They wanted also a guaranteed half-day's work. The companies in their difficulties had pushed the casual system to its very limits; it was too far for the dockers.

It was said above that the movement of 1889 was overdue. This was true in more senses than one. Not only were there long-standing grievances in the port, but there existed also an organisation which had been campaigning for some time for their redress. The Tea Operatives and General Labourers' Association had been established in 1887.[8] It had been formed as a result of a wage reduction imposed by the East and West India Dock Company upon tea workers at the Cutler Street warehouse. The latter had convened a meeting of tea workers generally and out of this assembly the new union had been created. It was not a conscious revival of the Labour Protection League, but there were no doubt men amongst the tea workers who remembered the earlier union.[9] The new society's leading spirit was an ex-sailor named

Benjamin Tillett, who had attended the first meeting as delegate from the Monument Quay Warehouse.[10] Tea workers as a whole tended to regard themselves as somewhat superior to ordinary dock labourers, but Tillett counteracted any tendency for the new organisation to become preoccupied purely with sectional problems. As the union's Secretary, he had set about converting it into a comprehensive organisation for all port workers. Tillett was indeed a remarkable personality, and he was to play a crucial role in the future development of waterside unionism. He had settled down in East London after an early life spent mainly at sea. Unable to obtain admission to the Stevedores' Union, he picked up a living at various docks and wharves and eventually obtained a preference for work at the Monument Tea Warehouse. He also acquired a knowledge of that staple East End trade, shoemaking. It was this craft which gave Tillett his first experience of trade unionism, for by 1887 he was a member of the Boot and Shoe Operatives' Union. No doubt it was partly on the strength of his experience of union affairs that his workmates elected him as their secretary. But Tillett had in any case other qualifications. He had made strenuous efforts at self-education, and at one time cherished a secret ambition to become a barrister. He was certainly possessed of very considerable natural ability, although this was to some extent offset in the early days by certain physical disadvantages, for he was a small man with rather poor health and suffered from a serious impediment of speech.[11] The last disability Tillett certainly conquered, for he was to become the great orator of the waterfront. He was a flamboyant character, a man of grand gestures, sweeping generalisations, extravagant denunciations and considerable vision.[12] He could give expression, as no others could, to the pent-up emotions of men who felt themselves abused and misunderstood by society at large. In some respects, however, Tillett's personality was to prove a liability as well as an asset in the task of developing waterfront unionism. He was an unstable man; highly emotional, over sensitive to criticism, and lacking in application. Tillett was no administrator, and it was fortunate that from the very beginning of his union career he could rely on the assistance of Harry Orbell, a friend and workmate, who became President of the Tea Operatives.[13]

From its inception the Tea Operatives' Union bore the imprint of Tillett's personality. He was not interested in rallying merely the

warehouse workers. The whole port was to be his stamping-
ground. As a sensitive man he was genuinely appalled by the
degradation of waterside life; the sight of men fainting at work
from undernourishment, of men 'picking the rubbish heaps in a
furtive search for any kind of eatable', of men struggling like
savages for work at calling-on times.[14] The following outburst in
an address to the public in 1887 was characteristic: 'I cannot
wonder that men lose the dignity of their manhood when they are
driven helter-skelter to the gutter by a system that degrades and
imbrutes.'[15] 'Dignity' and 'manhood' are words that recur
constantly in Tillett's writings and speeches; for him, trade
unionism existed above all to restore to the labourer his self-
respect. It was this approach which drove him to regard his tiny
union not as an agency of sectional interest, but as an instrument
of propaganda, which would expose both to the public and to the
dockers themselves the degradation of the waterfront. Tillett thus
rarely lost an opportunity to put his case before the public. He
gave evidence before the 'Sweating Commission', he attempted to
interest a number of M.P.s in his work, he publicised the mis-
management of the port by the dock companies, and he attempted
to obtain the co-operation of the established trade union world.[16]
The work of organisation was conducted like a political campaign,
and embraced the entire port. The campaign was started at
Tilbury where working conditions were worst. Later on there
were regular Sunday meetings at the East India Dock Gates,
evening meetings 'across the water' at Bermondsey and Rotherhithe, and early morning meetings at the Albert and Victoria
docks. 'From Tilbury to the up-town docks, at the gate and on
the quayside, at the approaches to the wharves, and at street
corners, we began our constitutional propaganda.'[17] Tillett's
closest associate in the early days of this campaign was, surprisingly,
Tom McCarthy, the Secretary of the Amalgamated Stevedores'
Union. McCarthy was by no means at one with his membership in
the interest he displayed in Tillett's activities. He was, like Tillett
himself, an exceptional figure. A London Irishman from Limehouse, he had begun his working life in the decaying Thameside
shipbuilding industry, and after losing his employment there he
became a carman. Finally he took to the waterfront, joining the
Stevedores' Union in 1879, and becoming its secretary in 1885.
McCarthy had far reaching ideas about the role of trade unionism

in the port, and during the 1889 upheaval he was to leave his own exclusive organisation to become an organiser in the newly created Dockers' Union.[18]

The years 1887-9 were generally favourable to trade union growth, as trade gradually picked up after the depression of the mid-1880s. These were the years in which Havelock Wilson's Seamen's and Firemen's Union grew from nothing in July 1887 to forty-five branches at the end of 1888,[19] and the latter year saw also two new organisations of port workers founded at Swansea and Cardiff.[20] Yet despite all the enthusiasm of Tillett and McCarthy, the Tea Operatives did not at first reap any significant benefit from this rising tide. There was certainly plenty of discontent in the port, especially among the dockers of the north bank, and innumerable small-scale strikes occurred in the late eighties. Yet Tillett was unable to permanently harness the forces of rebellion to his society, and the union suffered from the beginning from an acute instability of membership. Members would be gained at a particular centre, there would be a strike for improved conditions, and as soon as the desired improvement had been gained the men drifted out of organisation. Membership fluctuated between about 800 and 300 and it seemed impossible to stabilise it.[21] The biggest effort staged by the society was at Tilbury, where a month's strike was organised to bring the minimum rate there up to the level prevailing elsewhere in the port. The strike was a failure.[22] In truth the message of trade unionism was falling upon exceedingly stony ground. There were several reasons for this. One fundamental difficulty concerned the general character of the waterside labour force. Casual employment created a turbulent, unbridled race of men. They were ready enough to strike, but they were less ready to pay regularly into a society and submit to its rules. A Dockers' Union official in the 1890s once referred to the men as being of 'the roughest and most desperate nature imaginable, and very difficult to manage'.[23] Without control of hiring procedures it was almost impossible to build up a stable membership among such a labour force, and of course Tillett's union had no such control.

Beyond this general factor, however, was another problem relating more specifically to the situation in London. During the course of the 1880s trade unionism on the London waterfront had acquired a rather unsavoury reputation, due to the activities of a gang of ruffians who specialised in the control of bogus labour organisations.[24] Thomas Kelly and Samuel Peters, the chief figures in this movement, had established a headquarters in Whitechapel, and had proceeded to build up a whole network of bogus organisations. The services of these associations were for hire during all the various political controversies of the decade. They provided audiences and gangs of thugs to break up meetings. The activities of Kelly and Peters were largely centred on London's dockland, and the 'unions' controlled by their group included bodies with such titles as the Dock Porters and Sugar Warehousemen, and the Docks and Riverside Labourers' Council. Tillett's Tea Operatives' Union, set up in 1887, was immediately suspect. It was taken by liberal observers for yet another bogus creation, and Tillett was severely handled in the columns of the *Star* newspaper. If Tillett thus encountered opposition from disinterested observers, he encountered still more from those whose vested interests were affected. The men who made a living out of bogus unions could hardly have welcomed the intrusion of a bona fide organisation into their sphere, and Tillett has described in his memoirs how in the first twelve months of the union's existence its meetings were constantly wrecked by rowdyism or broken up by gangs of hired thugs.[25] The atmosphere of the East End in the 1880s was thus scarcely favourable to the growth of a bona fide dockers' organisation. The dockers themselves must have distrusted the intentions of the new body, accustomed as they were to the activities of Kelly and Peters in the 'working class movement'. Trust is an essential ingredient in working-class organisations, and after a decade of Kelly and Peters trust in the integrity of union officers did not come easily on the London waterfront. It must be said, however, that while the activities of bogus organisations undoubtedly did much to discredit the name of trade unionism in the East End, another more favourable influence was also at work. The Social Democratic Federation was extremely active in London, and brought together a number of talented working-men, some of them from skilled trades, who were interested in establishing unionism among the masses of ordinary labourers. These men were to play a crucial part in leading the movement of 1889.[26]

At the beginning of 1889 Tillett could see precious little return for all the effort he and a few others had put into organising the dockers. His interest was turning to the organisation of the workers at the great Beckton gas works in East Ham, and in fact the Tea Operatives already included among its members Will Thorne, an outspoken gas stoker at Beckton and a member of the Social Democratic Federation. When Thorne launched a gasworkers' union in March 1889 Tillett became actively involved in the organisation of the new body, and in fact stood against Thorne in the election for the general secretaryship of the union in June. Thorne won the election easily.[27] Unlike the Tea Operatives, the Gasworkers' Union made rapid headway in the spring and early summer of 1889, and the story of the union's successful achievement of the eight-hour day is well known.[28] Success continued, however, to elude Tillett. He had failed to attain office in the gas stokers' organisation, and his own union was stagnant. His affairs were in fact rapidly moving towards a crisis. In so far as his little union had achieved any foothold in the port, it had done so in Poplar, among the employees of the East and West India Dock Company. The basic grievance of these men concerned the working of the plus system, and on 7 August Tillett had taken the matter up in a letter to the Dock Company. The letter was ignored, and Tillett felt his union to be too weak to take action.[29] His hand was, however, forced in a dramatic and unexpected way.

The organisation of the gas stokers at Beckton had inevitably had repercussions in the Victoria and Albert dock systems, which were located near by. Some dockers at these systems had in fact applied to join Thorne's union, but the latter body made a decision not to extend organisation to the dockers.[30] However, a tugman named Harris, who worked in the Albert and Victoria docks, and was a friend of Thorne's, determined to form a new waterside union.[31] Why such a step should have been necessary, with Tillett's union already in existence, is not really clear. Nevertheless on 3 August 1889 Harris presided at a meeting in Canning Town, with the object of launching a new union for 'the permanent and extra-permanent hands of the Dock Company'.[32] About 3000 people were reported as being present at the meeting and John Burns (an engineer prominent in the Social Democratic Federation) and Mr Walsh (of the Seamen's Union) spoke on behalf of the new organisation. It soon became clear that Harris intended to extend his union to include dockers outside the Victoria and Albert district. He was certainly aware that trouble was brewing over the plus system at the docks of the East and West India Company, and no doubt saw this as an opportunity which his union could not afford to miss. On Saturday, 10 August, he sent a telegram to Will Thorne asking him to be present at the South West India Dock on the following Monday, in order to assist in the organisation of the dockers working at that centre. As arranged, the gas stokers' leader arrived at the South Dock on Monday, 12 August, at calling-on time, where he was met by Tom McCarthy.[33] McCarthy and Thorne both made rousing speeches exhorting the men to form a union, and refuse to go into work that morning. Eventually they collected a gathering of rebellious dockers and led them off in procession in the direction of adjacent dock systems. Now all this was taking place in the 'territory' of the Tea Operatives' Union, and the events of the morning were duly reported by union members at a meeting in the tiny branch rooms at Wroot's Coffee House. The members of Tillett's union were furious at the intervention of Thorne, who had taken the affairs of the dockers into his own hands and completely ignored the existence of the Tea Operatives' Union. It seemed as if the union, after years of campaigning in the docks, had had the initiative snatched away from it at the crucial moment. The membership demanded that the union call a strike at the South Dock immediately, and after some procrastination Tillett agreed. He had in any case no choice, for the movement initiated by Thorne had snowballed and the dockers in this sector were now determined on a stoppage. By Wednesday, 14 August, the South Dock was at a standstill. Few could have guessed at the time that it would be mid-September before the dockers at this system again 'shaped-up' for work. Even fewer could have foreseen that the outmanœuvred Tea Operatives would by then number 18,000 members.

The immediate origins of the 1889 strike were, as we have seen, of a somewhat confused and controversial nature. Looking back at the end of the struggle, John Burns saw the strike as developing out of the successful movement of gas workers, and saw Harris as the man who forged the link between gas stokers and dockers.[34] In this connection it will be remembered that Burns played a part in Harris's attempt to form a new union in August 1889. Will Thorne, not surprisingly, took the same view as Burns. Tillett, on the other hand, makes no mention of Thorne or Harris in his autobiography, and indeed he had good reason to ignore their contributions, although at the time he was only too well aware of the threat they posed to the existence of his own union.[35] The feeling that existed between Tillett and Harris was well brought out in an incident that occurred three days after the commencement of the strike. The Tea Operatives held a meeting at Canning Town with the object of persuading the Victoria and Albert dockers to join in the strike of their brethren upstream and form a branch in Tillett's union. Harris's union had of course originated in this district, and Tillett lost no time at the meeting in attacking it as a 'union of dock officials'. This charge was hotly disputed by a section of the audience, but by this time Tillett's union had acquired some prestige and it had the majority of the meeting solidly behind it.[36] After this incident Harris's rival union vanishes from sight.

If Tillett's organisation did not take the initiative in beginning the strike, it quickly recovered its position once the strike had commenced. As the only really established union of dock labourers in London, it became the focal point of their revolt. Now that the Rubicon had been crossed, Tillett gave a vigorous lead. McCarthy, who after many months of supporting Tillett had played such an ambiguous part in the events of 12 August, returned to Tillett's camp. More important still, Tillett immediately got in touch with Tom Mann. Mann was, like Burns, an engineer by trade and a Social Democratic Federation member. He was also working at this time for H. H. Champion's paper, the *Labour Elector*. Tillett had met him some time before, and recognised his great talents as a labour organiser. His was indeed to be a large part in the developments that lay ahead.[37] Tillett, McCarthy, Mann—these three were the original strike leaders. A year later they were still together; Tom Mann as President, Ben Tillett as General Secretary, and Tom McCarthy as Organiser of the Dockers' Union. Burns, on the other hand, came late on the scene, and when the strike was over played little part in the organisation of the Union. He has a large place in the history of the 1889 strike, but not in the development of dockers' unionism. As for Will Thorne, he quickly faded from the waterside scene: perhaps he had done quite enough on 12 August.

2

The strike that began on Wednesday, 14 August, concerned at first only the dockers in the employ of the East and West India

Company, and it arose out of that company's peculiar piece-work system. Tillett had, however, formulated a programme of demands relevant to north bank dock workers generally—that is, employees of the London as well as the East and West India Company.[38] The most important demand was that both the plus and contract systems be abolished. Beyond this Tillett put forward three proposals aimed at reducing the purely casual nature of dock employment. First came the demand that the half-day should be the minimum length of employment. Next came the request that taking-on times be reduced to two per day. Finally there was the demand that overtime be penalised by raising the difference between the day and night rates to two pennies instead of one. The claim for a minimum day rate of 6d per hour was also made, and although this claim subsequently attracted much attention it was not at the outset regarded as crucial, for those dockers working under the contract system were already on this rate. Tillett's target was, essentially, the system of dock employment.

Dockers employed by the London Company tended at first to hold aloof from the movement led by Tillett. At the London and St Katherine's docks the contract system operated as a divisive force among the men. No doubt the majority were opposed to it, but the trouble was that many of the most active workers had been drawn off into the ranks of the contractors, and these had a vested interest in the continuance of the system. It is also possible that the men at these docks recalled the events of 1880, when their own strike had been unsupported by the dockers of the India Company. Resentment at this fact may well have lingered on. But it was the legacy of the contract system that was really important. Even when the men at the London and St Katherine's docks finally joined the strike, their allegiance to the common cause was extremely shaky. Throughout the stoppage the area proved a constant source of anxiety to the Strike Committee, and the picketing was less effective here than at any other centre.[39] After the strike was over the area presented further problems to the organisers of the newly created Dockers' Union. The contract system and its attendant corruption had divided and demoralised the men; this was the unpleasant fact that union organisers had to face. At the other dock systems of the London Company—the Victoria and Albert—the problem was not so great. The contract system was less deeply ingrained. Furthermore there was not the extreme poverty among the ordinary casuals that was found further upstream, for these docks were the most prosperous in the port. This factor of course influenced morale and capacity to organise. At first, however, the Victoria and Albert dockers, like those at London and St Katherine's, hesitated to commit themselves to a strike alongside the men at the India docks. On Friday, 16 August, three days after the stoppage had begun, Tillett's union convened a meeting in West Ham aimed at persuading these men to join the strike and form a branch in the Tea Operatives' Union.[40] The meeting was divided on the merits of strike action, for the men had no specific grievance outstanding, and it was decided to postpone a decision until the Sunday, when a mass meeting had been scheduled to take place outside the East India Dock gates.

If the dockers of the London Company were slow to follow the lead given by Tillett's union, the latter organisation did at least gain one incalculable advantage very early on in the strike—the support of the stevedores. Such support was vitally important on two counts. First, a stoppage of stevedores was capable of severely disrupting the working of the docks, thus strengthening the dockers' hand against the companies. Secondly, as experienced unionists, the stevedores could bring to the dockers' cause administrative skills that were of the utmost importance in the organisation of successful strike action. On the face of it, the early involvement of the two stevedores' unions on the side of the India dockers was rather surprising, for they had no demands to make of their own employers—the master stevedores—and came out purely in sympathy. Furthermore, they were putting at risk working conditions that were the envy of most port workers. The manifesto issued by the two societies proclaimed that they took action 'not to inconvenience the brokers, shipowners, or master stevedores, as our quarrel is not with them, but we feel our duty is to support our poorer brothers'.[41] No doubt altruism was one factor in the stevedores' decision to strike, but alone it is not a sufficient explanation of their action. The basic point was that in their work and in other activities the stevedores existed in close proximity to the India dockers. Stevedores worked alongside dockers in the enclosed docks, and their organisation was centred in Poplar where the Tea Operatives' Union also operated. Thus it was not easy for them to avoid involvement. When the East and West India Dock Company introduced blacklegs into the docks to replace the strikers, the stevedores were forced to decide whether or not it was proper for them to work alongside such men. Many of them thought it was not, and by the first Friday of the stoppage these men were already out in sympathy. However, the leadership of the two stevedore societies was at first divided as to whether or not official support should be given to the dockers. Tom McCarthy, the Secretary of the Amalgamated Union, was an ardent supporter of the latter's cause as we have seen, but other leaders were more cautious. On the evening of Saturday, 17 August, the councils of the two societies met at the Wades Arms in Poplar to finally resolve the matter one way or another.[42] The excitement in the street outside was intense, and inside the issue was hotly contested; in the end McCarthy's party won the day and an official strike was declared. Local pressures had proved too strong to resist.

The action of the stevedores changed the character of the stoppage entirely. Until the Saturday it had hardly extended beyond the employees of the East and West India Dock Company, but once the stevedores came out a much more general strike was foreshadowed. The stevedores gave the movement prestige and substance, and others would now be encouraged to follow where the original strikers led. On Sunday, 18 August, a mass meeting that had been previously arranged took place at the East India Dock gates. It was attended by large numbers and was extremely effective as a demonstration of strength; further stoppages could now be confidently expected for the following Monday.[43] Monday did indeed see a vast extension of the strike. The dockers at the Victoria and Albert systems came out as did also those at London and at St Katherine's. The men at Millwall began to turn out, and down at Tilbury Tillett and Orbell were able to persuade many of the men to leave work. While still far from port-wide in scope, the strike was well on the way to becoming so. Monday, 19 August, was important for another reason. On that day the first of the great processions that were to become so characteristic a feature of the strike took place. Its march into the City, while much less imposing than many that were to take place in the days ahead, gave the metropolis its first glimpse of the unfolding East End drama.[44] The great orderly processions were to become a vital part of the strategy of the strike. They maintained the discipline, morale and enthusiasm of the strikers, but their chief value was as a source of favourable publicity. Such publicity was crucial, for, lacking union funds, the strikers depended from the beginning on outside financial assistance in order to hold out against the companies.

On 21 August the Lightermen's Union threw in its lot with the strikers. This was an event of the greatest importance in view of the role played by the lighterage trade in the functioning of the port. Unlike the stevedores, however, the lightermen did not strike primarily in sympathy with the dockers, for they had demands of their own to press. The same was true of numerous other groups who struck during the week beginning 18 August.[45] Steamship workers and corn porters on the south side had recently suffered wage reductions, now they struck to recover the old rates. The wharfmen and warehouse workers likewise had their own demands to make when they joined the movement. By Thursday, 22 August, the stoppage was port-wide. It had become an immensely complex affair, reflecting the great diversity of the waterside labour force. It had even spread beyond that labour force as normally defined, to include sailors and the ship-repairing tradesmen. The employers of the port had allowed things to drift. They had underestimated the seriousness of the movement, had made no efforts to obtain a settlement, and had not bothered to compete with the men in winning over the Press and public opinion. They, and in particular the joint committee of the London and India docks, had brought the world's greatest port to a standstill.

The great growth of the strike movement presented a tremendous challenge to the men's leaders. During the first days of the stoppage the Tea Operatives' committee had to manage by itself, operating from Wroot's Coffee House in Poplar. The most important function it had to perform was the organisation of relief for the strikers. Unless this was done, hunger would quickly drive the men back to work. Funds began to come in from outside after the first Sunday of the strike, and the Tea Operatives formed a finance committee on the following Tuesday to deal with the distribution of relief. The committee broke down almost immediately, however, for, while Burns and Mann made a point of attending its first meeting, only one of the other five members put in an appearance (namely, Harry Kay, an old member of the union). The committee did make some attempt to get a system of relief going, but the position was very far from being satisfactory.[46] Meanwhile, of course, the stevedores had come out on strike, and they formed their own strike committee which met at the Wades Arms (also in Poplar). The stevedores quickly showed themselves to be competent administrators, and tacitly they began to assume the direction of the movement. The *Star* wrote on Thursday, 22 August: 'The Stevedores' Council is rapidly assuming the position of a sort of Parliament in this huge strike of riverside men. Last night there were upwards of 20 deputations from different bodies to consult them; they sit till after midnight.'[47] The leading role of the stevedores' unions in the conduct of the movement received formal recognition at the end of that week. It was then agreed to amalgamate the Tea Operatives' committee with that of the Stevedores to form one United Strike Council, which was to meet at the Wades Arms. The newly created council was representative of all the groups involved in the strike—dockers, stevedores, lightermen, sailors, and many others—but it was the stevedores who really ran the administrative machine. It was they who dominated the work of the all important finance sub-committee of the council.[48]

The finance committee was able to evolve fairly quickly an efficient system for the distribution of relief. Even before the formation of the United Council it had been decided to administer relief not in the form of cash payments, but by issuing food tickets (the money being paid direct to food suppliers). The committee now established eight district relief centres from which these tickets would be distributed, each centre being placed under the control of a district committee. The system was not infallible, but it worked sufficiently well to maintain the strike intact. As the stoppage went on the main problem ceased to be one of distribution, and attention then became focused on the crucial question of the flow of funds from outside. The distribution of relief was vitally important, however, not only from the point of view of maintaining the strike intact, but also in the light of its contribution to union growth in the port. Only a tiny proportion of the waterside labour force was organised at the commencement of the stoppage. Once the strike got under way it was inevitable that the enthusiastic atmosphere would lead to a great increase in union membership, but, given the character of the waterside labour force, it was likely that this growth would stop short of total port-wide organisation. The administration of relief made possible the compulsory enrolment of port workers, and operated in this respect as a substitute for control of hiring procedures. Thus, at the district relief centres, union cards were issued in return for the payment of 2d (entrance fee and weekly contributions being suspended for the duration of the strike). After a short period of time the presentation of a union card became the necessary credential for obtaining a relief ticket. This linking of relief to union membership was certainly an effective way of creating a union shop, and over 20,000 union cards were issued in this fashion during the course of the strike.[49] The system had its drawbacks. Many of the cards were taken by that class of demoralised casuals described in a previous chapter, and once work was resumed these men created problems. According to one union officer, at the time of the resumption in September 'hundreds were sent off because they would not work'.[50] The great majority of men issued with union cards during the course of the strike were nominally enrolled in the Tea Operatives' Union, as this was the only general waterside union existing at the time the strike commenced. Throughout most of the stoppage, however, the Tea Operatives remained a largely paper organisation, without a proper branch or district structure. Its leaders—Tillett, Mann, Orbell, Kay and others—were kept fully preoccupied running the strike, and not until work was resumed could they devote their attention to the real task of union organisation.

Apart from the crucial question of relief, the most important challenge to the strike leaders was provided by the introduction of blackleg labour. The dock companies were quick to enrol strike-breakers once the dispute began, and in fact continued in this policy right up to the very day on which a settlement was reached.[51] The outsiders were offered permanent employment at £1 per week. The only way in which this policy could be combated was by effective picketing, and from the beginning the picket lines occupied much of the attention of the strike leaders. According to Burns there were at the height of the stoppage as many as 3000 pickets in operation, some of them operating from boats in the river.[52] Burns was of the opinion that the sailors and firemen made the best pickets. Like the stevedores, these men had come out early on in sympathy with the dockers, and their work on the picket lines complemented perfectly the work of the stevedores in administration.[53] The achievement of the pickets was, however, uneven. At Tilbury they achieved remarkable feats in keeping the strike-breakers out, and success in this quarter owed much to the generalship of Harry Orbell.[54] The London and St Katherine's docks, on the other hand, had a very bad record. In all, the number of blacklegs imported into the docks ran into several thousands, although in many cases the pickets were able to persuade the strike-breakers to come out again.[55] It may be said that the picket lines held, but only just.

The establishment of the United Strike Council at the Wades Arms had seemed at first to provide an effective strike leadership that was acceptable to all the multifarious groups that made up the riverside labour force. However, it quickly encountered trouble on the south side of the river. The men there felt that insufficient attention was being paid to the area by the Wades Arms committee. The south-side men certainly had a case. The strike council, like the public at large, tended to see the strike as essentially concerned with the condition of the London and India dockers. This preoccupation was not only the result of the fact that the stoppage had its origins in this sector; it was reinforced by the circumstance that up until the strike all the branches of the stevedores' unions were situated on the north bank. Union stevedores well understood the grievances of the north-bank dockers, alongside of whom they were accustomed to work, but they had little knowledge of conditions across the river. The general ignorance of conditions on the south side was unfortunate because these conditions were substantially different from those on the north bank, and the same remedies could not therefore be made to apply on both sides of the river. Surrey men were commonly paid by piece rather than time rates, and what was more important, they were split up into numerous occupational groups each of which had its own set of working conditions. This was quite unlike the north bank, where masses of dock and wharf labourers were more or less lumped together under basically similar systems of employment. The complexity of the situation was to some extent recognised by the leaders on the north bank, for on Tuesday, 20 August, when the strike was just beginning to assume port-wide proportions, the leaders of the Tea Operatives called a meeting at the Assembly Hall, Mile End Road, 'to collect further information as to the rate of pay received by the different sections of riverside men, and to draw up a standard rate for these sections'.[56] However, in the general rush of events, this task was not carried through. Demands had been formulated on behalf of the north-bank dockers, as we have seen, but the strike committee failed to devise a programme for the Surrey men. There were other sources of friction between the two banks. The south-side men, for example, suspected that they were not getting their full share of relief tickets.[57] But basically the problem was, as one of their leaders said, that 'the various sections of waterside labour on the south side were unable ... to get their special grievances attended to or even understood'.[58]

In the end the United Strike Council decided to grant full autonomy to the men across the water, and at the beginning of September a separate South Side Strike Committee was set up. The committee met at Sayes Court in Deptford and had full powers to conduct the strike on the south side, being subject to Wades Arms only in matters of general policy.[59] As a further gesture to the Surrey men Tom Mann was dispatched across the river and his services were placed at the disposal of Sayes Court.[60] Mann did much to raise morale on the south bank, and he also acted as a liaison officer between the two strike committees. In time the Sayes Court Committee proved itself capable of doing what neither the Tea Operatives nor the Wades Arms Committee had been able to do. On 10 September it presented concrete demands on behalf of all the numerous south-bank sections. An enumeration of the various sections involved is sufficient to indicate the complexity of the situation; separate claims were put forward on behalf of Deal Porters, Lumpers (outside), Stevedores (inside), Overside Corn Porters, Quay Corn Porters, Trimmers and General Labourers, Weighers and Warehousemen, Granary Corn Porters, and finally Steamship Workers.[61] The south bank certainly presented a special problem and we shall have cause to return to it at a later stage.

The crisis of the strike was reached at the end of August. The cause was shortage of funds, and without adequate finance the strike could not be continued. Hunger was already beginning to affect morale. The joint committee of the two major dock companies had so far shown little readiness to make concessions, and the rest of the port employers had followed the committee's lead. The dominant personality on that committee was a Mr

Norwood, who displayed the greatest hostility towards the men's cause. The radical *Star* newspaper, which was strong in support of the men, remarked of Norwood: 'He is in appearance and manners the very embodiment of the insolence of capitalism. He is stout, well-fed, and arrogant.'[62] With funds running out, and with the employers apparently adamant against concessions, the strike committee at Wades Arms felt that the position had become desperate. The only way out that it could see lay in an extension of the strike beyond the waterfront, thus provoking a really major crisis in the life of the metropolis. It was a desperate remedy for a desperate situation. A manifesto was drawn up calling on the various trades in London to strike in support of the port workers. The committee was encouraged to believe that these trades would respond to the call by the fact that in its early days the stoppage had shown strong signs of spreading beyond the waterfront, and the Wades Arms Committee had then been obliged to restrain this tendency, partly on the grounds that many of the potential strikers were unorganised and would, therefore, require relief.[63] As it was, London coal porters and carmen were already out on strike.[64] However, when it came to the point, the strike leadership was divided on the wisdom of issuing the so-called 'No-Work Manifesto'. Although there appeared to be little alternative, some feared that it would alienate public opinion and thus finally dry up the flow of outside funds. There was also the fact that some of the London unions had shown little enthusiasm for sympathetic action; this being the case, the strike call might well turn out to be a fiasco which would only expose the weakness of Wades Arms. Thus, although the manifesto was in fact issued on the 30 August, it was withdrawn almost immediately.[65]

There was another factor behind the sudden withdrawal of the 'No-Work Manifesto', a factor that quite miraculously altered the entire situation. On 29 August, the very day on which the manifesto was drawn up, news arrived from Australia that the Brisbane Wharf Labourers' Union was sending £150 to the London strike fund. In itself this was not particularly significant. The point was that the Brisbane donation marked the beginning of a steady stream of funds from Australia. The reasons which led the Australian unions to make this tremendous contribution to the London dockers' cause need not concern us in this study, but there can be no doubt that their contribution made the difference between victory and defeat. From the beginning of September onward the strike leaders had no need to worry further about the problem of relief; massive financial support from Australia banished the spectre of defeat through hunger.[66] Taking advantage of this situation, the strike leadership quickly switched its tactics. The processions into the City were abandoned and all efforts were now concentrated on the picket lines.[67] If the infiltration of blacklegs could be kept down to a minimum victory was now a distinct possibility.

Chances of victory were all the greater during the opening days of September in view of developments in the employers' camp. Norwood's united front was beginning to crumble. The alliance of wharfingers and dock companies had been at best an uneasy one, and its break-up was perhaps not surprising. The wharfingers' peace offensive was launched by a Mr Lafone, and he and John Burns (acting for Wades Arms) arranged terms which raised the men's rate from 5d to 6d per hour, with 8d for overtime. There was, however, a problem impeding any resumption of work at the wharves on these terms. The lightermen refused to work anywhere in the port until their own demands and those of port workers generally had been met. The business of the wharves was very largely dependent upon lighterage, so that the attitude of the lightermen threatened to nullify any independent agreement with the wharfingers. However, those wharves receiving short-sea shipping could resume business on a limited scale, and on 5 September some lightermen agreed to work at the wharves, so that on that date the agreement came into partial operation.[68] At about the same time the men at several of the independent tea warehouses resumed work—also on an agreed 6d and 8d rate. The *Star* thought that this was the beginning of the end; surely the dock companies and their allies would not hold out for much longer.[69] On 5 September, the day on which the Lafone Agreement came into operation, the Lord Mayor intervened in the dispute (which was now running into its fourth week). Henceforward the Mansion House became the centre of intensive efforts at mediation, efforts which were to culminate in the signing of the so-called Mansion House Agreement.

The tortuous negotiations which led up to this agreement need not concern us. Norwood and the joint committee did not give way easily, nor did the Master Lightermen or the south-side employers. So far as the joint committee was concerned, it accepted that it would ultimately have to give way on the main points of Tillett's programme, and devoted its energies to postponing the date on which the new conditions would come into operation. In the end, with the tactful assistance of Cardinal Manning, a compromise was found concerning the date upon which the new rate of 6d and 8d was to come into force.[70] Consideration of what was to replace the plus and contract systems, which were to be abolished, was, however, postponed. This was to be the subject of a separate agreement to be negotiated at the end of October.[71] A rough settlement having been hammered out for the north-bank dockers, it remained to deal with the lightermen and the multifarious groups represented by the Sayes Court Committee on the south bank. Both the Lightermen's Union and the Sayes Court Committee stuck rigidly to the letter of their original demands, but at last, on Saturday, 14 September, a final settlement was reached. Needless to say it was a settlement distinctly favourable to the men, although there remained many crucial details to be worked out in the aftermath of the stoppage. The resumption of work was fixed for Monday, 16 September, but for the moment it was a time for celebration, and on the Sunday a mass rally was held in Hyde Park to mark the triumphant conclusion of the dispute.

3

The 1889 strike resulted in an expansion of trade unionism throughout the port of London. The chief beneficiary of this process was undoubtedly the Tea Operatives' Union, whose membership grew from a few hundred at the start of the strike to nearly 18,000 at its close. The position at the end of the stoppage was, however, not regarded as entirely satisfactory by the leaders of this society. They had naturally hoped that, in so far as unorganised workers could be enrolled as trade unionists, they would be enrolled as members of the Tea Operatives' Union. So far as workers on the north side of the river were concerned, this hope was to a considerable extent realised. On the south side, however, events had taken a different turn. During the course of the strike the Surrey men had gone beyond the establishment of a separate strike committee, and had in fact begun to evolve their own union, independent of the Tea Operatives. Thus at an early date they eliminated the possibility that all unorganised workers might be brought within the one dockers' union.

In the latter part of August 1889 branches had begun to spring up in the districts south of the river.[72] It was here that the strength of the old Labour Protection League had been concentrated, so that there existed a tradition of organisation among the lower grades of workers which was not present on the north bank.[73] The pockets of organisation which sprang up south of the river in 1889 were deliberately modelled upon the 1872 union. They called themselves 'Lodges of the Labour League',[74] and, in the manner of 1872, the men were organised in autonomous branches based upon occupational groupings. These branches were represented upon the Sayes Court Committee, and, after the strike had ended, they turned that committee into the executive council of a separate south-side union.[75] The continuity with 1872 was reflected in the title of the new organisation—the South Side Labour Protection League (S.S.L.P.L.)—and a further connection with the movement of 1872 is to be seen in the linking to the new organisation of the overside corn porters' branch, the sole survivor of the old union on the south side.[76]

The emergence of an independent union on the south bank was a constant source of friction, for the Tea Operatives' Union had hoped to make a clean sweep of all unorganised port workers. It had, in fact, formed some branches south of the river, and these were struggling with the league for supremacy there in the autumn of 1889.[77] By late November, however, it was obvious that the S.S.L.P.L. had come to stay, and Tillett's union therefore agreed to accept the existence of the Surrey organisation.[78] The conflict between the two unions was significant, not because the S.S.L.P.L. was a particularly dangerous rival to the Tea Operatives, but because it represented an attempt to revive an earlier form of association. Tillett and his friends did not see the matter in this light. From their point of view, the formation of a separate union on the south bank merely created needless disunity among dock and wharf workers.[79] The Surrey men, on the other hand, could claim with justice that theirs was the really authentic union for London riverside workers, and that Tillett's society constituted a new and alien element on the waterfront.[80] To understand this point, it is necessary to compare the constitutions of the two unions and the fibre of their organisation. Like its predecessor of

1872, the S.S.L.P.L. adopted an extremely decentralised structure which left the branches as almost completely autonomous units, a structure that accorded well with conditions on the waterfront.[81] In the first place it took account of the widely varying conditions of employment, and of the consequent desire of the men to keep trade matters in their own hands. It also made possible the integration of different groups, some of which operated job monopolies while others did not have this advantage. Thus the overside corn porters, with their restrictionist policies, would not have merged themselves in a unitary organisation which opened their sphere of employment to all members. They were, however, prepared to unite themselves with ordinary wharf workers in a body which preserved their sphere of employment intact. The decentralised structure of the S.S.L.P.L. thus allowed it great flexibility in the matter of recruitment. It could contain exclusive job monopolies, such as those of the overside men and the steamship workers, and yet recruit among general labourers within the port industry, and even outside it. With a General Secretary— Harry Quelch—who was a member of the Social Democratic Federation, the S.S.L.P.L. thus formed an interesting bridge between the old and new elements in waterside unionism.[82]

The Tea Operatives' Union, in contrast to the league, represented in its expanded form a complete break with past tradition. At a meeting held in mid-September 1889, at the new union headquarters in Mile End Road, the Tea Operatives' Association converted itself into the Dock, Wharf, Riverside, and General Labourers' Union of Great Britain and Ireland (Dockers' Union being the abbreviated title).[83] At the same meeting Tom Mann was elected as the union's President and Ben Tillett as its General Secretary. Until his resignation, in September 1892, Tom Mann remained the dominant figure in the union, and so great was his influence that when he resigned it was feared that the organisation would fall apart.[84] Mann like Harry Quelch of the S.S.L.P.L. was a member of the S.D.F., but, unlike Quelch, he had no real roots in dockland. He had been trained as an engineer, and his heart remained in the engineering rather than the port industry.[85] Mann's interest in waterside unionism sprang from his passionate concern for downtrodden labour generally, and as leader of the Dockers' Union his policies were sweeping and sometimes high-handed. As an outsider, and an impulsive one at that, he occasionally encountered the most ferocious opposition from port workers, and on one occasion he told Burns that he was forced to carry a revolver to protect himself.[86] Nevertheless his personality was such an engaging one that he won in the end the whole-hearted support of his members, and his departure in 1892 was regretted throughout the organisation.[87] Mann's unfamiliarity with the waterfront was, however, a real handicap. It was almost certainly his decision that the Dockers' Union should adopt a rigidly centralised constitution, in defiance of all past practice in London and other major ports.[88] This policy of centralisation would have been impossible to implement but for the weak fibre of organisation on the north bank. Although the Tea Operatives' Association had enrolled 18,000 members by the end of the great strike, it was still in late September almost entirely without a branch or district organisation. The reason was that its large member-ship knew next to nothing about the workings of unionism.[89] On the south bank branches had grown up spontaneously as the men revived the traditions of 1872. Among dock workers on the north bank, however, these traditions were much less strong and branch organisation had to be imposed artificially from above. The lack of cohesion among north-bank workers thus made it possible for Mann to launch his centralised constitution, for there were no sectional interests sufficiently developed to resist it.

While Mann and Tillett were anxious to establish strong central control in the new union, they nevertheless realised that organisation would not survive unless they were able to infuse independent life into its branches. It was hoped that as many members as possible would be drawn into branch activities, and that the latter would develop among the rank and file a genuine interest in trade unionism. Progress was very uneven. At first members tended to bypass the branch completely, and carry their grievances direct to the union executive.[90] There was so little experience of organised activity at local level that it was difficult for branches to achieve an independent existence, and only too often they became merely the instrument through which dues were collected and forwarded to the Central Office.[91] It was often long before even this function was efficiently performed, and there were plenty of cases of defaulting branch secretaries. The burden of infusing life into branch organisation rested on the shoulders of the two union organisers, McCarthy and Orbell. Without these two the union would indeed have fared badly. For all their other qualities, neither Mann nor Tillett were good at routine adminis- tration, and both were easily sidetracked into participating in activities unconnected with the union.[92] Officially the two organi- sers were delegated to 'educate the members in the routine work of the union, and to encourage and develop an intelligent interest on all labour questions'.[93] In fact these two men were hopelessly overloaded, and much of their time had to be given to the handling of disputes and negotiations. With Mann's departure in 1892 things became still worse, for Tillett was constantly away from the Central Office and the burden of keeping the organisation going fell almost entirely on the Organisers.[94] In this situation the viability of branch organisation came to depend largely upon the calibre of local leadership, and it was fortunate that in many cases this was a good deal better than might have been anticipated. Posterity has not dealt kindly with these men. Crowley in his study of unionism at this period has conveyed the impression that the new unions were rotten at the core,[95] and in painting this picture he has relied heavily upon the memoirs of union leaders who were less than generous to their rank and file.[96] Corruption and irresponsibility there were of course, but they were only part of the picture. Booth's patient survey of the local organs of the Dockers' Union reveals another side, it shows a body of local officers struggling with genuine idealism to develop among their members a belief in the principles of unionism.[97] It was typical of Tom Mann's generous nature that he was one of the very few to pay tribute to the work of these little-known figures.[98]

The efforts of Mann and others to give the Dockers' Union a real rather than a paper existence was not without its ironic side. Wherever a section of the men established a vigorous unionism, it manifested the greatest opposition to central direction. The Wapping wharf workers were a case in point. Wapping was a compact neighbourhood, dominated by London Irishmen. Unionism took root quickly among this coherent group, and the district soon became the most active in the union. Under the leadership of a capable district secretary, Mortimer Costello, the men opened union premises of their own, containing a local office and social club.[99] The exceptional coherence of this group, however, made them especially articulate in asserting their special interests. Wharf labourers had benefited less than the dockers

from the settlement that terminated the great strike.[100] Immediately after the strike the wharf men began to take matters into
their own hands.[101] Wapping took the lead, and struck at a number
of wharves in quick succession, at each of which they were successful in obtaining their chief demand—meal-time payments. The
committees of the four Wapping branches then took the initiative
in drawing up a separate agreement to cover the conditions of
wharf labourers, and they were successful in securing the adhesion
of the largest local wharfingers to these new terms. The example
set by the Wapping men was soon taken up by the wharf workers
on the south side. Meal-time payments was the chief issue at
stake, and in the last weeks of 1889 a succession of strikes took
place on the Surrey side, in which isolated wharves were forced to
concede payment. The stoppages were entirely unofficial. The
movement culminated in a protracted strike at Hay's wharf,
beginning in January 1890. The union reluctantly gave official
sanction to this strike but, it being the slack season, the men were
badly beaten. The whole affair was, however, highly significant in
that it revealed the capacity distinctive sections had for playing
havoc with central control. Again, in the autumn of 1891, the
Wapping men were once more to demonstrate their independence.
Then the men at the Carron and Hermitage wharf came out
unofficially and conducted the strike and negotiations with scant
reference to the wishes of Mann or other union leaders.[102]

The centralised structure of the Dockers' Union found its
justification only with respect to the north-bank dock workers, for
the inexperience and instability of this group rendered any form of
branch autonomy out of the question in the early days of organisation. Centralisation was, however, not adopted by the union's
leadership merely in order to suit conditions in this sphere. Mann
had no patience with traditional forms, and was determined to
make a fresh start. For him centralisation was the essential pre-
requisite of strong organisation,[103] and from this position he
would not flinch. In the opinion of Quelch, the Labour League
branches would have been prepared to join the Dockers' Union
had they been granted a substantial degree of autonomy.[104] Thus
in a broad sense Mann and Tillett failed to carry the south side
with them because they underestimated the diversity in the
economic and social life of the port, and the older traditions of
unionism that went with it. The extent to which the Dockers'

Union broke with past practices on the waterfront is well illustrated by the question of branch meeting-places. In all other unions
the branches met at the local public house; in the Dockers' Union
this was discouraged.[105] Mann regarded the union not merely as
an industrial, but also as an 'educational' institution.[106]

The south side was not the only sector of employment which the
Dockers' Union lost to another organisation. There were many
other groups in the port, some of them of considerable strategic
importance, who preferred to organise themselves outside the
big union. The result of this development was an endless proliferation of small societies. The steamship workers were a case in
point. While some of these men joined the S.S.L.P.L. and a few
in Wapping joined the Dockers' Union, the remainder formed a
society of their own. This society had three branches, each one
significantly being completely autonomous.[107] Like the steamship
workers, the ballast heavers and the non-freemen preferred to
form small societies of their own during the strike rather than
align themselves with existing unions. Further instances of
fragmentation occurred among two other occupational groups of
comparatively recent origin, the crane drivers and tugboatmen.[108]
Some crane drivers were recruited by the Dockers' Union and
S.S.L.P.L., but considerable numbers joined either one or other
of two small societies set up in the East End during the strike.
These were the Amalgamated Society of Engine Drivers and
Firemen (Land and Marine) and the Amalgamated Protective
Union of Engine Drivers, Crane Drivers, Hydraulic and Boiler
Attendants. The tugmen's position was even more chaotic. The
lightermen's and non-freemen's societies both recruited deck
workers, while engine-room men were recruited by the two
societies catering for waterside mechanics. In addition to these
societies a separate Tugboatmen's Union claimed to recruit all
tug workers whatever their occupation. The final touch of disunity among port workers was provided by the men in the coal
and ship-repairing trades, all of whom were organised apart from
the main body of port workers.[109]

The new Dockers' Union had not only to face the fact that it
had failed to make a clean sweep of all hitherto unorganised port
workers. There was also the circumstance that the most skilled
workers in the port continued to remain separately organised,
as they had been since 1872. What was more, the strike had

immensely strengthened these established unions. The enthusiasm of 1889 made unionists of hitherto unorganised stevedores and lightermen, as well as of dock and wharf workers, and their unions emerged from the struggle with a greatly enhanced membership. Before the strike the two Stevedores' Unions had a combined membership of 2500 distributed among seven branches.[110] By the end of 1890 the two unions had amalgamated, and there was a membership of over 4000 distributed between thirteen branches.[111] The United Stevedores' Union takes much of the credit for bringing about this expansion. Not only had it enrolled many new members, but it had eliminated the differences between its own working rules and those of the Amalgamated Society, thus permitting a fusion of the two bodies. It had done this in the lower docks by forcing the big shipping companies to recognise the society preference, and also to pay the 14s night rate.[112] At the Surrey docks, where the lumpers had been enrolled, rates were raised up to the standard of 8d per hour daywork, and 1s per hour overtime—the customary rate for stevedores.[113] The lightermen's organisation also expanded rapidly as a result of the strike, and swept in all those rivermen in the upper reaches of the Thames who had clung to the old Turnway societies for so long.[114] Among these new recruits was Harry Gosling, the future President of the National Transport Workers' Federation.[115]

The trade union structure of the port of London as it had emerged from the great strike was bewilderingly complex. Numerically the Dockers' Union dominated the scene. By July 1890 it had a membership in the Thames area of 25,531, organised in seven districts and sixty branches.[116] Strategically, however, the new union was desperately weak, especially when compared either with the league of 1872, or even with the contemporary National Union of Dock Labourers in Liverpool. Whatever these two unions may have lost by their decentralised structure, they had gained by being able to embrace, however loosely, under one executive the great range of skills employed on the waterfront. It was perhaps a lasting misfortune that the 1872 league could not be fully revived in 1889, for the fragmentation of waterside organisation, deplorable as it was, was not to be overcome by insistence on centralisation. Unity would never be achieved on the waterfront without far reaching concessions in the direction of branch autonomy. If the Dockers' Union had made these concessions it might still have failed to embrace all unorganised port workers, and it is virtually certain that it would have failed to embrace organised groups such as stevedores or lightermen. Even so, it would certainly have strengthened its position in some directions, and, above all, would have done much to pave the way for an ultimate alliance of interests. Instead of this, it clung to its centralist principles, and attempted to use its great size to expand its sphere of influence by force.[117] In the end this policy brought only isolation and weakness. Furthermore, it created a gulf between the smaller occupational unions and the Dockers' organisation which was never properly bridged.

Next to the Dockers' Union in size, and closest to it in character of membership, came the S.S.L.P.L.[118] This union reached a membership of 5000 just after the strike, though some of these were not port workers. Of its eighteen branches in 1891, seven were of grain workers of various types, and this core of workers in a common trade and locality gave cohesion to the society. It was, however, a pale shadow of the league of 1872, and, because of its restriction to the south bank, it was destined to play only a minor role in the development of unionism in the port. 1889 marked the beginning of a new era in the port in more ways than one. It saw not only the revival of mass unionism, but the triumph of a new kind of mass unionism. The S.S.L.P.L. was in a sense still-born, for the type of organisation which it symbolised received in 1889 a permanent defeat.

5 A House Divided: Unionism after 1889

OCTOBER 1889 to October 1890 constituted a harvest year for the London port worker. Charles Booth described the case of a man who, having drifted through a number of jobs, turned to the docks just after the end of the great strike. The man obtained work there, and for a whole year averaged 45s a week, working heavy overtime, often until 10 or 11 o'clock at night.[1] Work was more plentiful than at any time since 1872, for not only was there the backlog from the strike to make up, but also trade continued to be exceptionally brisk through the first half of 1890.[2] The abundance of work at the port was the principal foundation upon which the new mass unionism rested. The men had money in their pockets to pay their union dues, and the shortage of labour forced upon employers a tacit recognition of the unions. In the elation of success few stopped to question the basis upon which it rested. There were, however, some wiser spirits who did attempt to analyse the position. Among them was H. H. Champion, at one time secretary of the S.D.F., and now the editor of the *Labour Elector*, the official organ of the Dockers' Union. In November 1889 he wrote warning the unions that their recent successes were due to the briskness of trade, and that this situation would not last.[3] Champion was of course right in his pessimistic predictions. The spectacular gains of 1889 largely wasted away in the less favourable economic environment of the 1890s,[4] and by the end of 1900 the level of organisation was not much better than it had been in 1880. It would, however, be a mistake to draw too sweeping a conclusion from this setback. On the surface the framework of the trade cycle appears to be decisive in the fortunes of waterside unions, yet it was only partially so. The decline of unionism after the boom of 1889–90 was not a uniform process; some groups within a single port fared better than others, and the position as between different ports varied even more. In some places organisation was destroyed, in others it was merely weakened. Thus, within the general framework of the trade cycle, other forces were at work, and these must be examined.

The necessity for a careful consideration of the base upon which port unionism rested is illustrated by the contrasting fortunes of organisation in Britain's three major ports. In Hull the union's strength did not slowly waste away over a decade, as in London; it was destroyed by a powerful employers' organisation in seven weeks.[5] In Liverpool, on the other hand, organisation survived intact at the South End right through into the new century. Thus in 1904 the National Union of Dock Labourers still enjoyed recognition, still enforced a union preference, and continued to regulate completely the conditions of work.[6] At the same period, in London, the Dockers' Union was virtually extinct. Only at the North End of the port of Liverpool had the National Union lost its influence, and this was the sphere where employment was controlled by the large shipping companies.

The above contrasts lead to one inescapable conclusion. While the trade cycle determined the bargaining power of organisation, and dictated when the men could move from defence to attack, it did not determine whether an organisation survived or not. The final arbiter of the union's destiny was the employer and his policy towards organised labour appears to have depended on the scale of his business concern. In London only one group of employers consistently recognised trade unionism throughout the period from 1872 to 1914—namely, the small master stevedores.[7] In Liverpool it was the same, and unionism only achieved stability at the South End because there the work was also dominated by small concerns. It was not the skill of their employees that was decisive in enforcing recognition upon these small men. Thus men performing precisely the same work for large shipping companies could rarely extract permanent recognition.

The size of the employing concern appears to have been decisive in the fortunes of waterside unionism for two main reasons. In the first place, the size of the firm determined the degree of contact between employer and employed. In large concerns there tended to be an appalling lack of sympathy between the two sides, a circumstance which also owed much to the casual basis of employment in the industry. This want of sympathy sometimes resulted in behaviour of the most extravagant kind, and of this behaviour the following quotation may serve as an example. The author of this remarkable piece of invective was the labour correspondent of the leading shipowners' journal, *Fairplay*.

> The simple docker alone, for whose purpose a turnip would answer for a head, and a round of beef for brains, must have everything regulated for him, so that he, the ignorant and sometimes drunken, may be raised by the State, at the expense of the ratepayers, to the level of beings as superior to him in intelligence as can possibly be.[8]

The men, for their part, tended to behave with an utter disregard for the interests of their employers, and on the big shipping-lines cases of theft and drunkenness recurred with monotonous regularity.[9] In this atmosphere of total alienation neither stevedores nor dockers were able to stabilise organisation. In smaller concerns this climate of ill-will was much less evident, and organisation was therefore able to strike lasting roots. Given this difference in atmosphere between large and small concerns, the second factor influencing a union's position comes into play. Unlike the small man, the large companies had the resources to break organisation at will. Nor was this all, for the large companies increased their power still further in September 1890 by joining together to form the Shipping Federation.[10]

The Shipping Federation was an alliance of large shipping companies, and its principal object was the destruction of union power on the waterfront.[11] It was formed, as we shall see,[12] largely as a result of the militant tactics pursued by the sailors' organisation, but the counter-attack which it launched affected all waterside unions alike. The federation had a masterful general manager in the person of George Laws, and an effective labour department was built up that was capable of supplying sufficient blacklegs to break most strikes. The strength of such a federation lay in the fact that it rendered employers to some extent independent of the local labour market. This power was well illustrated in London in 1900. In that year trade was booming and labour was scarce. In this favourable situation many dockers came out on strike. Yet the strike was utterly defeated, because the Shipping Federation was able to import blacklegs from places as far away as Swansea, Liverpool, Shields, and even Rotterdam.[13] Against such a power as this no union could stand.

The conflict between mass trade unionism and the large port employers centred upon the key issue of union monopoly. It was this issue which gave to industrial relations on the waterfront their peculiarly uncompromising atmosphere. Whenever trade was good, and organisation far advanced, waterside unions immediately insisted that employers should employ only members of their organisation.[14] So it had been in 1889. At the very beginning of the Dockers' Union's existence Ben Tillett had announced his intention of enforcing a union monopoly.[15] This monopoly was to be achieved by inducing employers to permit an inspection of union cards before the men were taken on for work. In thus insisting upon its right to influence hiring procedures the new union was treading the same path as that followed by the stevedores in the 1870s and 1880s.[16] The demand for such control was not the product merely of belligerence; it was in fact the only way in which an organisation could hope to stabilise its position. Like the early Stevedores' Union, the Dockers' Union needed to control employment both in order to enforce discipline among its turbulent membership and to restrict entry to waterside employment. In the case of the Dockers' Union this latter requirement was of crucial importance, for in the sphere of employment which it had organised natural restrictive influences, such as the skills attaching to a particular type of work, were largely lacking. Thus in the winter of 1889–90,[17] and again in August 1890,[18] the London districts of the union were instructed by the executive not to take any more new members. Restrictionist policies were, however, useless unless the union controlled hiring procedures. It was no good restricting union entrance if employers were able to go outside of the pool of union labourers when taking on men for work, and in times of bad trade, and nearly always in winter time, there were plenty of outsiders available. The union had thus to ensure that its monopoly was adhered to every day and at every calling-on stand, and this could only be done by a regular inspection of cards.

While the closed shop was an interest all waterfront unions had in common, it was absolutely unacceptable to the large-scale employers. It is true that in boom periods they might be forced to concede to the unions' influence over hiring procedures, as in 1889 and 1911. The concession was, however, purely tactical. To the large employers union monopoly represented an intolerable limitation on their freedom of action. The unions tried to sweeten the pill by being selective in their recruitment of members, thus ensuring that union workmen were good workmen. The Stevedores' Union had, as we have seen, adopted this policy since the 1870s,[19] and after 1889 it was taken up by the Dockers' Union. In August 1890 the executive of the latter organisation issued a directive, 'that no men known to be physically weak or otherwise incompetent, to be accepted under any consideration'.[20] Employers, however, remained unimpressed by the advantages of restricting themselves to union-selected labour. They dressed up their objections in a lot of talk about 'freedom' and the 'free' labourer but in fact their grounds of resistance were solid enough. They felt, sometimes not without justification, that union monopoly was fundamentally incompatible with effective work discipline. Employers in the late nineteenth century depended for a quick dispatch of shipping, not upon mechanisation, but upon a pliable labour force, worked at top speed for long hours.[21] They did not get this where unionists had a monopoly of the work. It was not merely a question of restrictions imposed by the working rules of the unions; the whole temper of the men changed when they had mass organisation to support them. It was a fact that during the period of complete organisation in London—from October 1889 to October 1890—the performance of the port's labour force declined considerably.[22] The rank and file of the new mass organisations had found themselves in a position of unaccustomed strength, and they had exploited this strength to the full. The chief objectives of the men were to have as many men employed as possible, and to spin out the work for as long as possible. In view of the chronic underemployment on the waterfront at most times this reaction was scarcely surprising. It was, however, extremely embarrassing for the unions, and especially for the Dockers' Union, the organisation chiefly involved. The union supported the men in their demands for increases in the numbers constituting gangs, but it found that the slowing down in the tempo of work hopelessly compromised it in its dealing with employers. Such 'ca'canny' practices were bound to generate among the owners a most determined resistance to union monopoly. Tom Mann issued several appeals to his members in order to get them to work more energetically.[23] He even showed himself prepared to sponsor a new system of working—the 'co-operative' system—by which the minimum time rates would be abolished and the men left to stand or fall by their earnings on a piece-work basis.[24] It was, however, all to no avail. The men held the whip hand during the 'harvest year' and they knew it. 'Ca'canny' apart, incessant unofficial stoppages disrupted the running of the port in this period of mass organisation, and the corn gangs of the Albert Dock earned a special notoriety in this respect.[25] The Dockers' Union was quite unable to control its turbulent and unbridled membership, and this fact put a lever in the hands of large employers, who only awaited an opportunity of breaking the power of organisation. Mr Hill of the Wilson-Hill Line told the Royal Commission on Labour in 1891 that he could not work his ships properly so long as the union had a monopoly of employment. The only way to restore control, in his view, was to introduce the threat of 'outside labour—free labour'. In his own words: 'non-unionists give us more control of the men.'[26]

The issue of union monopoly was thus the central problem dominating industrial relations on the waterfront. The crucial importance of this issue had much to do with the violent fluctuations in the fortunes of waterside unionism. It produced an uncompromising atmosphere in which each side felt bound to insist not upon a partial, but upon a complete victory. Given the oversupply of labour on the waterfront, complete victory was bound, sooner or later, to rest with the employers.

The urgency of the unions' demand for monopoly, and of the employers' resistance to it, both sprang from the instability of mass organisation on the waterfront. The Dockers' Union needed control of hiring procedures because, in the absence of any cohesion or traditions of organisation among its members, it had to enforce membership in order to achieve stability. In the long run the union hoped, by means of the educational work to which it attached so much importance, to replace coercion by a genuine allegiance to trade union principles. The tragedy was, however, that it was not given sufficient time in which to develop a real and lasting influence upon its membership. The large employers of the port made no distinction between unionism in its present form and unionism as it might be in the future. Only Colonel Birt of the Millwall Dock Company recognised the positive role that organisation could play in improving the calibre of the labour force, and he gave the union delegates the maximum encouragement.[27] Elsewhere employers, perhaps not surprisingly, took the short-term view. They identified organisation with reduced productivity and therefore sought to crush it. Their victory, like their viewpoint, was a short-term affair. When mass organisation revived in 1911, after twenty years of impotence, the same problems recurred as in 1889. Once more complaints were made that the men were out of control, that they were breaking agreements, and that the unions could not enforce discipline. Yet how could the unions be expected to enforce discipline when some of them, like the Dockers' Union, had been virtually extinct in London for a decade? How could men be 'reasonable' when they had no experience of any proper machinery for the redress of grievances? The whole thing was a vicious circle which became more and more intractable as the years went by and relations became more embittered. Mass organisation was never given a chance to develop roots in London, and this fact lay at the heart of the port's labour troubles. This was why Tillett called the port 'the great unmanageable',[28] and why Bevin said that it was calculated to break the heart of a trade union organiser.[29] Only the stevedores' sector provided an element of sanity. Here a group of small employers had consistently recognised organisation, and as a result a stable, reliable labour force had grown up, with a standard of workmanship unrivalled in the port. It was true that the stevedores had been recruited from sources different to those of the ordinary docker, but this does not invalidate the point. Some stevedores worked, not for the contractors, but for the big shipping companies, and many of these concerns consistently opposed the union. In this sphere industrial relations were as bad as anywhere in the docks, as we shall see below. In any case, the Stevedores' Union had had to deal in its early days with a membership as turbulent as that of the Dockers' Union in 1889.[30] Unlike the latter organisation, however, it had been granted the inestimable benefit of time.

2

The brief history of mass organisation in London after 1889 was played out against the stark background of the struggle for power at the calling-on stands. All the port unions were involved in this struggle and none came out unscathed. In particular, however, the battle tended to centre upon four organisations— the Stevedores' Union, the Dockers' Union, the National Amalgamated Sailors' and Firemen's Union, and the Lightermen's

Union—and it is upon these that attention will be focused. Although space has forbidden a full study of the Sailors' organisation, that union has been included here because its fate was intimately bound up with other waterside unions. There is also a special reason for the inclusion of the Lightermen's Union. The role of the lightermen in the struggle of the 1890s is a somewhat secondary one, but it is of importance in view of developments in 1911–12.

The Stevedores' Union had traditionally enjoyed recognition from the master stevedores of the port and it continued to do so after the 1889 strike. Some tension was indeed caused when the master stevedores formed themselves into the London Master Stevedores' Association, and the union at first refused to recognise the association.[31] This uneasiness was, however, soon overcome. The source of instability in the stevedores' organisation lay in fact outside the ambit of the L.M.S.A. 1889 and its aftermath had wrought a great change in the old Amalgamated Society of 1872, for the amalgamation with the United Stevedores, and the general expansion of organisation, had greatly extended its sphere of influence.[32] Prior to the great strike the jurisdiction of the society embraced only those master stevedores on the north bank who were engaged in loading ocean-going vessels. After the strike this sphere of influence was extended in two directions. First, it came to embrace those master stevedores at the Millwall and Surrey docks, whose work was largely concerned with unloading operations, especially the unloading of timber. In this sphere the society achieved lasting stability, for the masters on the south bank, like those on the north, proved amenable to the union's influence. The other major extension in the society's jurisdiction occurred at the downstream docks, where the large shipping companies performing loading-work were forced to recognise the union. As a result of extension in these two directions the society achieved a monopoly of all the shipwork performed in the enclosed docks, with the single (but important) exception of the discharging operations conducted by the dock companies. At the downstream docks, however, the society was unable to consolidate its position. Once again the problem of mobility asserted itself,[33] especially at Tilbury, and shortages of stevedores at that dock occasionally resulted in dockers loading oversea vessels.[34] However, the greatest source of instability downstream resulted from the character of the employers in

Trade Union leaders: Harry Gosling of the Lightermen (right) *and James Anderson of the Stevedores—respectively President and Secretary of the National Transport Workers' Federation*

*Ben Tillett: two studies of the Dockers' leader before and after a
conference at the Board of Trade, 1912*

this region. Several of the large steamship companies had loaded their vessels with non-unionists prior to the great strike,[35] and they greatly resented the reassertion of the society's power. The latter insisted that foremen should be society members, and that the men should be taken on outside the dock gates, where cards could be inspected and the union preference enforced.[36] For a while the large shipping companies accepted this situation, but there was little chance that this acceptance would prove permanent.

The position of the Dockers' Union generally resembled the most unstable sector of the stevedores' organisation. From the termination of the great strike until February 1891 the affairs of this union in London were dominated by its relationship with the joint committee formed for the management of the docks of the London and East and West India companies.[37] This enormous concern employed over 11,000 of its members,[38] and three out of the six London districts of the union were entirely dominated by joint committee employees. The Dockers' Union was indeed severely handicapped by having to face so powerful an employer, and from this standpoint was more unfavourably situated than any other waterside union in the country. Everything depended upon the ability of the organisation to extract an enduring recognition from this gigantic concern, for without that it had very little chance of achieving stability. After the termination of the dock strike the joint committee showed some willingness to recognise the new mass unionism. The financial crisis of 1888, and the great strike of the following year, had dealt the dock managements some severe blows and in the autumn of 1889 they were above all anxious to restore normal working to the port. The influence of Mr Norwood gave way to the more flexible régime of Mr Hubbard.[39] To Smith and Nash, whose history of the strike appeared in December 1889, it seemed that the joint committee had 'heartily recognised and encouraged the union'.[40]

The monopoly successfully established by the Dockers' Union in the joint committee's docks depended of course upon the organisation's ability to regulate calling-on procedures. This was the real significance behind the agreement covering piece-work, which was signed with the joint committee on 25 October 1889.[41] The Mansion House Agreement, which ended the great strike in September, had provided that the old 'contract' and 'plus' systems of work should be replaced by new piece-work arrangements;[42]

these new arrangements were the subject of the October agreement. This latter agreement was of crucial importance, and operations at the joint committee's docks were largely regulated by it until 4 November 1890, when it was terminated by the companies. The new system of piece-work was arranged on similar lines to the old plus system. The men now had a guaranteed minimum of 6d during the day and 8d overtime; in addition to the minimum they could earn a plus calculated on a tonnage rate. However, in order to obviate the old disputes as to whether the plus was calculated fairly or not, the men employed on a job were allowed to elect a 'workers' representative'. Ostensibly the main duty of the representative was to check that the plus rates were accurate and were fairly distributed among the men. The agreement, however, gave to the representative certain other functions, and these were to prove of paramount importance. Among other things the representative was entitled to be present at, and to assist in, the calling-on of men for work. In fact this meant that the representatives were to inspect union cards and block all non-unionists from employment, and this is precisely what they did.[43] At first the union's interpretation of the role of representatives was not challenged by the joint committee, and under this régime the organisation of the casual north-bank docker was rendered complete. There were, however, two groups of joint committee employees whose situation was different from that of the casual man, and who presented severe problems to union organisers. These were the two permanent grades of dock workers; the foremen and the permanent labourers. The Dockers' Union failed to extend its monopoly from the casual to the permanent grades, with ultimately grave consequences to itself.

In the aftermath of the 1889 strike large numbers of foremen and permanent labourers refused to join the Dockers' Union, and even strike action at Tilbury and elsewhere failed to compel their membership.[44] In resistance to the pressures exercised by the Dockers' Union both groups formed their own societies—namely, the Association of Foremen and Clerks of the Docks, Wharves and Warehouses,[45] and the Permanent Labourers' Mutual Protection Association.[46] The separate organisation of these two groups sprang from a similar source. Both groups lived a life remote from that of the dock casual. They enjoyed a regular weekly income, lived in neighbourhoods away from the waterfront, and normally subscribed to benefit schemes run by their employers.[47] The regularity, benefits, and status of their occupation were not to be lightly risked, and membership of a casual labourers' union certainly was a risk. As a foreman told the Labour Commission: 'It would not do for foremen and clerks to strike. You see we have a good deal to lose.'[48] The casual, for his part, despised the 'perm' and his way of life. He was regarded as a subservient being, 'who would work, if told to, for 2d an hour and a good kicking'.[49] Yet the Dockers' Union needed the foremen and permanent labourers. The foremen were a crucial group, who took on the men for work, determined the make-up of gangs, and dictated the pace of work operations. The labourers too were important, for what would happen if ever the joint committee decided to increase the proportion of its work done by permanent staff? If this sphere was left outside the ambit of the union it might prove dangerous indeed. Failure to extend its monopoly to these grades was, in fact, to prove disastrous to the Dockers' Union.[50]

It was not only the failure to enrol the permanent grades that quickly brought instability to the Dockers' Union. The joint committee began in the winter of 1889–90 to have second thoughts about union monopoly in the casual sector. Whether the early concessions had been merely tactical, or whether the committee was genuinely disillusioned with the results of union influence, it is difficult to say. Probably there were differences of opinion within the committee itself. It is certain that the dock authorities were becoming anxious about the deterioration in work performance, and were beginning to lay the blame for this deterioration upon the union. This changing climate was reflected in increasing tension at the calling-on stands. Tom Mann, the union's President, wrote to his old comrade Burns in February 1890: 'The Dock Company is making strenuous efforts to get us in a serious difficulty. They are now determined not to recognise the men's representatives and are taking on non-union men. This means serious trouble.'[51] At Cutler Street warehouse the union called the men out for four days over the employment of non-unionists. The strike was consciously regarded by the executive as a test case in the enforcement of its monopoly. 'We do not intend at any time', they said, 'to allow the thin end of the wedge in.'[52] In the summer of 1890, with trade still prosperous, the union found it easier to defend its monopoly, and in a clash over the examination of cards at the upstream docks it emerged victorious in July.[53] It was, however, clear that the joint committee had withdrawn from its earlier position of acquiescence. As long as trade continued good organisation was safe; otherwise, its future was precarious indeed.

The situation in the seafaring trades had much in common with that in ordinary dock employment, and it was in fact the seamen's organisation that brought the whole issue of union monopoly to a head in the port industry. The National Amalgamated Sailors' and Firemen's Union, founded in 1887,[54] differed little in its basic strategy from the organisations of port workers. It claimed a complete monopoly of ordinary seafaring employment for its membership, and enforced this claim vigorously against both employers and rival unions.[55] As a further step, it limited entry to the occupation by the imposition of high entrance fees.[56] Like the waterside unions, it was much preoccupied with the enforcement of its monopoly through control of hiring procedures. In pursuit of this aim it agitated for a re-constitution of the Local Marine Boards.[57] These boards controlled the Mercantile Marine Offices where sailors were signed on, and they were largely dominated by shipowners. The union claimed equal representation on the boards with the shipowners. The union's drive for monopoly centred, however, chiefly upon its efforts to enrol ships' officers, and it was this policy which provoked shipowners into active resistance. Ships' officers, like dock foremen, were an occupational group of the greatest significance, for they played a crucial role in the selection of men for employment. Sometime after the establishment of Wilson's sailors' organisation, a union was started for Certificated Officers.[58] In April 1890 the sailors' and officers' unions reached an important agreement.[59] The seamen undertook to take action to force the officers into their appropriate union, while the officers' union promised that its members would refuse to employ any men unless they were members of Wilson's Union. The seamen were certainly as good as their word, and the union issued an instruction that members were to refuse to work on a ship unless the captain and other officers were members of the officers' union.[60] This agreement between the two unions was the last straw for the shipowners. They complained that the forcible organisation of the officers undermined the discipline of the ship and therefore its security. The Officers' Union they regarded as a mere satellite of Wilson's Union, and in this connection they pointed to the fact that Wilson was himself Honorary General Manager of the officers' organisation, besides being General Secretary of the Seamen.[61] As the year 1890 progressed so the resistance of the shipowners to the tactics of the sailors stiffened. The journal of the shipping interest, *Fairplay*, began a long sustained attack upon the N.A.S. and F.U., an attack which came to embrace waterside unionism in general. Meanwhile shipping companies subsidised the creation of rival unions composed chiefly of malcontents ejected from Wilson's Union.[62] Finally, in September 1890, came the creation of the Shipping Federation, a body specifically dedicated to the destruction of the Sailors' Union. The irreconcilable hostility of these two national organisations had become the dominant feature of industrial relations in the ports of Britain, and the magnitude of the conflict was such that waterside employers and unions generally became enmeshed in its toils.

The Lightermen's Union had tradition on its side and benefited from operating in a labour market partially protected by the licensing and apprenticeship regulations of the Watermen's Company.[63] The influence of the society had, however, been hampered from the beginning by the cohesion of the employers' interest,[64] and to this disadvantage must be added another. The size of the average lighterage firm grew very considerably in the latter part of the nineteenth century (a number of these firms were not primarily lighterage concerns at all, but were wharfingers who ran a lighterage department in addition to their other activities). This development went hand in hand with developments in technique, which quite altered the character of the trade. Larger barges were employed, and tugs were used to tow them.[65] These changes reacted unfavourably upon the lightermen. They quickly destroyed, for one thing, the personal relationship between master and men which had once existed in the lighterage trade,[66] and continued to exist in the stevedoring trade. The changes also affected the lightermen's livelihood. In days gone by, barges had been navigated singly; now they were towed in groups by tugs and each barge had a carrying capacity almost double that of its predecessors. These innovations meant not only an all-round contraction of employment, they meant also that the masters had less need of the lightermen's skill in navigation. Thus it was that lighterage companies made increasing use of unqualified labour, even defying the licensing regulations of the company. Both unlicensed non-freemen and apprentices were paid at a lower rate than the qualified men, and employers often used them in the work of navigation, thus contracting the freemen's field of employment still further.[67] These developments greatly weakened the influence of the union, and after the 1889 strike the organisation made a powerful attempt to stabilise its position. In contrast to the master stevedores, the master lightermen had not in the past accorded society men a preference in employment. This the union was now determined to enforce. As in other waterside trades the key to the situation was the foreman, who had the responsibility for hiring labour. Thus the union attempted forcibly to enrol these men in its ranks. Like the Dockers' Union, however, it failed in this attempt, and, again following the parallel of the docks, the foremen formed a society of their own—the Amalgamated Society of Foremen Lightermen.[68] The future of organisation in the lighterage trade thus remained precarious, and over the years this sector was to develop into the greatest trouble spot in the industry.

3

The mass organisation established in 1889 had come to rest upon very slender foundations by the autumn of 1890. In almost every sphere the resistance of the employers to union monopoly had stiffened, and only the continuing buoyancy of trade had allowed the unions to retain their influence over hiring procedures. Good trade was, however, an asset upon which the unions could not count for long, and in the second half of 1890 the great boom had already begun to slacken off.[69] The winter of 1890-1 was to be crucial. Winter was always a time of weakness for waterside unions, for bad weather created unemployment in outdoor trades generally. Builders' labourers and others flocked down to the waterside looking for work.[70] In the previous winter employers had been unable or unwilling to take advantage of this situation. Now, however, things were different.

The joint committee was the first to take action. At the beginning of November 1890 it terminated the agreement of October 1889.[71] Workers' representatives were swept away, and the committee insisted that in future the men should be taken on inside the gates, where no union delegates would be able to examine cards. The monopoly of the Dockers' Union at the north-bank docks was shattered by this blow. Tillett commented with bitterness: 'I do not doubt that the dock companies wish to revert to the old system if possible, and have the men fighting at the gates for work like dogs'.[72] The action of the joint committee nearly precipitated a general strike of the union, and on Monday, 3 November there were widespread unofficial stoppages.[73] After hours of heated discussion, however, the executive decided not to call an official strike.[74] The risk of defeat was considered too great, and it was thought more advisable to ride out the winter passively, in the hope that the summer would strengthen the union's position. The action of the joint committee, however, weakened the union fatally, for once the control of hiring procedures was removed great numbers of men drifted away.[75] Furthermore those who remained loyal to the organisation ran the risk of victimisation now that the monopoly could not be enforced. Large numbers of prominent unionists were, in fact, boycotted by the officials of the joint committee in the winter of 1890–1.[76]

There was worse to come. In the turbulent aftermath of the 1889 strike the joint committee found that it was losing money on the discharging service which it performed for the shipowners. In the autumn of 1890, therefore, it began to prepare far-reaching changes in employment policy. By mid-November the essential features of the new arrangements were clearly to be seen. The committee announced its intention of handing over discharging operations to the shipowners at the beginning of the New Year; in effect it intended to pass the responsibility of labour management over to the shipping companies who, incidentally, were none too keen to receive it.[77] The committee intended, however, to retain control over sectors of employment in the upstream docks, where dock work was closely linked with warehousing business. In these latter sectors it was proposed that the work should be largely performed by permanent labourers, and the committee began to increase its permanent staff in November 1890.[78]

Permanent labour was universally regarded by casual port workers as a weapon in the armoury of employers.[79] Such a view was not without justification for, together with the loss of the power of inspection, permanent labour virtually killed the Dockers' Union in the upstream docks. The essential idea behind the joint committee's labour scheme[80] was that the bulk of the work should be performed by two classes of labourers: permanent men, and registered weekly labour. This latter category was to be employed on a casual basis, but was to be paid by the week and to have next preference in the work after the 'perms'. Outside these categories the real casuals were formed into preference lists, and were taken on for work according to their number on the list. In order to maximise the employment received by the two weekly grades, they were to be rendered mobile over the whole area of joint committee employment, thus breaking down the numerous submarkets that had existed hitherto. In this way a comparatively small number of men would receive virtually regular employment; on the other hand, a considerable number in the casual grades would receive scarcely any work. The scheme took some time to become completely effective, but a start was made in the winter of 1890–1. From the joint committee's standpoint the system had many attractions. It was hoped that it would greatly improve the calibre of the labour force, and the whole scheme resembled, in fact, a gigantic process of sifting, in which only the most efficient labourers were permitted to enter the two privileged grades. From the point of view of unionism, however, this system had another aspect. It gave to the committee powerful sanctions against its employees. Decasualisation only brings security to a port worker if it is universal in extent; if it is only partial, then the weekly labourer knows that only the favour of his employer stands between him and the ranks of the chronically under-employed casuals. This explains why decasualisation was regarded by many port workers literally as a system of slavery; a system in which a man was reduced to an abject dependence upon the whims of the employer. It also explains why the permanent system was felt to be incompatible with trade unionism.[81] The permanent grades had from the beginning been the weakest sector of the Dockers' Union's monopoly, and any substantial increase in the amount of port work performed by these grades was regarded as a clear threat to organisation. In the autumn of 1890, before the termination of the old agreement, the Dockers' Union apparently received an assurance that no major change was contemplated with respect to permanent labour. In November the committee began gradually to increase the number of weekly labourers, and the new places were offered at first to regular dockers, many of them unionists. In the absence of any notification by the management that large-scale changes were intended, the union advised its members to reject permanent places if offered.[82] Consequently the committee brought in a number of outsiders to fill the new vacancies, and, once started, this process went on relentlessly. The consequence was that unionists were largely confined to the lower ranks of the classified lists, and so received an ever decreasing share of employment.[83]

The introduction of outsiders to fill the new permanent places was obviously disastrous to the union, and it might be supposed that the union had only itself to blame for this development, as it had advised non-acceptance of permanency. The matter was, however, not quite so simple, for the organisation had good reason to suppose that permanency would prove incompatible with union membership. Thus by the summer of 1891 there was some evidence to show that where regulars had accepted permanent positions they had had pressure brought to bear upon them to leave the union.[84] In any case, the condition of admission to the weekly grades discriminated against union men, by fixing thirty years as the maximum age for appointment.[85] This restriction operated against the regulars who had followed up dock work over a number of years, and it was precisely from this class that the union drew its strength. To many unionists this regulation must have appeared as a deliberate attempt at exclusion. Their suspicions that the new arrangements were aimed primarily at breaking up the union were strengthened by the activities of the Permanent Labourers' Union. This body had been regarded from the beginning as a company union, and the activities of its officials in cajoling Dockers' Union members to transfer their allegiance were suspected of being inspired from the Dock House.[86]

The labour policies of the joint committee destroyed the influence of the Dockers' Union at the upstream docks. It would, however, be a mistake to assume that these policies totally destroyed the influence of the union in the port of London.[87] The influence of the joint committee was not universal throughout the port, and the organisation was able to cling on in those sectors outside its ambit. From February 1891 onwards these latter sectors included the biggest and busiest group of docks in the port, as in that month discharging operations at the Tilbury, Victoria and Albert docks passed finally into the hands of the shipping companies. The dockers at the downstream systems, however, quickly found themselves in conflict with some of their

new employers, for by February 1891 the long-awaited struggle
between the seamen and the Shipping Federation had already
commenced.

4

The conflict which engulfed the downstream systems in February
had its origins back in the previous September.[88] In that month
the Sailors' Union blocked the vessels of the British India Line,
following a failure to extend its monopoly into the sphere of ship-
repairing. Faced with this stoppage, the British India Line took
steps to replace the unionists by 'free' labour. The problem was
how to engage these non-unionists. The Mercantile Marine
Offices were the normal centres for the engagement of crews, but
the union naturally picketed these centres. Shipping companies
were, however, permitted by law to sign on their crews on board
ship, and the British India Line thus introduced the practice as a
way of evading the union monopoly. The device clearly corres-
ponded with the practice of taking on dockers and stevedores
inside the dock gates. Throughout October and November the
British India Line dispatched its ships with 'free' crews, who had
signed the articles on board ship, and the practice spread to two
other companies—the Shaw Savill Line and the New Zealand
Shipping Company. The Sailors' Union in London was quick to
sense the threat which the spread of this practice implied.[89] The
Tidal Basin Branch of the union was affiliated to the United
Labour Council, a federal body formed out of the old 1889 Wades
Arms Strike Committee.[90] Most of the smaller occupational
associations of the port were affiliated to the council, though both
the Dockers' Union and the S.S.L.P.L. had remained outside.
The Tidal Basin branch of the Sailors' Union now sought to
mobilise the resources of the council against the three offending
shipping companies. The sailors pointed out that although the
'free' labour menace as yet only concerned themselves, if the
shipowners 'were successful in this, their first step, they would
speedily extend their operations to the other unions'.[91] With this
in mind, the council agreed to assist the seamen, and on 3 December 1890 it issued the well-known Wades Arms Manifesto. The
manifesto called upon all affiliated members to cease work upon
the three lines until the latter agreed to desist from signing crews
on board.[92]

The Wades Arms Manifesto was a highly significant and controversial document. Significant, because it marked the beginning of a long struggle between the unions and the Shipping Federation. Controversial, because there were serious chinks in the armour of the U.L.C. which its leaders had not foreseen. In response to the strike call, the coal porters came out to a man, but the stevedores did not, neither did the dockers, who were not affiliated to the U.L.C. and therefore not officially involved. At the end of the year 1890 the strike was confined to sailors and coal porters.[93] The failure of the stevedores to respond to the manifesto was the source of much acrimony. The confusion arose from the fact that affiliation to the council was by the branch, and, on the evening that the decision to strike was taken, only three or four out of a total of thirteen stevedores' branches had been represented.[94] The Stevedores' Union thus claimed that it was not bound by the manifesto, and formally decided to remain at work.[95]

The gauntlet of 'free' labour thrown down by the shipping companies proved in the event to be a challenge that official union policy could not evade. In practice, first the stevedores, and then the dockers, found that a policy of neutrality towards the sailors' struggle was unworkable. A week after the issue of the manifesto the Shipping Federation imported Kentish fishermen and farm workers into the Albert Dock to take over the coaling work of the three lines.[96] The presence of blacklegs in the dock generated tensions that could not be contained for long. On 10 February 1891 the storm broke. On that day the stevedores at the British India Line struck against federation labour. The council of the Stevedores' Union sat from 8 p.m. until 2.30 a.m.; when the meeting closed the decision had been taken to call stevedores out from the lines where Federation men were employed.[97] Not long after, the dockers at the firms in dispute also came out.[98] In mid-February 1891 it looked very much as if the dispute would become general throughout the entire port. The Shipping Federation certainly prepared for such an eventuality, and put its depot ships in trim, ready to receive a fresh batch of labourers from the provinces.[99] The strike was not, however, extended beyond the three original firms and the Wilson-Hill Line (which had become involved in January).[100] The various unions involved certainly considered the possibility of extending the strike, and the Stevedores actually drew up a manifesto calling all their members out.[101] The Stevedores' Union, however, was deeply divided within itself, and inter-union co-operation was also at a low ebb. Furthermore, the Dockers' Union had already taken a severe blow at the hands of the Joint Committee, and was in a mood of the utmost caution. In view of the Shipping Federation's refusal to negotiate,[102] and the inability of the unions to extend the area of the stoppage, there was no choice but to close the dispute, and this was done in March 1891. The strike had resulted in crushing defeat.[103] In December 1890 'free' labour had constituted an immediate threat only to the seamen; now it menaced all port workers alike. At the end of the strike the three lines continued to work with 'free' labourers, supplied to them by a Free Labour Office at the Albert Dock. In July 1891 there were 850 men registered there, and they performed stevedores', dockers' and coalies' work indiscriminately.[104]

The dispute at the downstream docks reacted more severely upon the Stevedores' than upon the Dockers' organisation. This was due to a fundamental difference in the character of the two unions. The Stevedores' Union still in 1891 enjoyed recognition from the majority of employers in its sphere. These employers, mostly master stevedores, recognised the society preference and submitted to the union's working rules. The Stevedores' Union had thus a fixed standard to defend, and because of the need for uniformity it was bound to make an absolute distinction between society and non-society firms.[105] The Dockers' Union, however, being a union of recent origin, had no elaborate code of rules to defend. Furthermore, a union preference had become for the dockers the exception rather than the rule by the spring of 1891. The big union was thus more flexible than the Stevedores in adjusting itself to the new situation at the Albert Dock.

The Stevedores' Union had always found difficulty in enforcing its conditions upon the large shipping-lines, and the three lines involved in the sailors' dispute were, no doubt, only too ready to break with the Stevedores as well. After the termination of the dispute, the continued presence of 'free' labour at the Albert Dock encouraged other companies to be more assertive. In this environment the union found it increasingly difficult to enforce its code of working rules. In June the P. and O. Line broke with the union over the issue of double-time payment for work on holidays. The unionists were locked out and 'free' labour intro-duced to the work.[106] This was the fifth major steamship company

to break with the society since February. Even the master stevedores began to exhibit a disconcerting degree of independence,
and on one occasion their association actually threatened the
introduction of federation labour.[107] Constantly browbeaten by
employers with the threat of 'free' labour, the Stevedores were
induced in July 1891 to undertake the revision of their rules. The
process was a lengthy one, but by the spring of 1892 the new rules
were complete, and had been accepted by the Masters' Association and other employers. By this time also terms had been
arranged with the Shaw Savill Line.[108] The British India, P. and
O., and New Zealand lines, however, still remained firm in their
refusal to come to terms with the society. Not until the summer of
1911 were they again forced to submit to the rules of the Stevedores' Union, and then they broke free once more in 1912.

The breach in the Stevedores' Union monopoly at the Albert
Dock generated serious tensions inside the organisation.[109] The
dispute with the shipping companies affected chiefly the members
of the three society branches in West Ham. After the closure of
the dispute in March these men were forbidden to re-apply for
work at those firms where federation men were employed. For a
member to seek work in a non-society firm was illegal according to
union rules, and men could be expelled for such an action. This
rule hit the men at the three downstream branches very hard
indeed, and several attempts were made to get the executive to
lift the ban on federation firms, without success however. In the
end numbers of men defied the society and went to work at non-
society firms. The shipping companies were quite prepared to
employ these experienced stevedores, but they retained a substantial core of 'free' labourers at work, as a kind of standing threat
against any renewal of union activity. Thus in November 1891
the work of the British India Line was reported to be split evenly
between imported labour and old hands who had returned.[110]
The men who returned to the federation lines were, however,
invariably lost to organisation, for they were outlawed by the
society. This rigid adherence to rule reflected the fact that the
Stevedores' Union was essentially dominated by the older branches
in the upstream districts. Here the men were employed by master
stevedores, who continued to recognise the union. The policy of
the society was thus geared above all to the maintenance of the
standards recognised by the master stevedores, and it was feared

that any concessions to the downstream members would be exploited by the masters to lower standards generally. While there was logic in this policy, it obviously did not appeal to the downstream members for whom employment was becoming ever more scarce due to the proliferation of federation firms. The downstream branches wanted not only a removal of the ban on non-society firms, they wanted also to extend organisation to the federation labourers,[111] for without this extension it was impossible to bring pressure to bear on the recalcitrant companies. The Dockers' Union made considerable progress in enrolling 'free' labourers on the New Zealand and Shaw Savill lines,[112] and the downstream stevedores clearly wished their union to follow suit. The society's executive would, however, have nothing to do with this policy, for the reason that it threatened the uniform standard and the restricted labour supply in society firms. The whole situation was very reminiscent of the 1880s, when the society had been equally reluctant to extend organisation into the sphere of non-society shipping companies.[113] The downstream branches differed from the rest of the organisation on one final crucial point—namely, co-operation with other unions.

The downstream stevedores' branches had ever since the termination of the 1889 strike shown a desire to work with allied organisations,[114] and this desire was only strengthened by the reverses in the winter of 1890–1. In this they differed greatly from the older sectors of the union. This difference within the union was largely responsible for the confusions in its external policy, confusions particularly marked at the time of the Wades Arms Manifesto and the later general strike manifesto. This ambiguity had been much increased by the fact that union leaders had tended to side with the minority party, and had espoused the more expansive unionism of the downstream branches. The difference between the old and new sectors of organisation reflected largely a differing experience of trade unionism. The older branches were very stable institutions, and had enjoyed, since 1872, recognition from their employers. In this sphere everything was regulated by custom and personal contact; it was a close-knit world, essentially insulated against strangers and change. Things had never been like this downstream, and trade unionism was experienced in a manner quite different from that in the old areas. The stevedores in the Victoria and Albert docks had had to fight like the dockers to enforce their control of hiring procedures. The downstream stevedores, in fact, felt themselves closer at times to other new unionists than they did to their brothers of the Society upstream. This divided loyalty had emerged clearly in February 1891, when the joint committee had abandoned discharging operations at the downstream docks. In its early days, when it enjoyed such numerical predominance, the Dockers' Union had behaved with great truculence towards the smaller unions, and in particular it had tried to extend its sphere of influence at the expense of the Stevedores.[115] The latter organisation had its chance of revenge when the joint committee decided to abandon discharging, for the society received several offers from employers who wished the stevedores to undertake the work. The union executive was certainly in favour of this extension of its influence, provided that employers paid the society rate for both loading and unloading.[116] In the event, however, the downstream stevedores refused to co-operate, on the grounds that discharging in the lower docks was properly the dockers' sphere of employment, and this they would not invade.[117] The incident was highly significant when seen in the context of the widening breach between the new and old sectors.

This breach within the Stevedores' Society came to a head in the autumn of 1891. The issue at stake was affiliation to the new federation of waterside unions. Federation was something that had been discussed ever since the termination of the great strike, yet in the autumn of 1891 it still had not been fully achieved. Waterside federations were never easy to achieve, for considerations of job monopoly and trade autonomy constantly raised obstacles to unity, and in London between 1889 and 1891 the obstacles were particularly hazardous. In the early days it was the Dockers' Union that impeded co-operation. Its numerical predominance in London, and powerful provincial organisation, fostered a feeling of self-sufficiency. Furthermore, like all the mass organisations formed in British ports in 1889, it really hoped to absorb the smaller unions in time, and thus create for itself a complete port monopoly. The Dockers' Union therefore ignored the sectional societies in London, and when these small unions formed the U.L.C. in January 1890 the Dockers stayed out, as did the S.S.L.P.L.[118] The winter of 1890–1 changed the attitude of the big union very considerably. The breach with the joint committee, and the falling off of trade, undermined the stability of organisation, and its vast membership began to melt away. In January 1891 the Dockers' Union therefore joined with the Sailors and the S.S.L.P.L. in forming a federal organisation,[119] but this body included none of the smaller associations, who remained affiliated to the U.L.C. This latter organisation embraced many groups with considerable strategic power, and it was clear that no federal body would be really satisfactory unless these key groups were included. In particular it was vital that the Lightermen and Stevedores be embraced. Now, however, the situation changed, for it was the turn of the small strategic unions to hold back. Again the winter of 1890–1 marked the turning-point. The strike in February 1891 shook the smaller unions, the Stevedores in particular, and the introduction of 'free' labour forced them onto the defensive. Yet the reaction of the Stevedores to this situation differed very markedly from that of the Dockers. The reason was that the Stevedores' Union, despite its reverses, still had much to lose. Its rules and monopoly were still recognised by the bulk of employers in its sphere. The Dockers' Union, on the other hand, had seen its monopoly obliterated everywhere except at the Millwall and Victoria docks.[120] The stevedores suspected that the big union intended to make up for its own lack of strategic power by federating with unions that had that power, and that it intended to use the smaller unions as a lever with which to restore its fortunes. In this suspicion the stevedores were of course correct. By the autumn of 1891 Dockers' Union officials were placing their hopes of recovery upon a comprehensive waterside federation, in which each union would assist the others in enforcing 100 per cent organisation.[121] Such an idea had few attractions for the old branches of the Stevedores' Union. They would be asked to jeopardise their own position in order to assist organisation in sectors where it was chronically weak. Such a bargain was too one-sided. The Stevedores' Society had already lost large areas of employment to 'free' labour due to its support for the dying Sailors' Union. It did not wish to lose any more ground. In September 1891 the Dockers' Union had finally succeeded in carrying out a merger between its own federation and the U.L.C.,[122] and it immediately called upon the new body to assist its Wapping members who were involved in a strike at the Carron and Hermitage wharf.[123] The Lightermen gave some assistance in blocking goods normally brought to and from the wharf in barges, but the Stevedores' Society refused assistance and cut off all contact with the new federation.

The decision of the Stevedores' executive to refuse assistance and to cut off contact was reached only by a casting vote,[124] although a subsequent ballot confirmed the verdict.[125] In taking this decision, however, the society brought the conflict within its own ranks to a head. The division between new and old within the union mirrored the wider division outside. It was not a conflict between new and old ideologies, but between stable and unstable forms of organisation, between unionism with nothing to lose and unionism with everything to lose. The downstream branches were falling apart under the attack of the shipping companies. They needed a flexible and expansive policy, above all they needed co-operation with the dockers, with whom they had so much in common. This their executive had denied them, and so they rebelled. By mid-December 1891 all three downstream branches had withdrawn their delegates from the council of the union, and it was February 1892 before they finally decided against secession. For a while there were rumours that the branches intended to amalgamate with the Victoria and Albert district of the Dockers' Union.[126] The downstream branches also attempted to alter the structure of the union, in such a way as would give them greater autonomy.[127] They thus hoped to be able to pursue policies felt to be relevant to their own particular situation. In this, as in other things, they had some support from the south-side branches of the union, which were also of recent origin. In the event, however, the dissident elements were unable to alter either the structure or the policies of the society, nor did they feel able to take the plunge of secession. Instead, the downstream sectors slowly decayed, so that by the mid-1890s the branches there were tottering on the verge of extinction.[128]

5

The period between 1892 and 1911 was a long one, but it did not fundamentally alter the pattern of unionism established by events in the winter 1890-1. Except perhaps in 1900 the condition of trade was never sufficiently buoyant to permit of a revival of mass unionism, and the upsurge of 1911 was as sudden as it was unexpected. The dominant economic development in the period

was the continued movement of trade downstream, and, in particular, the vast expansion of business at Tilbury after 1900.[129]
This movement naturally had important consequences for the
two main unions of dock workers—the Stevedores and Dockers.

At the upstream docks, the combined effect of trade stagnation
and the joint committee's decasualisation scheme was sufficient to
render impossible any revival of the Dockers' Union after November 1890. At the Albert and Victoria docks, however, trade
continued to grow, and only the growth of Tilbury after 1900 cut
this movement short. Furthermore at the Royal Docks the shipping
companies were the employers after 1891, and there was no
permanent labour problem. In this situation the Dockers' Union
survived remarkably well at the Albert and Victoria systems. For
a while it was even able to operate a monopoly at several firms in
the Victoria Dock.[130] Even without control of hiring procedures,
unionism continued to endure in this sector, although there was,
of course, a marked decline in membership.[131] Survival was
fostered by the flexibility of the organisation, and its willingness
to recruit members at firms where the union was not recognised.
At the end of the 1890s the Victoria and Albert district of the
Dockers' Union was the only one of the original six districts to
retain any real influence. Between 1893 and 1900 it was in fact the
biggest district in the entire union—including all provincial
areas.[132] The new century, however, brought a double blow. In
1900 trade was particularly brisk, and in the summer when labour
was scarce the Victoria and Albert dockers struck unofficially.[133]
They demanded from the shipowners the stevedores' rate of 8d
and 1s, and they also demanded that men should be engaged
outside the dock gates, in order that the union monopoly could be
enforced. The Dockers' Union recognised the strike as official on
14 June and attempted to enlist the help of other unions, particularly the Lightermen and Stevedores.[134] In this attempt the
union failed, and the Shipping Federation was able to defeat the
dockers with imported labour. The 1900 defeat obliterated the
influence of the Dockers' Union at the Victoria and Albert
systems. Furthermore a recovery was hard to stage, because after
1900 trade began to decline at the Royal Docks, as business was
transferred to Tilbury. By 1906 the Dockers' Union was virtually
extinct in London. In that year the single metropolitan district
had an income of only £89, compared with £1308 in 1900.[135] In

the years 1900 to 1910 the Dockers' Union was essentially a provincial organisation, and in 1908 even little Newport had an income nearly nine times that of the metropolis.[136]

The movement of trade downstream affected the Stevedores no less than the Dockers. In the first place it accentuated the problem of maintaining mobility within the society, and thus threatened the effectiveness of the union's restrictive policies. In 1904 attempts were made to improve mobility between the upper docks and Tilbury, and it was arranged that notices should be posted informing men of work available at society firms downstream.[137] It was not only Tilbury that was the problem. The increasing draught of vessels and the growth of the cement, paper and other riverside industries, meant that increasing numbers of vessels were taking in cargo at industrial wharves far downstream; at Purfleet, Greenhithe and Northfleet.[138] Not only was much of this work going to local non-union men; sometimes it was directed by local non-society firms who could offer cheaper rates than the master stevedores based upstream. In view of this situation, society firms began to ask the union for modifications in its prices in order that they could compete for contracts at the cement and paper centres.[139] Faced by these problems, the society decided in 1909 that it would have to extend organisation to the local labourers at these centres, and in 1910 it opened a branch at Northfleet.[140] With these local labourers enrolled, it felt it could close entrance once more, and attempt to level their conditions up to the standard of the Masters' Association. Thus its monopoly would be greatly strengthened downstream. Furthermore, in increasing its membership at the cement centres, it ran no risk of inflating the labour supply at the society firms in the docks, for the two sectors were separated by a considerable distance and there was little danger of an influx of new men into the upstream regions. In any case the intake of new members was strictly limited. These calculations, however, quickly went astray for once more the union had to reckon with the opposition of large-scale employers. The Associated Portland Cement Manufacturers did not carry on stevedoring work directly, but they had a powerful influence over the contractors who did do the work, and they tended to use this influence against the society. In January 1911 one society employer admitted to the union that the Cement Combine had forbidden him to use union labour to load cement, and that in consequence he had refused the job.[141] The Stevedores' Union was troubled by one other large employer in the downstream regions, an employer of much greater importance to it than the Cement Combine. Messrs Scruttons Ltd was a very large stevedoring firm which came to dominate loading and unloading work at Tilbury and other downstream centres. Although this firm was affiliated to the London Master Stevedores' Association, and thus formally recognised the Stevedores' Union, it took its obligations in this respect very lightly indeed. The firm was not above employing non-union labour in the loading of vessels, nor was it above evading the society's rules in other matters. By 1910 relations with this firm had become very strained indeed, for its policies threatened the whole future of organisation at Tilbury.[142]

6

The strength of the Dockers' Union in 1889–90 had lain in its sheer size. Once the falling off of trade permitted employers to remove the union's control of hiring procedures, this vast membership slowly melted away. The trouble was that the big union contained so few groups of strategic importance.[143] Unlike the league of 1872, it was unable to obtain a secure foothold in any sector of the port, and thus it drifted slowly towards total extinction. Realisation of this strategic weakness dominated much of the union's policy between 1891 and 1911. The Dockers' Union had been behind the efforts for a comprehensive waterside federation in 1891. In 1895 it tried to bring about an amalgamation between itself, the Stevedores' Union, the S.S.L.P.L. and the Liverpool dockers' organisation.[144] When this failed Tillett's union turned once more to schemes for federation, and in 1896 eagerly assisted in the formation of the International Federation of Ship, Dock and River Workers.[145] Finally, in 1910, the Dockers' Union took the initiative in forming the National Transport Workers' Federation.[146] In all this, union policy was directed towards securing the assistance of strategically placed groups of port workers. Until 1910 this policy singularly failed to improve the union's position, for between 1891 and 1910 neither the Lightermen nor the Stevedores would have anything to do with federation or amalgamation.

Throughout the period until 1910 the Stevedores remained adamant against joining any form of industrial alliance. In 1902 the society even refused to form a joint committee with the

Lightermen and Crane Drivers.[147] This isolation was not related to any narrowness of outlook on the part of James Anderson, the union's General Secretary,[148] or of his executive. In this period the union, in fact, greatly broadened its outlook. It joined the General Federation of Trade Unions,[149] affiliated to the Labour Party,[150] participated in local government,[151] carried out important internal administrative reforms,[152] and built up a fruitful co-operation with Sexton's Liverpool dockers' union on matters of general interest, such as safety regulations in the docks.[153] In this period also it gave monetary assistance on numerous occasions to all manner of organisations involved in disputes. Yet it would have nothing to do with an industrial alliance. The isolation of the Stevedores' Union in the port of London was based upon its singular position. It alone enjoyed full recognition from employers throughout the period, with all that this implied in security of employment and regulated conditions of work. The events of 1891 had seemed to suggest that the quickest way to lose this advantage was to become involved in industrial alliances. Support for the seamen in that year had brought the union's fortunes to the lowest ebb in their history. For months on end the society had been without funds, with the Secretary borrowing money from day to day in order to meet needs as they arose. By the mid-1890s the union had recovered its stability and confidence, and it was secure in the recognition accorded to it by the L.M.S.A. It was, however, determined not to risk its position again in propping up organisations without any real stability. This isolation was reinforced by the standing dispute with the Dockers' Union, a dispute which had been initiated by demarcation troubles in 1890 and 1891, and had flared up again when Tillett rashly accused the stevedores of blacklegging in the 1900 strike.[154] This was a charge difficult to forgive.

The division between stable and unstable unions was fundamental between 1891 and 1910. In the latter year, however, there were some signs indicating that this division might be overcome.

6 The Great Leap Forward, 1911

I

As mass organisation gradually withered away after 1891, the Stevedores and Lightermen had been left as the only unions of any real influence in the port. Neither of these two societies, as we have seen, were inclined for a long time to exert themselves on behalf of a revival of mass unionism. Thus when, in July 1910, the Dockers' Union invited these two organisations (among others) to a conference on federation,[1] it was something of a surprise when they agreed to attend. Both had resisted all overtures of a similar kind for nearly twenty years; why the sudden change in 1910? The point is important, for without the adhesion of the Stevedores and Lightermen the National Transport Workers' Federation could never have got off the ground in London.

It is not possible to be categorical in giving reasons for the change of policy by the two unions. The new attitude appears to have been the cumulative result of a number of pressures operating in the first decade of the century. In the case of the Lightermen, there was the fact that industrial relations in the trade had been steadily deteriorating over a long period of time.[2] A conciliation board, set up in the early 1890s, had quickly fallen through, and there had been serious strikes in 1900 and 1909. In this situation, the union had certainly been very conscious of the need to strengthen its position. Thus it had opened its ranks to the non-freemen in 1900;[3] no doubt the freemen realised that it would be easier to enforce their monopoly of navigation with these men inside, rather than outside, the jurisdiction of the society. In 1910 a further extension of the organisation took place, for in that year the sailing bargemen of the Medway were brought into the union.[4] A key figure in this development was Harry Gosling, the union's Secretary.[5] He was able, not without a struggle, to force his rather old-fashioned members to face reality and do something to improve the society's declining fortunes. A tribute to his success came in

1908, when the masters were induced to accept a code of working rules.[6] The Lightermen's Union had, however, to face a constant uphill struggle against employers most reluctant to accord it recognition. It is thus not surprising that by 1910 it was beginning to feel that sectional organisation was not enough, and that only a revival of unionism throughout the port would be sufficient to consolidate organisation in the lighterage trade. Certainly the progressive leadership of Gosling was a factor influencing policy in this direction. The lightermen wished to retain their separate organisation, but they were beginning to welcome the idea of a powerful federation able to back them up in their demands. 1912 was to dramatically illustrate this new situation.

In the case of the Stevedores' Union there were influences at work similar to those in the lighterage trade. Although the Stevedores, unlike the Lightermen, enjoyed a harmonious relationship with large numbers of employers in the trade, organisation nevertheless faced severe problems. In particular, it felt itself powerless to deal with large employers downstream, who either openly defied the union, or who recognised it in theory but defied its rules in practice.[7] There were the shipping companies, the Cement Combine and Scruttons Ltd. The continual movement of trade away from the old centres of organisation was making the recalcitrance of these firms serious. In order to re-impose its monopoly in these spheres the society needed sanctions more powerful than it possessed in its present form. By the summer of 1909, James Anderson, the Secretary, and other leaders had realised this fact. Big employers could not be coerced unless organisation was strong throughout all the grades of port workers. Scruttons employed dockers as well as stevedores; these would have to be organised. The question was, by whom? The Dockers' Union would have appeared to be the relevant society for this project. Since 1900, however, this union had been virtually moribund in London, and the Stevedores' Society had to some extent assumed the position of spokesman for London port workers generally. James Anderson thus served upon the Government Committee inquiring into the conditions of piece-work at the docks in 1907.[8] In 1909 he was appointed to the newly-created Port of London Authority.[9] These and other developments must have greatly raised the prestige of the society, and its aspirations. If there was to be a general reorganisation of the dock workers, then why should not the Stevedores undertake it? After all, the Lightermen had made a dramatic break with tradition in 1900, when they extended organisation to the non-freemen. The break with the past was easier for the Stevedores to make in the 1900s, because 1889 had greatly modified their basis of organisation. In that year they had enrolled shipworkers engaged mainly in discharging operations, at the Millwall and Surrey docks, and in fact in 1891 they had even attempted to oust the Dockers' Union from discharging at the downstream docks.[10] Thus the society could no longer be considered as confined to men engaged in loading; it had become open to shipworkers generally. Having come thus far it needed only one more step for the union to become open to quayworkers as well as shipworkers. In considering this point, it is necessary to remember that the downstream docker was moving closer to the stevedore in status in the years between 1891 and 1910.[11] Thus by 1909 the leadership of the society had taken the view, not only that organisation generally should be revived, but that the Stevedores' Society should undertake the task. This view was strengthened by a profound distrust of the leadership of the Dockers' Union,[12] and a consequent reluctance to see its influence re-established. In the summer of 1909 trade in the port of London was on the upgrade,[13] although unemployment remained high in the economy as a whole. Nevertheless, with the promise of improving trade, Anderson decided to embark on his project. On 29 July, therefore, the executive passed the following remarkable resolution:

> This Council [it ran] with a view to extending and strengthening the position of the Society is of the opinion that the time has arrived when the necessary steps should be taken to enrol as members all men engaged in the operations of loading and unloading vessels, or handling cargo on dock, wharf, or quay, in the Port of London, and strongly recommends that these steps be taken at the earliest opportunity.[14]

A ballot of the members was to be taken on the issue, after explanatory meetings had been held.

The decision of the Stevedores' executive to transform the union into an all-grade society was a bold and imaginative one. It was perhaps unfortunate for unionism in London that it did not succeed. Until 1911 the resolution of July 1909 remained virtually a dead letter. One new branch was indeed opened at Northfleet, as we have seen,[15] and at the end of 1909 there was a large intake of new members generally. Apart from Northfleet, however, all the new members were within the society's customary sphere of influence and subject to the customary conditions of entrance. Until 1911 the basic structure of the union remained unchanged. Failure to implement the resolution resulted largely from powerful internal opposition. The men in the old branches feared that an influx of new members from other spheres would threaten their own standards and employment. Thus the ballot on extension produced only a very narrow majority in favour of the executive's policy.[16] In view of this indecisive result the leadership quietly shelved the project in August 1910.[17] Even if they had felt able to press on with it, it is by no means certain that they would have met with much response from those they desired to recruit.

Although the Stevedores' Society had proved unable to undertake a revival of unionism in 1909, it necessarily remained interested in any proposals for a general reorganisation of the port. Trouble with Scruttons and the Cement Combine was coming to a head in 1910 and 1911, and it is significant that, within a month of the inauguration of the National Transport Workers' Federation (N.T.W.F.), the Stevedores' Society proposed that joint action should be taken against the Cement Combine.[18] The Stevedores thus responded, like the Lightermen, to Tillett's scheme for federation, and on 1 March 1911 the new body was formally inaugurated. At the commencement seventeen unions affiliated, and these included all the waterside organisations in London and the most notable provincial transport unions.[19] Implicit in the scheme for federation was the desire for a revival of organisation in the ports, and the new body began its existence with an all-out recruitment campaign.[20] In the case of the moribund Dockers' organisation in London, the need for a revival of unionism was self-evident. The Stevedores and Lightermen for their part had, as we have seen, come to accept the necessity for an all-round expansion of organisation. They were happier that this revival should be undertaken under the general auspices of a federation, rather than by the Dockers' Union unilaterally. The acceptance of the federal idea by these two unions was further facilitated by the fact that they were in a position to dominate the new body, in London at any rate. One of the biggest objections to federation in the past was that the smaller strategic unions would become mere instruments in the hands of a large unstable organisation. In March 1911, however, the Dockers' Union in London was still terribly small. Throughout the first half of the year its income in the metropolis was half that of provincial districts such as Bristol and Swansea.[21] Certainly organisation had been improving in London since 1909, and 1910 was in fact the best year since 1900.[22] Even so, the union had a very, very long way to go. In this situation, the Stevedores and Lightermen exercised the biggest influence in the new federation. Gosling, the Lightermen's Secretary, became the President of the N.T.W.F., and Anderson of the Stevedores its General Secretary.[23] In any process of reorganisation, or of joint industrial action, the two unions thus hoped that they would be able to exercise a powerful influence.

The creation of the N.T.W.F., and its organising campaign, did not at first yield any very striking results in London. Thus even on the eve of the great transport strike, in August 1911, around 50 per cent of port workers remained unorganised by any union.[24] The situation in the spring and early summer of 1911 in fact resembled the situation at the same time of the year 1889.[25] In both periods trade was becoming exceedingly brisk and unions were carrying on recruitment campaigns, yet at neither time did the propaganda campaigns yield dramatic and tangible results. In both periods it was strike action, or its immediate prospect, that yielded the harvest of recruits. On 12 April 1911 the Dockers' Union launched a campaign for a wage increase to 8d and 1s for ordinary dock and wharf workers.[26] The Dockers' Union had got the endorsement of the Stevedores for this claim,[27] and began organising meetings to enlist the support of the dockers in the movement. It was, however, the end of June before the claim was submitted to the employers.[28] Delay resulted from the continued weakness of the Dockers' organisation. If progress was slow, however, it had at least the advantage of being controlled. The unions could control their members and co-ordinate their policies. Above all, there was the hope that the future growth of organisation would be planned in a rational manner. The sphere of the Lightermen's Union was distinct and not subject to controversy. The spheres of the Dockers' and Stevedores' unions were not, however, clear-cut, and in the early 1890s demarcation disputes had embittered the relationship of the two organisations. In view of the Stevedores'

Society resolution of 1909, with its formal commitment to a general expansion, the danger of conflict was even greater now than in the earlier period. In May 1911, however, the Stevedores and Dockers agreed to confer together on their respective spheres of influence.[29] If mass organisation could be developed within this framework of consultation endless trouble and controversy could be averted. The danger was, that in a sudden upsurge of rank and file militancy, the unions would abandon this co-ordinating machinery and enrol members indiscriminately and without plan.

2

The period from July 1911 until the outbreak of war followed closely the pattern of events between 1889 and 1892. In both periods mass organisation was achieved suddenly, and in the midst of a great industrial dispute. There followed in both cases an uneasy period of union power and universal organisation, leading eventually to renewed industrial conflict and a resultant weakening of unionism. The issues and tensions in inter-union, and union and employer, relationships are strikingly similar in both periods. Behind the crowded industrial scene of 1911 and 1912, as in 1889 and 1890, lay the circumstance of a trade boom. Trade had been consistently on the upgrade in London since 1909,[30] and this fact had given some assistance to the efforts at reorganisation in the port. What made the summer of 1911 so particular, however, was the low level of unemployment in industry generally.[31] This circumstance removed all but the regulars from the waterfront labour market, and, with the docks now full, regulars found themselves in short supply. By July 1911 the *Daily News* was proclaiming, 'Unemployment touching bottom',[32] and indeed the situation was then more favourable to industrial action than at any time since 1900. The men, too, had every incentive to act. Prices had been rising continuously since 1896, but the rise was particularly sharp after 1905. In London, between 1905 and 1912, retail food prices increased by 11·4 per cent,[33] and this was a period that included two chronic years of unemployment, 1908 and 1909. Rising prices, unemployment, and, in the London port industry, stagnating wages,[34] must have created a mood of profound discontent. Yet the men remained for long unresponsive to the appeals of union leaders for recruits. Faith in industrial action developed slowly among the rank and file, and then only by experiment. When experiments began to yield results, however, the trickle of new recruits became an avalanche, and the unions were swept along by a spontaneous movement they were unable to control.

Faith in industrial action was certainly a doctrine preached more vigorously by union leaders in this period than at any time previous. Tom Mann had returned to England in 1910 a convinced syndicalist, and the creation of the N.T.W.F. was for him a first step towards the formation of an Industrial Union, which would be 'absolutely united for fighting purposes as one body'.[35] The Dockers' Union gave Mann every facility for spreading his doctrines among port workers, and at the request of the union's executive he conducted an organising campaign at various ports in July and August 1910.[36] Unlike Mann, Tillett was never a syndicalist in the strict sense, but at this period he was in sympathy with syndicalism's general mood.[37] In particular, he voiced the syndicalist's contempt for parliamentary institutions. When the dockers struck in August 1911, he proclaimed that the strikers 'had done more for labour in the past few days than Parliament would do in a century'.[38] He voiced also the belief that the interests of capital and labour were irreconcilable. 'The real fight', he wrote in 1910, 'is between wage-slavery and capitalist tyranny and dominance.'[39] With two such persuasive orators as Mann and Tillett at work on the waterfront in 1910 and 1911, it would have been surprising if port workers had remained unmoved by appeals to militant action. Yet it was the mood of syndicalism, not the doctrine, which made headway in the port and other industries. Perhaps only in the South Wales coalfield was syndicalism espoused by large numbers of men as a guide to revolutionary action by industrial means.[40] Elsewhere, its appeal was more vague, and the spontaneous revolt it helped to generate lacked defined political objectives. Furthermore, established union leaders were, in the last resort, concerned more with containing the revolt than with channelling it into revolutionary directions.

In London, as in other ports, it was the successful industrial action of the seamen, in June 1911, that really sparked the movement off. On 14 June the sailors at Southampton struck unofficially and the National Sailors' and Firemen's Union quickly called a national strike. Nearly all ports were affected by the sailors' stoppage, and at Hull, Goole, Manchester and elsewhere the dockers began to come out in sympathy.[41] By 27 June it appeared as if the London dockers might follow the example of the provinces. The spontaneous strike movement of June caught the N.T.W.F. by surprise. The Sailors' Union was affiliated to the federation, and on 1 June it had notified that body of its campaign for better conditions and had asked for support.[42] The sudden development of the seamen's strike movement, and its extension to the provincial dockers had, however, altered the whole complexion of the campaign. Suddenly the N.T.W.F. was faced with a major industrial crisis in the provinces, and the possibility of its spreading to the metropolis. Hurriedly a conference of the federation was called in London for 28 June, in order that some sort of policy might be formulated. Some shipowners had already conceded the sailors' demands and the conference decided that if the recalcitrant companies had not conceded terms by 1 July, then a further conference should assemble on 3 July in order that 'drastic action' could be taken against companies refusing a settlement.[43] 'Drastic action' clearly meant calling upon the London port workers for a sympathetic strike.[44] Whether the unorganised London men would in fact respond to such an appeal was a nice question, but if the evidence of other ports was anything to go by, then the chances seemed good.

At this point Ben Tillett decided to take a hand in proceedings. The Dockers' Union had been campaigning since the previous April for a wage increase, but in view of the continued weakness of organisation this claim had held fire. Now, with the sudden prospect of a widespread strike, Tillett acted. He was determined to tie his movement in with the planned sympathetic action. On 29 June, the day after the federation meeting, the Dockers' Union sent off letters to the P.L.A., Wharfingers, Shipowners and Granary Keepers, demanding the 8d and 1s rate for ordinary port employment.[45] The letters were in the form of an ultimatum, which was to expire on 3 July, the date on which the N.T.W.F. was to take the decision as to sympathetic action. The Dockers' Union was not the only organisation to take advantage of the situation in order to press demands on the employers. On 3 July the Association of Master Lightermen and Bargeowners received a letter from the Lightermen's Society demanding various alterations in the conditions of employment.[46] Seamen, Dockers, and now Lightermen therefore had claims outstanding. In the account that follows we shall, however, be dealing only with port workers strictly so-called—i.e. excluding the seamen.

On 3 July 1911 it seemed that there was every prospect of a port-wide stoppage in London. That day the federation was to meet to decide the issue. Even though the majority of port workers were still unorganised, there is evidence to suggest that many of them were prepared to abide by the federation's decision.[47] At the beginning of July the dockers at Hull, Liverpool and Manchester were all out, and it would be no surprise if London were to follow. Unrest in the port had been steadily mounting since 27 June. On 29 June the dockers working for the large shipowners at the Surrey Docks had begun a series of sporadic stoppages, and there was unrest also among the grain trimmers employed by the Port Authority.[48] However, in spite of these signs, there was no general stoppage at the beginning of July. The reason was that the employers, frightened by events in other ports, showed a willingness to negotiate. The P.L.A. arranged for a conference of employers to be held under its auspices, a conference which would take into consideration the various claims that had been put forward by the transport workers.[49] The N.T.W.F. was only too willing to take advantage of these signs of amenability, and it did not call for sympathetic action on 3 July. However encouraging were the signs of renewed militancy in London, the cold reality was that organisation was still weak. No one could be sure what the response to a strike call would be; it was best to negotiate and build up strength in the meantime. The first crisis in London had thus passed by 4 July. At that date the strikes in Hull and Liverpool were over, and the excitement seemed to be dying down. In London, and over the rest of the country, an interim period ensued. Apart from Cardiff in mid-July, there were no more major stoppages until August.[50] The movement was, however, far from over. During the crisis of early July the Dockers' Union had begun to recruit members fast, and the Stevedores had decided to act upon their earlier resolution to expand. In the weeks ahead organisation proceeded apace and enthusiasm mounted. Renewed crisis was inevitable.

After the first crisis of 3 July the threat of a total stoppage continued to remain just beneath the surface. It was this threat which induced the numerous port employers to consider negotiations with the unions. The idea of negotiating a comprehensive settlement was a new one in London,[51] and consequently presented many difficulties. If a general stoppage was to be averted, then no sector of employment could be left out. This meant getting together a fully representative conference. On the men's side this did not present too much difficulty, because the creation of the N.T.W.F. meant that there already existed a body representative of all London port workers. On the employers' side things were different. Although the various employers—wharfingers, ship-owners, short-sea traders and others—all had their own associations, there was no organisation able to speak for them all. The creation of the P.L.A. had, however, helped matters in this respect, for here was a public body that was capable of taking the initiative in bringing the employers together. It was thus under the auspices of the P.L.A. that a conference of employers was finally convened, and this assembly duly met the executive of the N.T.W.F. on 10 July 1911.[52] The employers represented at this conference were the P.L.A. itself,[53] the Shipping Federation, the Short-Sea Traders, the Wharfingers and Granary Keepers, and also the Master Lightermen. The London Master Stevedores' Association was not represented, because the Stevedores' Society had presented no claims against it. It was one thing to get this assembly together, but quite another to keep it in being until a fully acceptable settlement had been reached. This was the first time in the port's history that a fully representative gathering of men and employers had met one another across a table. The atmosphere was one of evasion and distrust,[54] for everyone knew that it was only the threat of a general stoppage that had brought them together.

The N.T.W.F. hoped to extract two major concessions from the employers. In the first place it hoped that it could induce them to recognise fully all the transport unions in London.[55] The Stevedores' Society was already recognised by the L.M.S.A., though not by some of the large shipping-lines. Apart from the Stevedores, no other union in the port enjoyed full recognition. Secondly, the federation hoped to establish a port rate of 8d and 1s. This claim would involve an increase of at least 1d per hour for all waterside workers except the stevedores, whose rate this already was. The claim did not apply to the lightermen, whose conditions were quite separate. The coal, corn and deal porters were also not involved, for they were paid entirely by the piece.[56] The claim was significant, not purely as a wage increase, but as involving the concept of a port rate. This idea of a port rate may be traced back to 1897, when the International Federation had begun a campaign on these lines.[57] A port rate meant simply that there should be one rate to cover the whole field of dock and wharf labour, certain special trades of course excepted. The object of the unitary port rate was to end a system whereby a man's wages depended not upon his work but upon his employer.

> The idea that was at the backs of our heads, [commented Harry Gosling], was that we should get a port rate for similar work, so that whether a man worked for Brown, Jones or Robinson, if he was doing the same work he got the same price.[58]

The idea was a realistic one. There were, it is true, considerable differences in skill between the various departments of ordinary port labour, but the differences in rates were rarely based upon them. They were based instead upon the nature of the employing concern.[59] Thus P.L.A. employees generally received 6d and 8d, whether they worked on the ship, quay or in the warehouse. Shipping company dockers at the Victoria and Albert docks received 7d and 1s. Labourers on short-sea vessels at upstream wharves received in some places 7d and 9d, in others 6d and 8d. The whole wage structure was a tangled mass of custom, and it had become a source of great discontent among the men. The uniform port rate would remove these discontents. It had another distinct advantage for union leaders. Whenever mass organisation was achieved in the port industry there were always disputes over job monopolies. Unions whose members occupied a privileged position refused to allow members of less favourably placed organisations to work in their sphere. There was thus no mutual recognition of union tickets, and this friction impeded inter-union co-operation.[60] If the whole sphere of ordinary dock work was subject to uniform conditions the establishment of a single federation ticket[61] would become possible. Furthermore uniform conditions would mean that no organisation would be able to extend its sphere of influence at the expense of another union by offering inferior rates. In the 1890s this problem of undercutting had caused much friction between the Stevedores and Dockers.[62] The uniform 8d and 1s rate was especially attractive to the leadership of the Stevedores' Society. If parity was achieved between

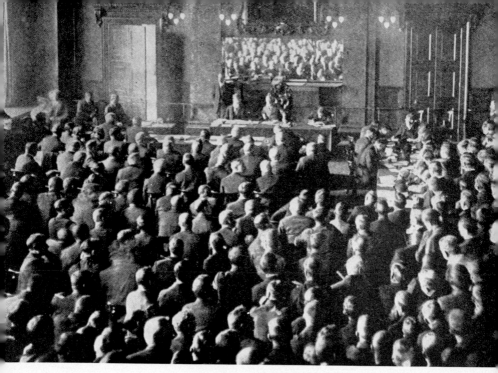

The 1912 crisis: the Clarke Enquiry in session (above); Tillett in his element on Tower Hill (below)

Mass unionism: the banners out on Tower Hill

L.M.S.A. conditions and dock conditions generally, then the way would be open for the expansion of the union into new spheres.

Recognition and a Port Rate, these then were the two basic aims of the N.T.W.F. They were not easy of achievement, and the objective of a port rate was compromised almost as soon as negotiations began. This was because the Short-Sea Traders' Association, after attending the conference on 10 July, refused to participate any further. 'They slipped out of it,' Gosling said, 'and therefore we could not make a port rate to cover everybody because they had gone.'[63] After the withdrawal of the Short-Sea Traders four groups of employers remained in the negotiations—namely, the Oversea Shipowners, the Wharfingers, the Granary Keepers, and the P.L.A. in its capacity as an employer. Of these four groups, the last three were similarly situated so far as wages were concerned. They all paid a basic rate of 6d and 8d, whereas the shipowners usually paid at least one penny more on day and overtime rates.[64] The problem of the federation was thus to get the P.L.A. and wharfingers to pay a larger increase than the shipowners, in order to bring both groups up to the 8d and 1s level. In this it was unsuccessful. The P.L.A. offered to its employees an increase of one penny on day and overtime rates,[65] but beyond this it would not go, and the three crucial conferences of 25, 26, and 27 July failed to alter the position.[66] This resistance of the P.L.A., and with it that of the Wharfingers and Granary Keepers, shattered the idea of a uniform 8d and 1s rate. It was not easy even to impose this rate on the Oversea Shipowners, who were already paying their dockers 7d and 1s. On 26 July this question was thrashed out. The federation leaders claimed that as shipowners sometimes employed stevedores to discharge at 8d and 1s, then why should they object to paying dockers the same rate for the same work? They claimed that the distinction between stevedore and docker had in most cases become meaningless, and that it was merely used, in Tillett's words,

> with a view to imposing a minimum or lesser rate upon what they [the shipowners] should choose to call the docker as distinct from the stevedore.[67]

In the upshot, the shipowners refused to concede the 8d and 1s rate at the conference, but agreed that the matter should be submitted to arbitration. Taking the July negotiations as a whole then, the N.T.W.F. had succeeded in obtaining some wage advances, but it had singularly failed to establish the uniform 8*d* and 1*s* rate.

The problem of union recognition proved as difficult for the N.T.W.F. as that of the port rate. Gosling and Tillett claimed afterwards that during the conferences of 25–27 July the employers had agreed to recognise unreservedly all the unions in the port.[68] This may be so, but it is quite clear that this recognition did not imply acceptance of a union monopoly. The shipowners especially were quite definite on this point, and they sought, and obtained, assurances from the N.T.W.F. representatives that no attempt would be made in the future to enforce such a monopoly.[69] The unionists were being less than frank in giving this assurance, but they were very uncertain of their own strength, and anxious not to throw away the chance of a settlement.

The settlement was finally reached late on 27 July. It was a provisional agreement, subject to ratification by either side. The settlement became known as the Devonport Agreement,[70] after Lord Devonport, chairman of the P.L.A. and chairman of the joint conference. It embodied wage increases on the lines outlined above. Men earning 6*d* and 8*d* were to be brought up to 7*d* and 9*d*, while men already earning this amount were, subject to arbitration, to receive 8*d* and 1*s*. The Lightermen's claims were not dealt with in this agreement. Their society had conducted negotiations with the master lightermen independently of the main conference, and in this sphere a separate provisional agreement was reached on 28 July.[71] In one sense the Devonport Agreement was a great achievement. It was the first time in the port's history that a general settlement had been negotiated without a general stoppage of work. There were, however, very serious defects. In the first place, it was not comprehensive. It did not apply to the men working for ship-owners in the short-distance trades. Nor did it embrace coal porters, tugmen, and other similarly specialist groups. Another serious defect lay in the fact that in no case had the 8*d* and 1*s* rate been conceded outright. This was the more serious in that this demand had been widely canvassed since the 1890s. In 1900 men had actually struck for the 8*d* and 1*s*,[72] and since that time the rise in the cost of living had increased the urgency of the claim. There was one final flaw in the agreement. The vital question of hiring procedures was left undecided. The agreement did contain a clause as follows:

Working arrangements and conditions in all other respects to remain as at present.

The shipowners were later to maintain that the clause was put in specifically to rule out a union monopoly.[73] In support of their argument was the fact that Gosling and others gave verbal assurances that no attempt would be made to enforce a closed shop. Yet it was quite obvious that, whatever was said about union monopoly, the waterside organisations would never tolerate indefinitely the practice of calling-on men inside the gates. It was certain that sooner or later they would demand that hiring procedures be modified in order to allow of at least a union preference, if not a monopoly. On the waterfront the form of the call-on was the most crucial factor in an organisation's influence, yet this was a problem that the Devonport Agreement left unresolved. It was the final and fatal evasion.

In concluding the Devonport Agreement the leaders of the N.T.W.F. made a serious miscalculation. The terms of the settlement were not good, but Gosling and the others felt that they were not strong enough to reject them. The strength of the unions had greatly improved since the beginning of the month, but there was still a long way to go. Furthermore the new battalions were composed of untried recruits, and there was no way of telling how they would respond to a call for action. The record of over twenty years of weakness and defeat did not make for optimism among the leadership.[74] The leaders of the N.T.W.F. thus felt unable to hold out for better terms, and they were prepared to be grateful that a settlement had been reached at all. In making this assessment, however, they completely misjudged the mood of the men, who threw the terms out and came out on strike. Before this startling development is examined it will be necessary to turn back to consider what had been happening in the unions themselves during the long period of negotiation.

The crisis of 27 June to 4 July had released the springs of activity in the port of London. Suddenly union organisers found that they were speaking to responsive, not apathetic, audiences. The good trade, the events in other ports, and the prospect of action were stirring emotions that had long lain dormant. The Dockers' Union, with its low entrance fees and subscriptions, and expansive outlook, was naturally the first to benefit from this change of mood.

It was not, however, the expansion of the Dockers that was the really significant thing in this period. Given the favourable environment, this was predictable. The really far-reaching development occurred in the Stevedores' Society. The leaders of this union had decided back in 1909 that it would be advisable to open up the ranks of the union so as to embrace port workers generally.[75] It was the actual implementation of the policy that was the difficulty. But in July 1911 the union executive decided to take the plunge.[76] It was a question of now or never. If the Stevedores' Society did not act, other unions would act in its place, and would cut it off from all its potential areas of expansion. In the early days of July, too, the leadership may have been encouraged by the prospect of an 8d and 1s port rate, for a uniform rate would do much to ease the process of expansion. The step remained, however, a leap in the dark, and no one could foresee where it would end.

In order to expand, the Stevedores' Society had to throw on one side its entry controls and its lingering conception of itself as a craft union. The high entrance fee was the first to go, and at the beginning of July organising delegates were instructed to use their own discretion regarding conditions of entry.[77] On 13 July the new entrance fee was finally fixed at a mere one shilling.[78] The drastic reduction meant that the Stevedores were able to compete with the Dockers for members on terms of equality. In its recruitment campaign the society naturally concentrated at first upon shipworkers in the oversea trades. To begin with, the union had a score to settle with the P. and O., the British India, and the New Zealand lines. These important companies had dispensed with union stevedores since 1891. Thus on 1 July delegates were sent to the Albert and Victoria docks to begin recruiting their shipmen. An obvious next step from here was Tilbury. The P. and O. used this dock as well as the Albert, and there were also other large companies there who used non-unionist labour for discharging and sometimes for loading as well, for, as we have seen, organisation was weak at Tilbury.[79] Here therefore was a great prize to be had for the asking, and throughout the month of July the Stevedores and Dockers competed vigorously with each other for a controlling influence.[80]

At the Royal Docks and Tilbury the society had at first recruited men it had long claimed the right to organise. It quickly became apparent, however, that the Stevedores were not going to confine their recruiting activities to shipworkers in the oversea trades. On 4 July the union first began to take an interest in the shipworkers in the short-sea trades.[81] These men worked in the upstream regions of the port, at the wharves and in the river. In 1889 they had founded a society of their own,[82] and in 1911 traces of this organisation still survived.[83] The Stevedores' Union now began a vigorous organising campaign in this sector, and by the end of July two branches had been established, composed entirely of shipworkers in the coastal and near continental trades. The most remarkable development of this period was, however, the extension of the society outside the sphere of shipwork altogether. This was a complete break with the craft traditions of the organisation. The change was first seen on 8 July, when a branch of deal porters was formed on the south side.[84] The deal porters were admittedly a somewhat privileged group, but their labour was nonetheless entirely confined to the quay. In the period that followed the union showed over and over again that it was prepared to expand into any sector of port work, including that of quay labour generally. There was one final change in the basis of the Stevedores' organisation at this time. Until 1911 the union was always regarded as a purely local organisation, with no ambition to extend its influence beyond the port of London. The months of July and August 1911 changed all this. The society had in 1910 developed a keen interest in the cement and paper traffic of the Thames,[85] and in 1911 it seemed natural to extend organisation to cover the similar traffic of the Medway. It was, however, not only interest in the cement and paper industries that led to this development. There was a general desire to recruit members wherever they could be found. Thus on 7 July the union even made an attempt to establish itself at Hull, but without success.[86] In turning to the Medway, therefore, the Stevedores were concerned not merely with the cement and paper trades, but with port work generally, and at Rochester it was the coal trade that formed the union's chief recruiting ground. By the middle of August 1911 branches had been founded at Rochester, Queenborough and Rainham.

This provincial activity was the culminating point of a remarkable period of expansion. The whole campaign was, however, a tremendous gamble on the part of the union's leadership. It generated powerful tensions inside the union, tensions that were becoming manifest by the middle of July. Inevitably also it created difficulties with the Dockers' Union, and already on 13 July Ben Tillett was complaining that the society was 'making members of sections hitherto not considered eligible for the Stevedores' Union'.[87] Finally, the extension of the society was to exacerbate greatly the problems of industrial relations in London. For a while, however, the strike movement of August swamped all these difficulties.

It is necessary at this point to put the activity of the Stevedores' Union into a broader framework, and to examine the general union structure that was emerging in the port at this time. Although at the end of July 1911 organisation was still far from complete, there had been sufficient development to indicate what kind of total picture would emerge. The structure was one which differed in several respects from that of the 1889–92 period. There was not, for instance, the fragmentation that characterised the earlier period. The tiny societies of Ballast Heavers, Steamship Workers, Non-Freemen and others had vanished, having been absorbed in a larger organisation. It was the older societies that had tended to benefit from this process. The Lightermen had thus absorbed the Non-Freemen back in 1900, similarly the Stevedores had taken over the Steamship Workers. Of course, a number of small societies remained, and many coal porters, for instance, chose to be separately organised, despite the efforts of the Stevedores and Dockers to enrol them.[88] Nevertheless the unmistakable trend was toward larger units of organisation. Unfortunately, however, the decline in the number of tiny, isolated associations had not produced a more rational trade union structure. While tiny occupational associations had tended to disappear, there had grown up an increased number of expansive societies, ready to recruit port workers wherever they could find them. In 1889 only the Dockers and S.S.L.P.L. had fitted into this category. Now, in July 1911, to these unions were added the Stevedores, the National Amalgamated Union of Labour (N.A.U.L.), and the United Order of General Labourers of London (U.O.G.L.). As a consequence of this development, the relative importance of the Dockers' Union in the Thames district was less in 1911 than it had been in 1890. In 1890, for instance, the Dockers had embraced great numbers of waterside workers in the Thames and Medway cement and paper district.[89] Yet in 1911 it was the Stevedores and N.A.U.L. who dominated these sectors. The same had happened in the short-sea trades, where the Stevedores again, and the U.O.G.L., had deprived the Dockers of much of their former influence.[90] The collapse of 1900 had thus permanently weakened the Dockers' Union in London, for while it recovered sufficiently to become much the biggest single port union in 1911,[91] its old sphere of influence was not regained. The Stevedores and Lightermen, on the other hand, were much stronger in 1911 than in 1890. On a comparison with 1890 both unions had increased their membership and extended their sphere of influence.

In the last days of July 1911 these developments were still at an incomplete stage. The process of reorganisation was still in full swing. It was at this juncture that the N.T.W.F. concluded the Devonport Agreement, and submitted it for ratification to a mass meeting on 28 July.[92] Gosling and Tillett recommended acceptance, but the men would have none of them. The terms were not good, and in any case the mood of the meeting was one of great excitement and turbulence. There were a few men already on strike, and the men as a whole looked for an improvement much more drastic than that provided for in the agreement. The leaders were thus sent back to get better terms. Lord Devonport, however, refused to modify the settlement by one jot. It was deadlock. Meanwhile the lightermen had also refused to ratify their own separate agreement, and had refused to settle for anything less than their original demand for a ten-hour day. Renewed negotiations on 1 August produced no result, and so here also was deadlock.[93] In view of the mood of the men, a large-scale strike had now become virtually inevitable.

It was the coal porters who began the process.[94] They had been excluded from the provisions of the Devonport Agreement, and on Saturday, 29 July, numbers of them began to leave their work. On the following Monday the movement continued, and by the end of the day 1000 coalies were on strike.[95] Events on the next two days were decisive, for the coalies were joined by the mass of the dockers working at the Victoria and Albert systems, and also by those at the Surrey Docks.[96] These men were employed not by the P.L.A., but by the Oversea Shipowners. Under the terms of the Devonport Agreement their claims for the 8d and 1s had not been granted directly, but had been submitted to arbitration. For this

arbitration the men refused to wait; they had waited fifteen years
for the 8*d* and 1*s* and that was long enough. There was also another
consideration. The men were taken on by the shipowners inside
the gates, a procedure greatly to the detriment of unionism, and
one which the Devonport Agreement did nothing to end. The
Victoria and Albert dockers thus determined to settle these two
points themselves. The whole situation was amazingly reminiscent of 1900,[97] when the dockers in this very sector had struck
unofficially, as they did now, for precisely the same two points.
Gosling of the federation and Orbell of the Dockers' Union made
strenuous efforts to induce the men to return to work, pending
the hearing of the arbitration, but they were unsuccessful. A mass
meeting of dockers was called for the evening of 2 August, in West
Ham where the revolt had its centre. The leaders of the Dockers'
Union and the N.T.W.F. decided to bend with the wind and
accept the inevitability of a stoppage. Tillett was the principal
speaker at the meeting, and although the previous day he had
publicly regretted the hasty action of the men,[98] he now warmly
commended them. The meeting resulted in an official call for a
general strike throughout the port of London.[99] The same
evening the executive of the Lightermen's Union called all its
members out in support of the demand for a ten-hour day.[100] The
1911 strike in the port of London may thus be said to have begun
in earnest on the morning of 3 August.

3

The manner in which the 1911 strike developed was unfortunate
and had lasting consequences. The N.T.W.F. and the Lightermen's Union had made a serious miscalculation in signing their
two respective agreements. They had not particularly liked the
terms, but had felt that they would not receive adequate support
from the men if they held out for anything better. When, after all,
the men showed fight, Gosling and Tillett could not conceal their
delight. On 2 August Tillett performed, as we have seen, his
remarkable volte-face, and even the cautious Gosling, who had
endeavoured to persuade the men to return to work, let slip to the
Press a statement about how delighted he was with the men's firm
stand.[101] This was perfectly understandable of course, but it was
nevertheless a disastrous beginning to the new era of collective
bargaining in the port, for the employers saw it as a distinct breach

of faith.[102] The union leaders had signed the agreements, and although these were provisional, they had promised to recommend their terms for acceptance by the men. Yet within a few days here they were exhorting the men to resistance and calling official strikes. The Master Lightermen were especially indignant, in view of the fact that they had offered to refer the dispute to the Board of Trade for settlement.[103] The shipowners also were indignant, for the official strike began on the very day on which Sir Albert Rollit was due to hear the arbitration case. In the strict sense, however, the employers were mistaken in their accusation of a breach of faith. Furthermore, on their side, the inflexibility of Lord Devonport had contributed much to the final breach.[104] Nevertheless Gosling and Tillett had laid themselves open to the charge of duplicity. The truth was, however, that they had little control over the forces which they were supposed to be leading. It was difficult to maintain a consistent position in negotiations with employers, and yet at the same time respond to sudden developments among their volatile supporters. Yet failure to do so helped to increase still further the distrust between the two sides of the industry.

The stoppage of port transport workers was not complete on 3 August.[105] At that date it was fairly general among dock and wharf labourers, lightermen and coal porters, but the stevedores still remained at work. Furthermore, the carmen, whose union was affiliated to the N.T.W.F., and who were later to become so closely involved in the struggle, had not yet come out. As with so many strikes on the waterfront, the claims of the men were far from clear. The lightermen had a specific claim outstanding, and the coal porters wanted a wage increase. As for the dockers, the only formal claim outstanding was the 8d and 1s for men employed by oversea shipowners, and this was being arbitrated upon by Sir Albert Rollit. Behind these spoken demands, however, remained two others not so clearly formulated. First, there was the issue of whether men should be taken on inside or outside the dock gates, and secondly, there was the position in the short-sea trades. These problems did not, however, emerge clearly until later in the struggle. On Sunday, 6 August, Rollit announced the terms of his award. He had decided in favour of the men, which meant that dockers employed by oversea shipowners and contractors were to receive the 8d and 1s. The result of the arbitration was proclaimed to the men at a mass meeting held in Trafalgar Square on the same day.[106] Rollit's decision did not end the strike, which in fact became much more general in the days that followed. There were the claims of the coalies and lightermen still outstanding, and in addition there were the unspoken issues mentioned above. At the Trafalgar Square meeting the N.T.W.F. called upon all the sections to refuse to work until a settlement had been made which covered them all. Such a policy was not merely tactical, but was a test case for the idea of federation. The N.T.W.F., Gosling proclaimed, must be the organ for policy, and all the men must 'stick together' until the job was finished.[107] The huge audience in the Square responded, and agreed to remain out until a comprehensive settlement was reached. In the next few days the strike extended rapidly. The vast demonstration in Trafalgar Square had been the final touch, and it set London alight. The carmen now began to leave work in their hundreds, bringing with them the street affrays that always accompanied action in this sphere. By the Wednesday street traffic had been paralysed, and the executive of the Carmen's Union had submitted demands to their employers. Other sections also formulated claims and came out. Stevedores, crane drivers, tugmen, sailing bargemen, ship repairers, all were affected.[108]

The Stevedores' Society called its members out officially on the night of 7 August, to take effect on the following morning.[109] The background to this decision is of interest. The old core of the union had remained at work during the early stages of the strike. They were relatively satisfied with their existing agreement with the L.M.S.A., and had not been involved at all in the July negotiations. As the strike grew after 3 August, however, it became increasingly difficult for them to remain at work. Furthermore a good case could be made out for using this opportunity to force the British India and P. and O. lines to recognise the union. The men working for these lines had applied to the society for assistance, and it agreed to respond. By 5 August unofficial stoppages were taking place, and the P. and O. in a panic agreed to recognise the society, the British India following in its wake a few days later.[110] Up until Monday, 7 August, there had been no question of the Stevedores terminating their agreement with the L.M.S.A. The rank and file of the union, however, were becoming restive. Nearly all other sections had put in claims for wage increases, and the

Rollit Award issued on 6 August had actually granted to many dockers the stevedores' rate of 8d and 1s. Many members in the old branches must have felt that the stevedores were falling behind, and that it was time for them to re-establish their position. Thus at a mass meeting on 7 August a resolution was passed demanding that the union rate be raised from 8d and 1s to 1s and 1s 6d. The same evening an official strike was declared, and the following day a list of demands, including the wage increase, was dispatched to the L.M.S.A.[111] The Stevedores' demand for an increased remuneration was perhaps inevitable, but it is highly likely that it did not represent official union policy. Anderson was out of London when the claim was made, and the suddenness of its emergence stamps it as a purely spontaneous development. The union's leadership may well have had reason to regret the issuing of the claim. There was already trouble between the old branches of the society, with their 8d and 1s rate, and the new members in the short-sea trades, who received only 7d and 9d.[112] It was hoped that the 8d and 1s could be obtained for the new members, thus maintaining uniform conditions within the society. Now that the stevedores in the oversea trades were demanding a further rise, the achievement of this end became much more difficult, for the Short-Sea Traders would be most unlikely to pay more than 8d and 1s, even if they paid that. Furthermore, if the old core of stevedores succeeded in obtaining their rise, it would shatter the N.T.W.F. ideal of a uniform rate for all men employed by shipowners and contractors. In view of these difficulties the union leadership did not emphasise the claim, and in fact resolved on 9 August that the society would be prepared to resume work on the old terms, as soon as other unions had obtained satisfaction.[113]

The day the Stevedores came out (8 August) also saw the intervention of the Government in the dispute.[114] The area of the strike had grown alarmingly since the Sunday and the food situation was becoming serious. The incredibly hot weather had much to do with this, for cargoes of foodstuffs were rapidly rotting away in the sheds and on the ships. The demands of the coal porters and lightermen seemed to be the most clearly outstanding, and the employers in these sectors were eventually induced by the Board of Trade to meet the men at the department offices. Shortly afterwards the Carmen and Sailing Bargemen were also brought into the negotiations. The bulk of dock and wharf workers were not included, as their grievances were supposed to have been settled by the Devonport Agreement and the Rollit Award. The discussions at the Board of Trade lasted from 8 to 11 August.[115] In view of the food situation the negotiations were conducted in an atmosphere of great urgency. Nevertheless many employers, especially the master lightermen,[116] entered into the discussions only with reluctance, and the fact that a settlement was reached so quickly was due largely to the genius of the Board of Trade conciliator, George Askwith. Finally, at midnight Friday, 11 August, the job was complete. Five separate agreements had been arrived at, in all of which the men received substantial gains.[117] The sections covered were the lightermen, the sailing bargemen, the carmen, the coal porters who discharged colliers and finally the coal porters who bunkered ships. The first two were signed on behalf of the men by the Lightermen's Union, the other three by the N.T.W.F. All were countersigned on behalf of the Board of Trade by George Askwith. While the negotiations had been in progress, the N.T.W.F. had approached the P.L.A., and had asked for an assurance that, in the event of a general resumption of work, all their permanent and registered labourers would be reinstated in their former positions.[118] Such an assurance was given in general terms, and so on 11 August, the negotiations being concluded, the N.T.W.F. officially declared the strike at an end.[119]

The agreements of 11 August did not, in fact, end the 1911 strike. It was typical of the anarchy of London that the dispute, after being formally declared at an end, should continue to run for another ten days. It had been confidently expected that Monday, 14 August would see a general resumption of work,[120] and indeed the bulk of the men duly reported for work on that day. A general resumption did not, however, take place. There were several causes of continued chaos. The first concerned the P.L.A. Despite the assurance that had been given, the Port Authority refused to reinstate about 3000 of their labourers.[121] In consequence of this action, the majority of P.L.A. employees came out on strike again, and the renewed stoppage was officially endorsed by the N.T.W.F. on 15 August.[122] An additional irritant in this sector was the question of meal-time payments, which the P.L.A., unlike the shipowners, refused to concede.[123] Eventually the difficulties in this sphere were smoothed over, but the renewed stoppage had scarcely improved an industrial climate already seething with distrust and ill-will.

The other sources of trouble were more intractable than that which concerned the P.L.A., and they had been steadily boiling away beneath the surface since July. None of the series of agreements that had been negotiated since that time had done anything to remove these potential sources of conflict. The most important concerned the old problem of union monopoly and its means of enforcement. This was an issue which concerned primarily the shipowners and the master lightermen. It was not an issue with the master stevedores, because they already recognised a union preference, and it was not an issue with the P.L.A., because their decasualised scheme of employment ruled out union control of hiring. The issue of union monopoly was bound to break out on the waterfront as soon as the various organisations became reasonably strong. All the London unions had grown steadily in July, and by mid-August the influx of new recruits had become an avalanche. In these months the Dockers' Union expanded its London membership from under 2000 to over 22,000,[124] and the number of branches grew from fourteen to forty-nine.[125] The Stevedores' Union increased its membership from 4000 to 8000, and branches from nine to seventeen.[126] The matter could thus be contained no longer. The establishment of a union monopoly depended upon union control of hiring procedures, and at the docks and wharves such control normally depended upon having the men called-on outside the dock gates. At the beginning of August the Victoria and Albert dockers had, as we have seen, tried to induce the shipowners to cease taking on men inside the gates.[127] Now the issue reappeared once more. The men returning to work on 14 August refused to allow themselves to be taken on inside the gates, and as the employers would not come outside for them, work remained at a standstill. Once again the N.T.W.F. stepped in to endorse the spontaneous action of the rank and file, and on 17 August it resolved that the men should be taken on outside the gates.[128] The stoppage over this issue concerned not only the dockers but also a section of the Stevedores' Union. Members of the L.M.S.A. always conformed to the society rule that stevedores should be taken on outside the gates, but two large shipping-lines, the British India and P. and O., did not conform. They had only agreed to recognise the society during the panic of the strike, and when work was resumed they attempted to take the stevedores on inside the dock. These men naturally stood out with the dockers.[129]

The lightermen were also involved in this issue of union monopoly, but their position was rather different. Working, as they did, all over the port, their control of hiring depended not upon where they were taken on, but upon who took them on. In short, upon whether the foreman was a unionist or not. Thus on Monday, 14 August many of the lightermen returning to work refused to take orders from foremen who did not hold a N.T.W.F. ticket.[130] The point about the N.T.W.F. ticket was that many foremen were members of the Foremen Lightermen's Union,[131] a very conservative body that was not affiliated to the federation.[132] The issue was therefore whether the foremen could be forced to join a bona fide union, preferably the Lightermen's Union. Meanwhile the master lightermen set their faces firmly against this attempt to enforce a monopoly,[133] and so within a day or so after 14 August the lighterage trade was again brought to a standstill.

The dispute over union monopoly threatened for a time to throw the whole port back into turmoil. The renewed stoppages were the more serious in view of developments in the provinces. There had been renewed trouble at Liverpool at the beginning of August, and by the 14 August this had flared up into a general transport strike in that city. Finally, developing out of the Liverpool strike, came the national railway strike on 17 and 18 August. There was even talk at this time of the N.T.W.F. calling a national strike for 22 August,[134] and so together with the railwaymen paralysing the entire national transport system. The situation was thus very grave indeed, and in London there was much talk of the military being used to break the dock strike. In the event, however, the Government did not resort to any drastic action, and instead intervened once more to conciliate the London dispute. Conferences were convened at the Home Office on 18 and 19 August and the issue of union monopoly was hammered out. Meanwhile the national railway strike was brought to a close, also on 19 August, and much of the excitement died down.

The discussions at the Home Office resulted in two separate agreements being reached. The first was signed on 18 August.[135] It was drafted as a supplement to the Devonport Agreement, and concerned the N.T.W.F. and the Oversea Shipowners. The second agreement was signed the following day, and applied solely to the lighterage trade. The agreement of 18 August was in many ways a distinct triumph for the unions. In it the shipowners at last conceded the point that men should be engaged outside the dock gates. This concession gave the unions every chance to enforce a card inspection at the calling-on stands, and so went a long way towards permitting a union monopoly. It is clear, however, that the shipowners conceded the point reluctantly, and only in face of strong Government pressure.[136] If the shipowners yielded on this issue, they remained adamant on one point. They would not tolerate the compulsory enrolment of foremen and tally clerks in the N.T.W.F. A clause was thus inserted in the settlement binding the unions not to insist upon foremen and tally clerks being federation members.

On 19 August the lightermen's agreement was arrived at, after discussions every bit as tough as those with the shipowners. This agreement provided that certain minor difficulties should be referred for decision to the Board of Trade. On the major issue of union monopoly, however, the master lightermen made no concession. Like the shipowners, they insisted that their foremen must not be forced to take the ticket, and a clause to this effect was embodied in the agreement.[137] The Lightermen's Society thus remained no closer than before to its goal of a closed shop, whereas the dockers had at least obtained the concession over calling-on procedures. The Home Office agreements of 18 and 19 August may be said to have ended the 1911 strike, for on the following Monday, 21 August, the bulk of the men resumed work. The issue of union monopoly was not settled, however, for neither side was ultimately prepared to modify its position.

There was another intractable problem in the port besides that of the closed shop, and it was one of the issues responsible for the prolongation of the strike after 11 August. This problem concerned the men in the short-sea trades. On 21 August, when work was resumed elsewhere in the port, these men remained on strike. The trouble here arose over the question of wage rates. Originally, before the Devonport Agreement, there had been two basic rates in this sector. The men employed by short-distance shipping companies or their contractors had generally been paid 7d and 9d. The short-sea men employed by wharfingers, however, had normally only received 6d and 8d. There was a reason for this differential, but it was based not on skill, but upon the situations of the two groups of employers.[138] The wharfingers performed precisely the same function in the port as the old dock companies, and their successor, the P.L.A. They discharged ships and housed and delivered the cargoes. The wharves and docks had competed vigorously with each other for business for over half a century,[139] and they had both traditionally paid the same wage rates. Their wage rates were lower than elsewhere in the port, partly because of the ruinous effect of their competition, but partly also because their widely ramified activities enabled them to offer more regular employment than shipowners or contractors. Lower wages, they claimed, were offset by more continuous employment. While the wharfingers' wage rates had thus been identical with those of the dock managements, the rates of short-sea shipowners and contractors tended to approximate more closely to the prices paid by oversea shipowners. Thus until the Devonport Agreement both oversea and short-sea shipowners paid a 7d per hour day rate. The wage structure that resulted from these circumstances was thoroughly unsatisfactory to the men, who were bound to judge their remuneration according to the nature of the work performed. A short-sea vessel was the same to them whoever was the employer responsible for her discharge, and the work should be paid for at the same rate. The men were perhaps ready to excuse the Port Authority's 6d rate, because P.L.A. employees were a distinct body of men working as permanent or preference labourers. It was the disparity at the wharves that was the source of grievance.

The union leaders of the port, mindful of this situation, had long campaigned for a uniform port rate, and had pressed for the 8d and 1s standard. In the event, however, the Devonport Agreement and Rollit Award only confused the situation still further. The wharfingers had taken part in the July negotiations, and were signatories of the Devonport Agreement. Under this agreement the P.L.A. and wharfingers had both conceded a rise of one penny, so that the men working short-sea vessels and employed by wharfingers received an increase from 6d and 8d to 7d and 9d. The difficulty arose, however, with the short-sea men employed by shipowners. Under the terms of the Devonport Agreement, the question of whether the employees of shipowners should receive 8d and 1s was referred to arbitration. However, the terms of reference of the arbitration specifically excluded shipowners in the short-sea trades, because this group had withdrawn from the negotiations at an early stage. Rollit duly awarded the 8*d* and 1*s* to the oversea men, but the short-sea men were left on their old rate of 7*d* and 9*d*. Thus a new anomaly took the place of the old. There was now a uniform rate for the short-distance trades, but there was also a marked differential between the employees of oversea and short-sea shipowners. For the latter group the situation was intolerable, and it was made worse by another factor. During July 1911 many of these men had become members of the Stevedores' Society.[140] The standard rate of this union was 8*d* and 1*s*, and membership of this organisation thus increased the resentment of men who had been denied the higher rate. The consequence of these developments was tremendous unrest in this sector of employment, and after 14 August many of the men refused to work unless the 8*d* and 1*s* rate was paid.

The N.T.W.F. eagerly took up the case of the men working in the short-sea trades. It hoped that it would prove possible to stretch the Rollit Award so that it would cover the short-sea as well as the overseas trades.[141] In this manner all men employed at loading or discharging ships, with the single exception of the P.L.A. men, would be brought upon a uniform port rate of 8*d* and 1*s*. (This is of course on the assumption that short-sea workers would be treated as a single group, irrespective of whether they worked for shipowners or wharfingers.) In the early stages of the strike the federation had not pressed this demand, but now it was brought into the open. A few firms in the short-sea trades agreed to pay the 8*d* and 1*s* and here the men returned to work.[142] The majority of firms, however, rejected the higher rate. It was not so much that these employers objected to the enhanced rate in itself; it was the consequences of such a concession that worried them. It was well known that the Stevedores' Union wished to bring the wages and conditions of its new members up to the level of the old branches.[143] If the Short-Sea Traders granted the 8*d* and 1*s* it was felt that this would be taken by the men as an indication that the Short-Sea Traders' Association intended to conform to the same conditions as the L.M.S.A. This was something the S.S.T.A. certainly had no intention of doing. The Stevedores' Union had already approached the L.M.S.A. with a demand for a wage increase.[144] Thus if the S.S.T.A. recognised the existing stevedores' rates, it might soon find itself faced with a further demand for an increase to the new rate paid by the L.M.S.A. Wages were not, however, the only consideration involved. The Stevedores' Union wanted not merely a uniform wage rate for its entire membership, but also uniform conditions. This meant that the S.S.T.A. would be pressed to recognise the working rules of the society; rules which included union control of hiring procedures. The issue of the 8*d* and 1*s* rate in the short-sea trades was thus exceedingly complex, for it was bound up with the character and problems of the Stevedores' Union.

On 21 August, when work elsewhere in the port was resumed, the Short-Sea Traders made a concession.[145] They offered to pay a rate of 8*d* and 10*d*—that is, a rate just short of the stevedores' standard. The majority of the men refused to accept this offer, and were encouraged by the N.T.W.F. to hold out for the original demand.[146] Thus on 22 August work in this sector was still at a virtual standstill.[147] The only way out was arbitration, but it was some time before the N.T.W.F. and the S.S.T.A. could agree upon the terms of reference. Finally, on 23 August, the two sides signed an agreement which provided that the question of the 8*d* and 1*s* rate should be settled by an arbitrator, to be appointed by the Board of Trade.[148] Even so, it was 31 August before work had returned to normal in this troubled sector.[149] The award finally appeared early in October, and was given against the men.[150] It was unlikely that this defeat would be accepted for long.

The agreement of 23 August was the last of the long series that had begun with the Devonport Agreement on 27 July. In all, nine separate agreements had been required to settle the affairs of the port. The main body of port employers, who had for so long held the unions at arm's length, now felt that they had gone to the very limit in making concessions to the men. Only the Government had induced them to go so far, and they would go no further. They therefore regarded the agreements as final, and were resolved that any further demands must be resisted. This spirit was perfectly embodied in the first clause of the 18 August agreement. 'Settlement to be final, and no fresh points to be raised after this agreement has been signed.'

This inflexible attitude was of course disastrously inept, but it was understandable. Because of the spontaneous nature of the 1911 uprising, the union leaders had never been sure of the mood of their constituents. As the movement had gained in size and intensity Gosling, Tillett and others had tended to step up their demands from week to week. The reflex action of the employers had been to insist upon a limit; to try to establish a point at which the mounting tide of union power could be contained. Hence, for them, the 'final' character of the settlements. Yet the settlements could, of course, never be final. The 1911 movement had created as many problems as it had settled, and if renewed conflict was to be averted, the maximum amount of patience and flexibility would be needed. If employers persisted in regarding every grievance of the men as just another indication of union aggression, then industrial war could not long be postponed.

The inflexible attitude of the employers in turn moulded the outlook of union leaders. The latter felt, rightly or wrongly, that employers were irreconcilably opposed to really strong unions. They felt, therefore, that their position was fundamentally insecure. Many could indeed remember what had happened to mass trade unionism in 1891, and there was the feeling that such a catastrophe could well happen again. Union leaders were not encouraged therefore to be moderate, but rather to press home their advantage to the limit. They distrusted the employers profoundly and regarded the latters' movements with the most exaggerated suspicions. Neither side of the industry therefore approached the settlements of 1911 in a rational, detached manner, nor were they prepared to judge each issue upon its merits. The peace that settled on the port in August was an uneasy one, and it did not require a prophet to forecast its speedy disruption.

7 The 1912 Strike: Origins and Aftermath

THE sources of future trouble in the port centred upon the two oldest organisations—the Stevedores and Lightermen. This was not an accident. When old organisations expand into new sectors of employment, they bring with them a whole series of problems. This is because they have fixed standards to maintain, and are consequently subject to considerable pressures both from within and without. Their older members will be fearful lest new recruits compromise hard-won gains, and employers will resist the intrusion into their domain of unions whose standards are high and conditions precise. So it was with the Stevedores and Lightermen, and the former organisation in particular suffered from its need to impose fixed standards.

The Stevedores' Society had occupied the centre of the riverside scene since at least the turn of the century, and the hectic organisation of July and August had not altered this situation. Of course, in these months the Dockers had greatly outstripped the society in numerical terms, but it had not supplanted it from its central position. This position was due to two factors. First the society, through its relationship with the L.M.S.A., operated a code of working rules far more advanced than those of any other organisation in the port. And secondly, since its expansion outside the sphere of the L.M.S.A., it sought to apply this code to a wide range of port employment hitherto untouched by its influence. As a result of these two factors, the society occupied the central role in a complex web of industrial relations. In order to examine this role it will be necessary to distinguish the various sectors of employment in which the union had members and to deal with each in turn.

The core of the Stevedores' Society was formed by the employees of the master stevedores. Conditions in this sector were regulated by collective bargaining between the union and the L.M.S.A.

Here the society enjoyed complete recognition and its influence was unchallenged by any rival organisation. When the great 1911 strike was terminated, the claim of the men in this sector for a wage advance was still outstanding. The machinery for adjusting such claims was, however, well-tried, and in the weeks that followed negotiations went ahead for a new settlement.[1] Finally, agreement was reached on an increase in pay, and minor points that remained in dispute were referred to the Chamber of Commerce Arbitration Board for decision. On 27 December 1911 the Board gave its award, and the new settlement was complete.[2] The new conditions entailed, among other things, a rise in the stevedores' basic rate from 8d and 1s to 10d and 1s. Piecework rates were also raised. The negotiations and settlement had conformed to a well established pattern that was not to be found anywhere else in the port of London. The society and the L.M.S.A. had evolved a system of industrial relations where adjustments in working conditions could be agreed upon in a frank and friendly manner. It was an atmosphere unique in the port. The changed character of the Stevedores' Union, however, gave to these negotiations a significance that they had not had before. Prior to 1911 this had been an autonomous sphere of industrial relations, set quite apart from circumstances elsewhere in the port. Now that the society had expanded outside the ambit of the L.M.S.A., however, things were different, and the agreement of 27 December had an impact that extended beyond the sector that it was intended to cover. The old core of the Stevedores' Society was still as stable as ever, but it was no longer a self-contained unit, insulated from outside developments.

In July and August 1911 the society had extended its membership beyond the boundaries of employment controlled by the L.M.S.A. In the upstream areas of the port it had enrolled the men working in the short-sea trades and also the deal porters. In the lower docks, it had enrolled the stevedores working for the non-society shipping lines. Finally, in the lower reaches of the Thames and in the Medway, it had recruited generally among waterside labourers. In all these new areas, its situation was greatly affected by the relationship it had long ago established with the master stevedores. There was in fact a constant interaction between the old and the new. Nowhere was this more the case than in the upper reaches of the port, where the society had recruited the short-sea men and the deal porters. The interaction between old and new was at its most intense in this region because it was here that they were in closest proximity. The bulk of the older branches were situated upstream, so that the creation of new branches in this region brought new and old face to face in what was potentially a single labour market. In view of this circumstance, the problems of the union's expansion are seen best in this region of the port, and it is therefore here that our attention will first be concentrated.

The creation of new branches of short-sea men and deal porters had caused trouble from the very beginning. The first problem came from within the society itself. Back in July 1911, when the first short-sea men's branch had been formed, the older branches had begun to protest against the creation of branches 'with one shilling entrance fee'.[3] The reason for the complaints was that the new members were looking for work at the places of call dominated by the established branches. The demand went up that the new members should have a distinctive union ticket, proclaiming their original calling, and thus debarring them from the old sector of the society. The strike of August 1911 halted this movement for a while, nevertheless the new members themselves had been disturbed by the uproar, and on 9 August they asked the executive for an assurance that their ticket would be recognised at all society places of call.[4] This assurance was given. However, when work was resumed after the strike, the trouble began over again. The short-sea men and deal porters had no preference in employment in their own occupations and many found difficulty in getting work. In any case, as we saw in the last chapter, at a number of short-sea firms the stoppage was prolonged after other port workers had returned to work. There was thus an influx of new members to the L.M.S.A. stands, and a storm of protest among the older members began again. In face of this storm the executive was forced to give ground, and on 21 August it resolved that the new branches should have 'separate colour cards and the names of the distinct trade or calling to be printed on the outside'.[5] As a result of this resolution, the branch of deal porters seceded from the society,[6] disgusted with the policy of discrimination. The short-sea men, however, continued to remain within the union.

Expansion had thus created a very difficult problem for the leadership of the union. If new members were to be retained they must enjoy equal rights with the older stevedores. Yet the older members would be bound to resist this equality as long as the new members worked under inferior conditions to themselves. The only solution was to bring conditions in the new sectors up to those prevailing with the L.M.S.A. This meant not only raising wage rates, but securing the union preference in the new sectors. Without this there was no reciprocity. New members could benefit by coming on to the old calling-on stands, but old members could not benefit by going to the new sectors. To make expansion work there had to be uniform wage rates and a uniform union preference. The deal porters were gone, but the men at the wharves remained. The society must bring the standards of these men up to the level of the L.M.S.A. As regards wage rates, everything depended at first upon the arbitration provided for under the agreement of 23 August.[7] If this were favourable to the men the S.S.T.A. would have to pay the same 8d and 1s as the L.M.S.A. Admittedly the latter were considering a further wage increase, but that was a hurdle that would have to be crossed when the time came. The achievement of immediate parity was the thing. Unfortunately, however, in October the award was given against the men.[8] The disparity thus remained and the society was therefore forced to retain the discriminating ticket. There followed a period of quiescence, until suddenly, at the end of October, the whole matter was again blown open by the well-known *Sea Belle* case.

The affair of the *Sea Belle* is meaningless unless it is placed against the background sketched above. At the time of the 1912 strike this affair was taken up by the unions as evidence of the employers' perfidy.[9] When the event actually took place, however, things were not quite so simple. The *Sea Belle* was a vessel belonging to a Mr Leach. Leach was also a wharfinger, and at the latter end of October 1911 his vessel docked at his establishment, Mark Brown's wharf. As a wharfinger Leach paid the men in his employ 7d per hour, according to the terms of the Devonport Agreement. Like most wharfingers, Leach dealt mainly with ships in the short-sea trades, but occasionally oversea vessels docked at his wharf, and the *Sea Belle* happened to be one of these. As usual his employees, members of the Stevedores' Union, were set to discharge her at the rate of 7d per hour. This time, however, somebody at the wharf decided to test whether a higher rate could be obtained for the work. The Stevedores' General Secretary agreed to take the case up, and the men at the wharf were advised to cease work on the ship.[10] The case put forward by the society was a very good one. Under the terms of the Rollit Award 8d and 1s were to be paid for oversea vessels where the employers were shipowners or contractors. This had originally been intended to apply to the large shipping-lines at the lower docks, nevertheless the fact remained that the *Sea Belle* was an oversea ship, and that Leach was a shipowner as well as a wharfinger. In legalistic terms the men's case was irrefutable. Leach, however, felt that the Rollit Award had never been intended to apply to the wharves. He therefore refused to pay the 8d and 1s and at first refused arbitration as well. Meanwhile the boycott of the vessel continued and the matter became serious. The P.L.A. took the vessel into dock, but the liaison between the Stevedores' and Dockers' unions was excellent, and the Port Authority's employees all refused to touch the ship.[11] The matter dragged on throughout November, and the Board of Trade intervened in order to end what was becoming a major threat to industrial peace. At long last Leach agreed to arbitration, and the question was referred to the Lord Chief Justice for decision. Predictably, he decided on 27 November in favour of the men being paid 8d and 1s. The whole business was, however, more complex than this outline would tend to indicate.

It is clear that the *Sea Belle* affair was not spontaneous, but was the result of deliberate union policy. This must be the case, for plenty of oversea ships had docked at Mark Brown's wharf in the weeks that preceded the *Sea Belle* incident, yet no question had then been raised of the legality of the 7d rate. It was only after the Short-Sea Trades Award had gone against the men that the matter was raised, and it is unlikely that this was pure coincidence. What did the society hope to gain from the affair? It is certain that the Stevedores' Union and the N.T.W.F. leadership hoped that the affair would establish a uniform 8d and 1s rate for work on all oversea vessels, at docks, wharves or wherever. For the Stevedores this would mean a step in the direction of levelling up the wharves to the conditions of the L.M.S.A. For the N.T.W.F. it meant a step towards a port rate for similar work. It was further hoped that if the wharves could be induced to accept an 8d and 1s rate for oversea ships, it would be easier to get them to pay that rate for short-sea ships. There is also evidence that the Stevedores' Society attempted to use the incident to push things a good deal further.[12] Apparently, at the Board of Trade Conference on this incident, the society suggested that the position of its members lay outside the framework established by the July and August agreements. That, as members of the Stevedores' Union, they were bound solely by the working rules of that union; working rules arrived at in conjunction with the L.M.S.A. The obvious implication of this line of reasoning was that the wharves should conform to the standards of the L.M.S.A. Leach himself was perfectly aware of the predicament of the Stevedores' Union, and of its need to establish uniform conditions among its members.[13] He regarded the incident as a manœuvre on the part of the unions, and this accounts for his prolonged resistance to the men's demands.

The Stevedores' Society and the N.T.W.F. failed in their attempt to utilise the *Sea Belle* incident, just as they had failed earlier to stretch the Rollit Award to apply to the Short-Sea Traders.[14] In the *Sea Belle* incident they won the arbitration case, of course, but Lord Alverstone's decision proved to be of no value at all. It had been hoped that his award in the *Sea Belle* case would be taken to apply to all oversea vessels using the wharves. These hopes were vain. Leach had been vulnerable because he was a shipowner as well as a wharfinger, and therefore came strictly within the provisions of the Rollit Award. Many oversea ships, however, were discharged at the wharves by wharfingers, and these could claim to have nothing to do with the Rollit or Alverstone Awards. Their scales of payment had always been closer to the P.L.A. than to the shipowners, and they steadily refused to be bound by the *Sea Belle* decision.[15] Thus, after all, only Leach emerged as being bound by the decision, and he duly respected the terms of the award. Some attempt was indeed made to induce the wharfingers to adopt the 8*d* and 1*s* rate for oversea ships. The United Order of General Labourers, which had members at the large Hay's wharf, attempted to get the full backing of the N.T.W.F. in bringing pressure to bear on this concern. This was in January 1912.[16] The Stevedores supported them in this movement, and the N.T.W.F. sent a deputation to Hay's wharf, but they were not even received by the management.[17] The issue was still open when the 1912 strike commenced.

The *Sea Belle* incident thus brought the unions no closer to their avowed objectives. Indirectly, however, it did have a powerful effect, for it unleashed once more the discontent in the short-sea trades. Things had been fairly quiet since the end of August, but militancy now revived. At the time when the *Sea Belle* had first been blocked the Stevedores' executive had abandoned its discriminatory policy, and resolved 'that similar cards be issued to all branches'.[18] This move had no doubt been made in order to reinforce the loyalty of the new members in the coming dispute. It was, however, one thing to pass such a resolution, quite another to see that it was properly implemented. What in fact happened was that the rank and file of the old branches began to refuse to work with the new members, thus nullifying the council's resolution in practice.[19] In consequence of the action of the old branches the members in the short-sea trades became extremely restive. They realised that they would never have equal status with the older members until their conditions were the same, and so they began to press for direct action to achieve this end. By 8 November Branch 11 (one of the two short-sea branches, the other being No. 13) had passed a resolution urging the union executive to give one of the big wharves a fortnight's notice of coming under the 'Stevedores' Rules and Rates of pay'. Anderson, however, was not yet prepared to go this far. As Secretary of the N.T.W.F., as well as of the Stevedores, he had been a signatory of the agreement covering the Short-Sea Trades. He felt 'it would not be policy to break away at the present time', and suggested that after a decent lapse of time a proper campaign should be inaugurated by the N.T.W.F.[20] The men, however, were not prepared to wait. The internal pressures in the society were too strong, and the men were determined to come under the Stevedores' rules and rates of pay. In December 1911 a whole series of unofficial stoppages began in the short-distance trades, and by January 1912 the disruption in this sector of the port was assuming serious proportions. The position had become particularly acute in January, because in that month the new agreement with the L.M.S.A. came into operation. This meant that the new branches were further than ever from parity with the old, and thus discontent mounted to the breaking-point. By the middle of the month a whole series of wharves were in dispute, and the Board of Trade intervened once more to sponsor negotiations. An attempt was made to get together a conference between the S.S.T.A. and the Stevedores' Society, and the men were instructed by the union to resume work while negotiations were going forward.[21] The looked-for conference did not, however, materialise. The employers knew that the men wanted conditions on a par with those of the L.M.S.A., and they had no intention of granting these conditions. In face of the employers' resistance, the problem of increased rates in the short-sea trades tended to subside for a while, and trouble in this sector was diverted onto another issue.

Parity between the old and new centres of the Stevedores' organisation depended not only upon uniform rates, but also upon equal opportunities for employment. The L.M.S.A. employed society foremen, and recognised the right of society members to be taken on before all others. In this sector it was a firm rule that no non-society men were to be taken on until all Stevedores' Union members had been cleared from the stand.[22] This was the essence of the union's power, and the principal benefit that it conferred upon its members. In the new areas of organisation, however, this rule did not apply, and its absence was perhaps the primary source of tension between the old and the new centres. The disparity tended to increase the numbers competing on the old stands, for it was easier for a member to obtain work there than in the new sectors. It was therefore essential that the union preference should be extended to the wharves. This was a process with a dual impact. It affected not only the employers, but also the other unions with a stake in the area, for a society preference meant not only a preference over non-unionists but also over other unionists. In conditions of nearly 100 per cent organisation, as in the winter of 1911–12, it meant, in fact, primarily preference over other unionists. This issue thus had powerful implications for inter-union relations.

The society preference, unlike the uniform rate, was something that the Stevedores' Union could hope to enforce even in the face of powerful opposition from the employers. The union took the matter up in earnest in November 1911. This was a time when the executive had just restored the 'similar cards',[23] and when tension between old and new was at its height. Something had to be done to achieve parity, or at least keep new members off the old places of call. Thus outdoor delegates were appointed to visit the wharves and insist 'on our own members being taken on first previous to members of other unions'.[24] It was a hard job, but where the men were taken on outside the wharf gates, and where a majority were society members, a card inspection could do the trick. Employers,

however, very often insisted on the men being taken on inside the
wharf, and the delegates were debarred from trespassing on the
firm's premises.[25] In such cases it was impossible to ensure that
society men were given the preference. By February 1912 the issue
of the society preference at the wharves had come very much to
the fore. In that month there were stoppages at several wharves,
where men came out in protest against members of other unions
being employed in preference to stevedores.[26]

The attempts to enforce the Stevedores' preference at the
wharves created considerable tension in inter-union relations,
because it meant discriminating against the cards of other organisations. At the wharves the unions chiefly involved in this process were
the old S.S.L.P.L.,[27] the U.O.G.L. and the London Carmen's Trade
Union. The inclusion of the last organisation may seem surprising,
but it contained many men who occasionally sought for temporary
employment at the waterfront. The other two organisations both
had a considerable number of members regularly working at the
wharves. The issue of non-recognition of cards had always been an
impediment to co-operation among organisations in the port
industry, and so it was now. At the conference of the N.T.W.F.
in February 1912 the issue was hotly debated,[28] and it is clear that
the controversy centred largely around the policy of the Stevedores'
Society. The Carmen's Union at this, as at subsequent conferences,
headed the attack against the monopolistic policies of certain
federated unions, and it was the Stevedores' Union that it had
principally in mind. The Carmen were supported by the Gasworkers' Union, whose main grievance was against the Dockers'
Union, because the monopolistic policies of that organisation in the
Victoria and Albert systems prevented gas workers from obtaining
seasonal work at the waterfront. An attempt was made to establish
the principle of equality in employment for all federated organisations, but the Stevedores and Dockers received enough support
from provincial waterside unions to enable them to smother the
movement. The same issue recurred again, however, at the
N.T.W.F. Conference in June.[29] The protagonists were also
precisely the same. Once again it was clear that the Stevedores'
policies constituted a powerful element in the controversy. The
Secretary of the U.O.G.L. supported the Carmen and Gasworkers, and his speech clearly referred to the Stevedores' Society
when he stated that a number of his members had lost their

employment the previous year through the preference in work being given to 'one particular union'. Once again, however, the advocates of the 'One Man, One Ticket' principle were defeated. The Stevedores, Dockers, and National Dockers all opposed them, and most other waterside unions followed suit. There is, however, evidence that the rank and file of the less entrenched unions some-times tackled the situation in their own way. Thus in May 1912 the Stevedores' Society complained to the N.T.W.F. that the members of the Labour Protection League and the U.O.G.L. were coercing stevedores to break the union rules.[30] It is possible that this meant that society members were being forced not to insist upon a card inspection. Whatever the actual case, the Stevedores' 'controlling interest' was being actively undermined by the rank and file of other organisations.

The trouble in the short-sea trades thus developed largely out of problems arising from the expansion of the Stevedores' Union. The need to obtain parity between the old and new sectors had been crucial. This need had involved the society in endless friction both with employers and with other unions. There had been constant disruption, revolving at first around rates of pay and centring later upon the achievement of the society preference. In March 1912 the issue was still unresolved. It could not go on indefinitely. At the end of the month, a member of the executive proposed that the S.S.T.A. should be given notice that the society intended to enforce its conditions in this sphere.[31] The issue was postponed for a month, but on 3 May it came up again. The executive passed a resolution inviting the S.S.T.A. to a con-ference 'with a view to the adoption of the Working Rules as accepted by the L.M.S.A.'.[32] This was the first time the demand had been submitted to the employers in black and white, and it was clear that drastic action was intended. On 14 May the society decided to press the S.S.T.A. for an answer to its proposal.[33] Things were moving towards a complete stoppage in this sector. In the event, however, it was the Lightermen, not the Stevedores, who started the 1912 strike, for by 14 May the dispute at the Mercantile Lighterage Company was already far advanced.[34] The affairs of the two societies had come to a head almost simultane-ously.

The dilemma of the expanded Stevedores' Society had been greatest in the upper regions of the port, for reasons that have already been outlined. However, the union's position in other areas exhibited features that were not dissimilar to those prevailing at the wharves. The situation at the lower docks was of particular interest, although it was only after the 1912 strike that developments in this sector dominated the affairs of the society. Unlike the wharves, the downstream docks fell within the traditional sphere of influence of the Stevedores' Society. Stability in this sector had, however, always been difficult to achieve owing to the opposition of the large shipping companies.[35] In the great period of organisation, in July and August 1911, the Stevedores' Society had set itself the primary task of forcing the recalcitrant firms in this region into conformity with the standards of the L.M.S.A.[36] The employees of these companies in West Ham had been organised in a new branch, No. 14, and the organisation at Tilbury had been greatly expanded. As a result of the 1911 strike the companies duly agreed to recognise the society and conform to its conditions, including the practice of taking the men on outside the dock. The Stevedores thus succeeded in restoring their control over loading work in the docks, and the L.M.S.A. conditions once again governed all firms performing this operation. Three of the big shipping-lines, however, could never really accept the permanence of the union's influence. They were the P. and O., the British India, and the New Zealand lines. These companies had defied the society between 1891 and 1911, and they accepted their defeat in the latter year with a bad grace. In consequence, the friction between the union and these three companies grew apace, and by January 1912 relations had become notoriously bad.[37] The same was true of the society's relationship with Scruttons Ltd of Tilbury. It was clear that these big firms would utilise any pretext in order once more to break free of the Stevedores' organisation. In May 1912 cases were reported where the British India Line and Scruttons Ltd had employed dockers instead of stevedores for loading purposes,[38] and the P. and O. had also occasionally resorted to this practice.[39] Inevitably this manœuvre created friction between the two unions, and the Stevedores complained to the N.T.W.F. that the Dockers' Union was overlapping into its sphere of influence.[40] The existence of two major unions in the docks, with differing rates and conditions, created an extremely difficult situation, for there was always the danger that employers might try to play the cheaper union off against the more expensive

organisation. The logic of the Stevedores' decision to expand in
1909 was thus clearly vindicated, and the failure to fully implement their resolution was to cost the union dear in 1912. By the
middle of May 1912 the relationship between the Stevedores'
Society and the big shipping-lines was drifting rapidly towards a
renewed breach. Thus when the lightermen came out on strike,
the downstream stevedores, like the short-sea men, were ready to
enter the fray once more. The consequences of this action were to
be disastrous indeed.

The final area into which the Stevedores' Union had expanded
consisted of the downstream wharves. The union's position at
these wharves resembled the situation in the short-sea trades, in
that men had been organised who had hitherto been completely
outside the society's sphere of influence. On the other hand, this
fact had not presented the same internal problems as had appeared
in the upstream districts. This was because areas like Northfleet,
Swanscombe and Queenborough were quite self-contained as
labour markets, so that there was no friction between the old and
new sectors, and no demands that the men at these wharves should
have separate union cards. As far as relations with employers were
concerned, however, the downstream wharves raised difficulties no
less than the upstream establishments. The society was bound to
try to level the conditions of these new recruits up towards the
L.M.S.A. standard, for several society firms contracted for work
in this sphere, and without a uniform application of their standard
they were at a constant disadvantage.[41] Thus in late August 1911
pay claims were submitted by the union on behalf of the men at
the cement wharves.[42] The Cement Combine, like the S.S.T.A.,
strongly resisted these claims, on the ground that the riverside men
in the industry could in no way be considered as stevedores in the
traditional sense. In view of this resistance the union threatened to
strike the cement wharves, but the Board of Trade intervened yet
again in order to bring the two sides together. The consequent
negotiations resulted in an agreement being signed between the
Stevedores' Society and the Associated Portland Cement Manufacturers Limited.[43] This was in the middle of September, and in
the following October the society negotiated another settlement,
this time to cover the men discharging paper pulp for Lloyd's
mills at Queenborough and Sittingbourne.[44] It is certain that a
considerable improvement in conditions was achieved by these

settlements, although it is probable that the improvement fell well short of the L.M.S.A. standard. The employers in this sector, as elsewhere, did not take kindly to the intrusion of the Stevedores' Union into their province. Already by May 1912 there were complaints that certain cement manufacturers were trying to evade the agreement of September 1911.[45] Furthermore, as in its other areas of expansion, the position of the society was weakened by the presence of other more flexible organisations. This time the union concerned was the National Amalgamated Union of Labour. In May 1912 cases were arising where cement manufacturers were replacing Stevedores' Union men by members of N.A.U.L., and once again the society was forced to protest to the N.T.W.F. about the overlapping of other unions.[46]

In its three areas of expansion the Stevedores' Society thus found itself at a disadvantage because of the high standards that it embodied. Employers in all these sectors were reluctant to accept these standards, and turned inevitably towards unions whose conditions were more amenable. It is a significant fact that in May 1912 the Stevedores' Union lodged complaints to the federation, about the conduct of other unions, in each of these three centres. At the upstream wharves the L.P.L. and the U.O.G.L. were involved, at the downstream docks the Dockers' Union, finally in the cement and paper area the N.A.U.L. was the organisation concerned. In all the centres into which the society had expanded there was tremendous friction, both with employers and with younger organisations. In May 1912 this friction was developing into open conflict in every sector of the union except its original core; only within the confines of the L.M.S.A. were industrial relations still conducted in an atmosphere of stability and harmony.

2

The one other old established major union in the port, besides the Stevedores' Society, was the Lightermen's Union. The Lightermen, like the Stevedores, were at the centre of trouble on the London waterfront. In one sense the tensions in the lighterage and stevedoring trades may be said to have sprung from a similar source. The Lightermen, like the Stevedores, had recently expanded into new areas of employment, and they encountered there the same reluctance of employers to submit to union regulations. There were in particular two sectors of employment where these tensions were clearly manifest. The first was in the sailing-barge trade. The Lightermen's Union had first opened its ranks to sailing bargemen in 1910,[47] and during the 1911 strike these new recruits struck along with the rest. At the termination of the struggle the bargeowners signed an agreement with the union, and under the terms of the settlement it was arranged that a schedule of rates for sailing-barge work should be drawn up at the Board of Trade. This task was finally completed at the end of 1911, but according to the terms of the original agreement the new rates were to operate retrospectively—that is, as from 21 August 1911. In fact the new rates scarcely came into operation at all. In May 1912 none of the firms of bargeowners had paid any of the back money due to the men, and a large number had not even bothered to pay the new rates as from 1 January. Employers had simply gone on as before, and had refused to acknowledge the authority of the agreement or of the society. Repeated applications were made both by the union and by the Board of Trade for the money due, but without effect.[48] In Gosling's words:

> They [Board of Trade] have not been able, and we have not been able, and you cannot get it unless you strike.[49]

This, as may be imagined, was a powerful source of grievance.

The second new sector of organisation where there was difficulty concerned work on the tugs.[50] Unlike the sailing-barge workers, the tugmen were employed by members of the Association of Master Lightermen. Organisation had, however, always been weak on the tugs,[51] and in 1911 there was still no collective agreement covering the men in this branch of work. At the end of the 1911 strike the men had returned to work without a settlement, but on their return they made application to the masters for a rise in wages. This application was generally granted by the employers, but on an individual rather than a collective basis. Thus the terms of the wage advance varied from firm to firm, and there was still no uniform rate for deck hands on tugs. This situation was obviously extremely unsatisfactory to the Lightermen's Union, and on 28 March 1912 it invited the Masters' Association to attend a conference for the purpose of arranging conditions of employment for these men. From the point of view of the Lightermen's Union this seemed to be a reasonable request, but the employers viewed things from a different angle. For them it appeared as the last of a long series of impositions, and, irrespective of the merits of the case, they were determined on principle to concede no more. They thus flatly refused to reopen the question of the deck hands. The union retaliated by submitting terms to the employers, and giving notice that the tug hands would terminate their employment on 26 April. In face of this threat the masters carried the matter a stage further, and threatened to lock out the whole of the lighterage trade if the deck hands ceased work. At this stage, as was now common practice, the Government intervened to keep the peace, and the notices of the men were postponed. The issue was still unresolved when the Thomas incident fired the fuse,[52] and so the lightermen came out on the issue of union monopoly instead of on the condition of the tugmen.

The issues of the sailing-barge workers and the tugmen profoundly disturbed the lighterage trade between August 1911 and May 1912. Both arose from the attempt of the union to extend its influence into new sectors, and from the refusal of employers to tolerate this extension. The really crucial issue in the lighterage trade, however, did not centre upon the newly expanded sectors of organisation. It concerned in fact the society as a whole, the old core as much as the new extensions. It is in this respect that the Lightermen's case differs markedly from that of the Stevedores. The crucial issue in the lighterage trade was the question of union monopoly. Union monopoly was fundamental to the policy of all waterside organisations. In August 1911 it had kept London port workers out on strike after most other grievances had been settled. As a result of the 1911 strike, the two other major unions besides the Lightermen had been able to go a long way towards achieving their objectives in this field. The Stevedores had long enjoyed a union preference at the hands of the L.M.S.A., and they had apparently been successful in August 1911 in enforcing this condition upon recalcitrant shipping companies. The Dockers' Union had also made big strides in this period. The Home Office agreement of 18 August guaranteed that shipowners would take on the men outside the dock gates. The Lightermen alone had made no progress. For them a monopoly depended upon unionist foremen, and this condition had been denied them by the Home Office agreement of 19 August.[53] To a proud craft organisation like the Lightermen's Union the position was intolerable. It was determined that the Masters' Association should accord it the same privileges as were accorded to the Stevedores' Society by the L.M.S.A. Until this was achieved there would be no peace. The irony of the situation was that the master lightermen had come to feel that any increased union power was entirely incompatible with the smooth functioning of the trade. Their distrust of the society was absolute.

After the stoppage of 1911 the lightermen had finally returned to work on 21 August. The trade remained, however, in a state of permanent crisis, and on at least three occasions between August 1911 and May 1912 the Masters' Association felt it necessary to notify their customers that a general stoppage was anticipated.[54] The question of the employment of non-unionists was a constant issue, and by December 1911 disputes upon this point were assuming critical proportions. In that month the Masters' Association invited John Burns (the signatory of the 19 August agreement for the Government) to intervene in the matter.[55] Nothing came of this initiative, however, but the non-unionist issue tended for a while to become a little less pressing. It revived at the very end of April 1912. The union delegates took up the case of an ex-foreman, named Thomas, employed since 1910 as a watchman by the Mercantile Lighterage Company.[56] Thomas was a founder member of the Foremen Lightermen's Union, a body not affiliated to the N.T.W.F. In view of the fact that he was now working as a watchman he should, in the eyes of the Lightermen, have taken a federation ticket. Thomas, however, was a foreman through and through and he refused on principle to take a N.T.W.F. card. In consequence, a union delegate, acting on his own initiative, asked Thomas's workmates to cease work, which they did. On 7 May the delegate approached the manager of the firm on the matter, but the latter insisted that any complaints should come formally through the Masters' Association. The Lightermen's Union, however, knew that it could expect little from formal procedures, and on 16 May it called all the men in the company out on strike. From then on events moved swiftly. The orders of the Mercantile Lighterage Company were handed over to other lighterage concerns, but the men in these firms naturally refused to do the work of the firm in dispute. They were thereupon discharged by their employers. The Lightermen's Society had already been threatened with a lock-out the previous month,[57] so in face of this renewed crisis it had little compunction about taking drastic action. On 19

May, therefore, the union called a strike of all its members. Within a few days the stoppage was general throughout the port of London and on the Medway.

The stoppage in the lighterage industry took place because neither side had anything left to say to the other. This is clear from the action of the Lightermen's Union, which made no use whatever of the formal negotiating machinery that existed in the trade. It is clear also from the action of the employers. On 17 May, before the general lightermen's strike was declared, Askwith had once again offered his services as a conciliator. In a long letter of reply the employers rejected his offer, giving at length their reasons for this decision.[58] They submitted that the Lightermen's Union was utterly faithless, and that it was useless to negotiate an agreement 'which would be wantonly set aside by the men as soon as it presented the least inconvenience to them'. 'As soon as one agreement is signed,' the employers claimed, 'fresh points are raised, and we have endless trouble.' They were determined, they said, to attend no more conferences. In this atmosphere of total alienation force was the only way out.

3

A general stoppage in the lighterage trade by no means meant that a port-wide strike would inevitably follow. The lightermen had struck before, without precipitating a general strike in the port. What was it, then, that in 1912 brought all other port workers out in their support? In the first place it should be said that the 1912 stoppage was not a spontaneous affair, like that of 1911, or even that of 1889. The 1912 strike occurred because the N.T.W.F. decided to make the dispute general, and because it commanded sufficient support among the rank and file to be able to translate its decision into effective action. The role of the N.T.W.F. in the 1912 dispute was thus crucial, and it is necessary first to briefly assess its position in London before turning to examine the reasons for its drastic action.

In the years before the First World War the N.T.W.F. was a reality in the metropolis in a way that it never was in the provinces. It had been formed at a time when effective unionism in the port of London was virtually confined to the relatively small organisations of stevedores and lightermen.[59] Outside of this limited sphere there was a vacuum, and it was the N.T.W.F. that stepped in to fill this vacuum in 1911. The immense growth of organisation in that year came simultaneously with the development of the federation itself, and the new recruits to unionism looked naturally to the N.T.W.F. as much as to their individual unions. The 1911 strike increased this tendency. While the Stevedores and Lightermen negotiated their own agreements, it was the federation who represented the vast bulk of hitherto unorganised port workers. In August it had signed agreements on behalf of dockers, coalies, short-sea men, and carmen. The federation itself then, rather than the constituent societies, had come to fill the void of disorganisation in London. After the 1911 strike, the authority of the N.T.W.F. remained, because there was no single union strong enough to replace it. In Liverpool the National Dockers were dominant, in Glasgow the Scottish Union of Dock Labourers, but in London no union had a controlling influence and federation was thus a necessity. A weak link in the federation's authority might have been caused by the two established unions, which were still jealous for their autonomy. In fact both unions were so deeply involved in trouble that the federal tie was vital to them. Thus in May 1912 the N.T.W.F. exercised considerable influence in the port. Without this unifying influence the lightermen's strike could not have been transformed so rapidly into a port-wide stoppage. A testimony to the federation's role is afforded by the actual manner in which the general strike was declared.[60] The Lightermen had ceased work on 19 May. On 21 May, after a meeting of the London District Committee of the N.T.W.F.,[61] the Dockers' and Stevedores' unions both passed resolutions pledging themselves not to perform any work which would normally be done by unionist lightermen. The executive of the N.T.W.F. was then called to London and, after conferring with the district committee, decided on 23 May to call a general strike in the port. It was in response to the federation's call, and not to any resolution of their own unions, that stevedores and dockers left their employment on the following day. The strike was effective within a day or two among waterside workers on the Thames and Medway, although the response of the Carmen was disappointing.[62]

The N.T.W.F. took an enormous risk on 23 May in calling for general strike action. What induced it to go to this length in supporting the lightermen? To the writer it seems that there was a kind of hopeless fatalism about the action of the federation leaders on 23 May. They genuinely expected a counter-attack by the employers sooner or later, and felt that eventually there would have to be another struggle. This at any rate is the overwhelming impression conveyed by Gosling's evidence to the Clarke Enquiry,[63] on 24 May, only a day after the decision had been taken. Gosling's charges against the employers make almost incredible reading today, yet the federation's President was normally a mild man and possessed of great integrity. His extravagant words at the enquiry obviously reflect the highly emotive atmosphere in which the decision to strike had been taken.[64] The Thomas case, small in itself, was well calculated to arouse among union leaders the feeling that the federation's existence was at stake. It concerned the crucial issue of the union monopoly, around which nearly all the great battles of the waterfront had been fought.[65] At the Clarke Enquiry Gosling declared quite frankly that the master lightermen were using Thomas as a tool. He was, Gosling declared, the thin end of the non-unionist wedge.

> He seems to me to be like a modern Canute who is being used by the Masters' Association to try to drive the tide of trade unionism back.[66]

Of course, these charges were entirely without foundation,[67] yet they were not so wild as might appear at first sight. There were plenty of precedents for ruthless counter-attack by employers. Had not the Shipping Federation, for instance, been formed in 1890 deliberately to break the power of the waterside unions? Had not the dock companies deliberately attacked the influence of the Dockers' Union, in 1890 also? In short, was not the federation entitled to believe that sooner or later the employers would seek to break its hold on the port? In 1890–1 the employers had broken down the power of the unions in piece-meal fashion. The N.T.W.F. existed to prevent that happening again. The union monopoly issue had always been a test case of a union's influence on the waterfront. Gosling claimed that the Home Office agreements of August 1911 had tacitly conceded the point to the men. The clause exempting foremen was, he suggested, a tacit recognition of the federation's right to insist upon the membership of all other workers.[68] Now the employers refused to recognise this monopoly, and he construed in this refusal a menace to the whole future of the N.T.W.F.

It seems certain that the N.T.W.F. leaders decided to fight the lightermen's case because they sincerely believed that the employers generally would force a showdown sooner or later. They lived in expectancy of a future conflict. This fatalistic attitude must be seen in the context of the general unrest throughout the port. In a number of spheres beside that of the lightermen grievances were coming to a head in May 1912. Perhaps any one of these could have begun the avalanche. The Stevedores' Union was on the verge of a complete breach with the S.S.T.A. in May. Its relationship with the big shipping companies and with Scruttons was also nearing breaking-point in this month. Similarly there were signs that its relations with the Cement Combine were in a process of rapid deterioration. Outside the Stevedores' ambit there were other grievances on the boil. In late March there had been trouble in the cartage trade through a breach of agreement by a master carman, and this had had repercussions in the docks.[69] Other specific points of tension included the claims the U.O.G.L. entertained against certain wharfingers, and a good deal of bad blood between the Dockers' Union and the P.L.A.[70] In most sectors of the port the unions felt frustrated in their aspirations, and they were ready to believe that in fighting the lightermen's case they were fighting their own. In their minds also was the glorious memory of the summer of 1911. The recollection of that easy victory encouraged them to press home their advantage, now, while trade conditions were still in their favour.

The decision to call a general strike in London was almost certainly influenced by another factor. The federation took the risk such action entailed because it was confident of victory. The reasons for this confidence did not derive solely from recent experience in the port industry. On 6 April 1912, less than two months before the London strike commenced, there had ended the most impressive demonstration of labour's power ever witnessed in Britain until that time. The 1912 Miners' Strike had been the first really national stoppage in the country's history. Its effects had been so drastic that the Government had rushed an Act through Parliament giving to the miners the substance of their claims. It would be strange if these events had not left a profound impression upon the leaders of a National Federation of Transport Workers. If necessity arose, could not they too clinch victory by national action? The idea was certainly attractive.

One of the biggest problems in a strike at a single port was that employers diverted vessels to other trouble-free centres. The 1911 stoppage had already illustrated the value of inter-port co-operation in resisting this manœuvre. Then the Southampton men had blocked ships diverted from London.[71] In a national strike all diversions would be impossible. Such a strike offered another advantage also. The biggest weapon employers had against the men in the port industry was the power to import strike-breaking labour. As long as disputes remained limited in scale, employers were able to get together sufficient 'free' labour to carry on a large amount of work. This was true even in times of good trade, as the 1900 London dockers' strike had shown.[72] If, however, there were a national stoppage the case might be different. In an article in the *Dockers' Record*, in August 1911, Tillett had attributed the success of the 1911 movement to the fact that there had been simultaneous stoppages in numerous ports. This fact, he suggested, had para-lysed the strike-breaking activities of the Shipping Federation. Tillett therefore drew the conclusion that the salvation of the docker lay in action on a national scale, and that the N.T.W.F. should be cherished as the instrument capable of achieving this national action.[73] It is quite clear that the N.T.W.F. contem-plated the possibility of a national strike from the very inception of the 1912 London dispute. On 24 May Gosling hinted at the Clarke Enquiry that such action was under consideration,[74] and the same day the Stevedores' Society passed a resolution in favour of a national strike.[75] It was obvious that the idea had been widely canvassed. The federation leaders thus commenced the London dispute with the idea that, in the last resort, they could clinch victory by calling a national strike.

The Government intervened at the very commencement of the 1912 strike, and straight away appointed Sir Edward Clarke to hold an enquiry into the origins of the dispute. The Clarke Enquiry was the first of a series of Government initiatives aimed at bringing the stoppage to a close. The men were responsive to the various proposals for a settlement put forward by the Government, but the employers were not responsive. The details of these proposals need not concern us, for they were all abortive, and in any case Lord Askwith has already adequately covered these negotiations in his book on this period.[76] The essential fact behind all these manœuvres was the steadfast refusal of the employers to accept anything less than the unconditional surrender of the N.T.W.F.

This attitude found its most powerful exponent in Lord Devonport, the Chairman of the P.L.A., and port employers generally tended to rest their case in his uncompromising hands. Against the determined resistance of the employers Government conciliators made no progress, and in the end they had no choice but to withdraw from the arena.

In this situation of deadlock it was obvious that the N.T.W.F. would play what it believed to be its trump card—a national strike. Thus, on 10 June 1912, the federation called upon the provinces to come to the assistance of the metropolis. The attempt at national action was, however, a complete fiasco. Only the provincial districts of the Dockers' Union responded to the strike call, and these received no support from organisations based in the provinces. Action in the provinces thus petered out within a few days of 10 June. After this disaster the London men were left to face certain defeat. The unpalatable truth was that the influence of the N.T.W.F. outside London was negligible. Inside the metropolis, however, the struggle went on, even though there could now be no hope of victory. The intransigence of the employers produced in its turn a determination on the part of the men to fight to the bitter end. By the end of June 13,000 'free' labourers had been drafted to the London waterfront, yet still the men clung on. The first serious signs of weakness occurred on the Medway, and on 18 July the men at Rochester began to resume work.[77] This collapse of resistance on the Medway inevitably had its effect on morale in London, but it did not yet break the strike.[78] It was the federation leadership who finally decided that the stoppage had to be ended. There were no funds left and further resistance only meant meaningless suffering. Thus on Saturday, 27 July they declared the strike closed and ordered a resumption for the following Monday.[79] Some men, however, were still not prepared for submission, and voted on the Sunday to stay out. Nevertheless Monday, 29 July saw considerable numbers of men applying for work at the calling-on stands. There was, however, no provision for the reinstatement of the strikers, and as a result serious disturbances took place between unionists and blacklegs.[80] In view of these riots it was well into August before a general resumption took place. It was a fittingly bitter end to one of the bitterest disputes in the history of English industrial relations. 1912 is remembered still on the London waterfront.

S.D.—7*

In May 1912 the N.T.W.F. had called a general strike, in the rather vague belief that its future was insecure unless it could extract from employers a recognition of union monopoly. In taking this decision it had greatly overestimated its industrial power. What would be the future of unionism now that this decision had resulted in unmitigated defeat? The defeat meant first of all a tremendous numerical decline in the London organisations. In the disillusionment and bitterness that followed the strike very many men abandoned their unionism.[81] The process must have been accelerated by discrimination against unionists at the call-on. The falling-off of membership was particularly marked in the Dockers' Union, a fact not surprising when the mushroom growth of July and August 1911 is recalled. The income of the union's London district was £6707 in the first half of 1912; in the second half it was only £2848. By the second half of 1913, despite the continued prosperity of trade, it had sunk to just over £2000. The war halted the decline, but even in 1916 the union's strength was very much below the level of early 1912.[82] In other unions decline was also marked. The Stevedores' membership fell from 8000 at the peak period to 5000 in 1914.[83] The 1912 defeat, however, had wider ramifications than merely numerical decline. It forced the London organisations back on the defensive, and in so doing inaugurated a new and anxious phase in their history.

4

The major issue at stake in the 1912 struggle had been union monopoly. It was clear therefore that the defeat of the men would result in a determined effort by employers to eradicate all vestiges of that monopoly. Thus when the men returned to work they were informed that they would be taken on inside the dock and wharf gates.[84] The Home Office agreement of 18 August 1911 was thus repudiated. This action obviously adversely affected the position of most unions, but it was liable to bear particularly hard upon an organisation of fixed standards and conditions. The only union so situated in London was the Stevedores' Society. Unlike other unions in the port, the Stevedores' Union had to face peculiarly intractable problems in adjusting itself to the post strike reaction. It had been the same in 1891:[85] now, however, the consequences of this adjustment were to prove more far reaching, and they form the principal theme running through union history in the final period before the outbreak of war.

The essential problem facing the Stevedores' Society was the fact that one section of employers recognised its rules, while the others did not. The L.M.S.A. had been prepared for a resumption of work on the normal conditions in June,[86] and when the return to work finally came at the end of July the majority of master stevedores reinstated society men and continued to recognise society rules. Outside of the ambit of the L.M.S.A., however, the employers refused to recognise the union and insisted upon taking on the men inside the gates. These employers fell into two categories. On the one hand there were the employers in the short-sea trades, and on the other there were the large oversea concerns at the Albert and Tilbury docks. Both groups had this in common. They had had the Stevedores' Society thrust upon them in the great movement of 1911, and had never really accepted its influence. Now that the men were defeated they were determined to rid themselves of the union for good. Unlike the Dockers' Union, the Stevedores could not just accept the flouting of its rules by a section of employers. There were vital reasons why, as we have seen, the society needed a uniform standard for all its members. In August 1912, therefore, it had to face an especially trying situation. At the time of the resumption of work the union sent deputations to all the firms which refused to take on the men outside the dock.[87] The deputations were ignored. The society then turned to the London Chamber of Commerce, which had arbitrated successfully so many of its disputes. This body agreed to communicate with Lord Devonport, in the hope that the latter would convene a conference of employers and men.[88] As might have been expected, however, Lord Devonport refused to do any such thing. There was thus no way out. Employers were determined to keep the union at arm's length.

The problems created by this situation were not quite the same in the two principal sectors involved, and it will be as well to consider the situation in the short-sea trades first of all. In the period between the two great strikes this had been the most unstable sector of the Stevedores' Union, because the society had been unable to achieve parity between the conditions of the S.S.T.A. and those of the L.M.S.A. In May 1912 in fact the situation had become so bad that a strike in this sector seemed possible at any moment.[89] When the men eventually came out in support of the lightermen, the original issue was not allowed to drop, for the men proclaimed their intention of enforcing the Stevedores' rates and conditions upon the short-sea traders.[90] The employers in this sector did not forget this fact, and in August 1912 they were ready for their revenge. The men returning to work were taken on inside the wharf, and were in certain cases forced to accept lower rates and worse conditions than those prevailing in May.[91] Thus the society was even further from parity than before. These developments were quickly reflected inside the union, as the old tensions between the old and new sectors flared up once more. Short-sea men, unable to get work in their own sphere, came onto the stands of the master stevedores. A chorus of protest then went up from the old branches. Resolutions flowed into the executive demanding that short-sea men should have distinctive working cards. Finally, cases began to occur where society foremen in the old sectors refused to employ men from the new branches.[92] It was August 1911 all over again. This time, however, there was no hope that the situation could be remedied by the achievement of parity. The Stevedores' Union, in response to pressure from the short-sea men, contacted the S.S.T.A. but the latter refused to recognise the society as representative of the men.[93] Strike action was obviously out of the question, and so the position was hopeless. Thoroughly disillusioned, the men began to drift out of organisation, until finally the principal branch of short-sea men, No. 11, was closed down on 15 July 1913.[94]

It was the end of a stormy chapter that had begun in July 1911. Events had shown that expansion without uniformity was impossible for the Stevedores' organisation. The union had struggled hard to achieve that uniformity, but the catastrophe of 1912 set the stamp of irrevocable failure upon its efforts. By the summer of 1913 it had ceased to take any interest in this sphere of the port. Meanwhile the conditions in the short-sea trades continued to remain hopelessly unsatisfactory, due to the wide range of rates and conditions prevailing in this sector. The U.O.G.L. took the matter up with the N.T.W.F. District Committee in 1913, and the latter made some effort to formulate a schedule of rates for the trade.[95] The Stevedores' Society was asked for its opinion on the matter but it declined to be drawn.[96] Its intervention in this sphere in 1911 had brought nothing but trouble, and it was determined not to become involved again.

The Stevedores' Union had resolved its difficulties at the wharves by tacitly abandoning organisation in this sphere. The problems at the downstream docks were, however, more intractable and dogged the history of the union down to the outbreak of war. They involved, furthermore, not merely the Stevedores but the Dockers also, and profoundly affected the future relationship of these two organisations. The docks were the traditional area of the Stevedores' Society's influence, and loading operations its historic monopoly. This monopoly had long been called in question by the more powerful employers, but in August 1911, as in 1889, it had been enforced throughout the entire field of export shipwork. The big shipping-lines and Scruttons chafed at this monopoly and the 1912 strike gave them the chance to end it. On 29 July 1912 the P. and O., British India and New Zealand lines, together with Scruttons Limited at Tilbury, all insisted that stevedores, like dockers, must be taken on inside the gates.[97] The Dockers' Union could adjust to this, as it had done in the 1890s, because it was flexible. The Stevedores' Union could not easily adjust, because the maintenance of L.M.S.A. standards was fundamental to its existence. The society expected its members to uphold these standards by refusing to go inside the docks to be taken on. On 6 August it decided that members chiefly affected by this situation should be supported by those men who were able to obtain work in accordance with the society's rules. Collecting-boxes were issued to branches 9 (Tilbury) and 14 (Albert) in order that a relief fund could be started.[98] The policy of rigid adherence to rule depended much on co-operation from the Dockers' Union. If the dockers allowed themselves to be taken on inside the gates the shipowners might put them not only to discharging work, but to loading also. In this way the Stevedores' position in the big companies would be undermined for good. Thus on 3 August the society's executive wrote to the Dockers' Union asking them to send delegates to prevent their members working at the P. and O., New Zealand, and British India lines.[99] This action did not, however, succeed, and by 11 August the society was protesting to the district committee that other organisations were permitting their members to go inside the docks to be taken on, and that as a result they were supplanting stevedores in loading operations. The union officials concerned admitted this to be the case, but stated that they were powerless to prevent the men's action.[100] In the

next few days the society desperately pressed home its complaint
to the Dockers' Union, and on 27 August actually used its own
delegates at Tilbury to prevent dockers going inside to be taken on
to work for Scruttons.[101] It was all, however, to no avail. The
discipline in the Dockers' Union was not equal to that of the
Stevedores, and in any case the former union had no high standard
to uphold.

The sight of Dockers' Union members gradually manning up
the work was bound before long to affect morale in the society
itself. Branch 14 at the Albert Dock held a ballot on the issue of
whether to remain out or not. The men decided that they would
continue to refuse the shipowners' conditions.[102] Discipline at
Tilbury, however, was not so strong, and the men decided that
they would go inside to work for Scruttons, P. and O., Orient, and
other lines. The executive sent delegates down to Tilbury to prevent the men going in, but the members repeatedly ignored the
instructions of the delegates and were determined to continue
work.[103] The union was now faced with a difficult problem. The
men at Tilbury had flouted the union regulation and were now
working for firms that did not recognise the society. Normally
this was an offence punishable by expulsion. Thus on 5 September
1912 the executive resolved that in future branch secretaries
should issue cards only to those members who abided by the rules
of the society.[104] The decision had been taken to enforce the strict
letter of the rules. Inevitably, in the conditions of the time, this
decision caused tremendous disaffection. Protests poured in from
members who had been refused tickets in accordance with the
resolution. Finally, a special deputation from Tilbury waited on
the executive on 17 September. They asked that, due to the
special circumstances at that dock, the rule should be relaxed.
Justifiably the deputation pointed out that unless they went inside
to be called on they would have no employment at all. The P. and
O. and Orient lines were already being worked by non-members;
if they stayed out now they would lose the remainder of the work
as well. Inevitably the union would be broken at Tilbury unless
they accepted the employers' conditions.[105] Faced with this position, the executive was in a complete quandary as to what to do.
Anderson was away sick most of the time, and there was no other
official capable of giving a powerful lead. The instinct of the
executive was to stick to a rigid enforcement of the rules, yet in the

case of Tilbury such a policy was clearly suicidal. Unable to give a decisive lead themselves, the leadership passed the question back to the branches, but still no clear-cut policy emerged. There were, however, many members at Tilbury whose patience with the society had reached its limit. Thus in December 1912 the bulk of the Tilbury branch broke away and formed a society of their own— the London Stevedores' Society.[106] As in 1887, the inflexibility of the Stevedores' Union had thus resulted in the formation of a rival union at the downstream docks.[107]

The price of this inflexibility was not yet fully paid in 1912, and 1913 and 1914 were to bring further setbacks. In June 1913 Scruttons took over the work of the Blue Anchor Line, and again the insistence was made that the men should come into the dock. Once again the society enforced strict adherence to rules and with-held tickets from members who worked under these conditions. By October 1913 the Blue Anchor Line was being worked by members of the Dockers' Union.[108] In 1914 the society continued to lose ground, for in May the owners of the White Star Line insisted upon the all too familiar conditions of engagement.[109] Thus the work of this company, too, was lost. The Stevedores' resistance to the employers' subversion of the society preference became the major issue in the port in the period before the out-break of war. Anderson had appealed to the N.T.W.F. Conference in 1913 for support for his union in resisting these attacks.[110] The matter was, however, referred back to the London District Com-mittee. The committee grappled with the problem, which not only threatened the position of the Stevedores, but threatened also to permanently embitter inter-union relations in the port. Other unions were deeply implicated in the matter, for it was their members who often took the place of the evicted stevedores. In view of the fact that most of its constituents were flexible organisa-tions, the district committee found itself reluctant to support the Stevedores' rigid adherence to rule. It clearly felt that the society was ill-advised to expel members working under illegal conditions, and thought that this policy inevitably weakened the fibre of organisation in the port and, incidentally, placed other less rigid unions in an embarrassing position.[111] In October 1913 the committee thus came up with a compromise. It suggested that first the society should restore to membership all those who had been expelled, and that when this was done the N.T.W.F. would give its full support towards resisting any further encroachments by the employers. From the Stevedores' point of view the scheme overlooked one basic fact. A number of the expelled members were now enrolled in the breakaway L.S.S. The union thus decided that the matter rested in the hands of the latter organisation, and that it would await an application for amalgamation from the breakaway union.[112] No such application came and the matter dropped. At the time of the White Star affair the Stevedores made further applications to the N.T.W.F. for assistance,[113] but in truth it was difficult to see what the federation could perform. Employers were adamant, and another total stoppage was out of the question. The battle for union monopoly had been taken up on the lightermen's behalf in 1912. The N.T.W.F. had in 1914 neither the inclination nor the power to fight the same battle for the stevedores.

5

The aftermath of the 1912 strike profoundly harmed organisation in London. It did this not merely in numerical terms. The lost membership could be recovered when times were more favourable, and indeed by the end of the war the level of organisation was back to what it had been in January 1912.[114] The solidarity that characterised the unions in the 1911–12 period was, however, never recovered. The reaction unleashed by the employers in August 1912 drove a permanent wedge in between the Stevedores' Union and the other port unions. The attack on the society's preference forced it back into ever narrower confines, while other less demanding organisations filled much of the territory it had vacated. Except for two Medway branches, at Rochester and Queenborough, all the Stevedores' gains of 1911 vanished. The deal porters, the short-sea men, the employees of the biggest shipping firms, were all lost to the society. Only the original core of master stevedores' employees really remained. The extended boundaries of 1911 were gone, and with them also went the wide horizons and large aspirations of the first decade of the century. Forced back in upon themselves, the stevedores became defensive in outlook, withdrawn, and alienated in some senses from other port organisations. This defensiveness had become clearly apparent by 1914. By this date the books of the society were closed once more, and financial difficulties were raising doubts about affiliation to the Labour

Party and even the N.T.W.F. As yet this movement had not gone far, but it was menacing nonetheless. The future of the London unions would be permanently damaged unless the Stevedores were integrated with other groups of port workers, yet the chances of this integration seemed to be receding into the distance. This was the real significance of the aftermath of 1912.

The most obvious manifestation of this unwelcome development was the attitude of the Stevedores' Society towards amalgamation. When the N.T.W.F. had been founded in 1910 it had been generally hoped that federation could eventually be transformed into amalgamation.[115] The events of 1911 and 1912 postponed any serious discussion of this project, for indeed there was scarcely time to get the federation properly organised.[116] The defeat of 1912 and the disastrous failure of the national strike brought the issue of amalgamation back into the forefront, and by the autumn of that year the federation had set up an Amalgamation Committee.[117] Tillett and the Dockers' Union were earnest advocates of the project,[118] but the Stevedores' Society at first ignored it completely. The majority of transport unions in London and in the provinces were, however, determined for a closer grouping, and when the N.T.W.F. Conference met at Newport in June 1913 this was the principal topic of discussion.

In all industries there are of course certain standard difficulties in the way of achieving an amalgamation of unions. Difficulties such as trade autonomy, for instance. In any industry involving port workers a further problem arose—namely, the problem of the protected labour market. Organisations of casual dock workers felt it necessary to protect the employment of their members from an influx of outsiders. Hence their insistence on the union monopoly. Hence also their refusal to recognise the tickets of other organisations. The N.T.W.F. contained among its constituents both waterside and non-waterside unions, and the two types were at constant loggerheads over the issue of the protected labour market. Non-waterside unions, such as the Gasworkers and Carmen, insisted that their members had a right to work anywhere so long as they had a federation ticket. The waterside unions, on the other hand (where they controlled hiring procedures), insisted that their preserves of employment must be inviolate, and that all of their members must be in employment before men of other organisations could be taken on. It was clear that if it had been difficult to combine the two types of organisation together in a federation, it was going to be even harder to reconcile their conflicting viewpoints in a scheme for amalgamation.

The leadership of the N.T.W.F. was well aware of the difficulties involved when it moved a resolution in favour of amalgamation at the Newport Conference.[119] The principal subject of contention at the Conference was whether the entire memberships of all the unions affiliated to the N.T.W.F. were to be amalgamated, or whether only the sections of port workers were to be joined together. The two purely waterside organisations that operated hiring controls were the National Dockers and the Stevedores. Both were strongly opposed to any amalgamation that went beyond the boundaries of waterside work. As the Stevedores' delegate put it: 'The river organisations do not want to be swamped by outside men.' The Seamen supported these two unions, and the general feeling was that amalgamation should embrace port workers alone. This scheme sounded very well in theory, but it was in fact totally unacceptable. Predominantly waterside organisations, like the Dockers' Union, contained also a substantial membership of men in outside industry. If a purely dockers' amalgamation was to take place it would break these composite unions in two. Furthermore, Ernest Bevin, speaking from his Bristol experience, assured the Stevedores and National Dockers that a composite amalgamation would not necessarily mean the flooding of the docks with outside labour.

> In the port of Bristol theirs [Dockers' Union] was the only union, they had all kinds of men in all classes of work, yet there was no trouble about lines of demarcation, and transfers were worked quite smoothly through a departmental system with different officers for each section. If it could be done locally it could be done nationally.

Despite this reassurance, opinion was still divided until Harry Gosling reminded the conference that they were asked only to vote upon the principle of amalgamation, not upon the exact way in which it was to be achieved. The vast majority of the delegates were certainly in favour of the principle, and so the resolution was carried.

The N.T.W.F. leadership regarded the Newport vote as a

mandate to press on with the amalgamation project.[120] Several unions in the federation were affiliated also to the General Labourers' National Council (G.L.N.C.),[121] and the executive of this body was also considering proposals for fusion. Thus in the latter part of 1913 the two organisations decided to combine their efforts, and a joint sub-committee was formed to draft a definite scheme. On 25 March 1914 the sub-committee was able to report back to a conference of the two executives, and the conference duly accepted its proposals.[122] These proposals envisaged a general labour amalgamation. That is to say, the entire memberships of the unions affiliated to the N.T.W.F. and the G.L.N.C. were to be joined together, whether they were port workers or not. Gosling, the President of the N.T.W.F., had not originally been keen on this idea. He was, after all, the Secretary of the Lightermen's Society, a purely waterside union with traditions similar to the Stevedores. He became convinced, however, that a purely waterside amalgamation was a practical impossibility, and that it would still be possible to safeguard the interests of waterside workers inside a general labour grouping.[123] The amalgamation proposals certainly paid special attention to these interests.[124] Two clauses in particular were designed to allay the fears of waterside men. One provided for the creation of semi-autonomous district and departmental sections within the union. The second clause provided:

> That means be devised to prevent the unnecessary migration of men from place to place and thereby pressing upon the available amount of employment at certain places at any given time.

The joint conference of the N.T.W.F. and G.L.N.C. executives having accepted these proposals, it had now to decide on the next step to be taken. It was agreed that a fully representative conference of all interested societies should be called to consider the proposals, and the date fixed was 8 July 1914.

On 8 July the 'Special Conference on Amalgamation' duly met at the Caxton Hall, Westminster, to give its verdict on the draft scheme.[125] The Seamen's and Stewards' unions had already opted out of the project, objecting on principle to the idea of a general labour grouping. Apart from this defection the conference was fully representative of all general labour and transport organisations (exclusive of the railwaymen). The ten clauses were gone through one by one, and the meeting showed itself very much in favour of the scheme; twenty-six unions voted in favour of the principle of the scheme, these included the Lightermen, the National Dockers, the Dockers' Union, the U.O.G.L., the Labour Protection League, and the Scottish Dockers. Unfortunately there were exceptions to this generally favourable mood. Two unions voted against the proposals; they were both provincial carmen's unions. Two were undecided: the Cardiff Coal Trimmers, and the Stevedores.

The Stevedores' Society was the only major port workers' union that failed to ratify the amalgamation scheme. Perhaps the society's exceptional position is to be accounted for by the fact that it lacked the vigorous leadership of the other waterside unions. Anderson was in 1914 but a shadow of his former self. Without vigorous leadership, perhaps the other port unions might have hesitated to commit themselves to the scheme. Certainly there were features about the entrenched waterside organisation that made amalgamation immensely difficult, and after the war both the Glasgow and Liverpool dockers were to have second thoughts about the scheme. It is difficult, however, to escape the conclusion that these inherent difficulties were accentuated in London by special pressures, and that these special pressures finally deterred the Stevedores from amalgamation. The Stevedores' Society, as we have seen, had been under constant attack by employers since 1912. In the face of this attack it had stubbornly refused to modify its rules, and so its frontiers had been gradually pushed back until the old nucleus of the society had been reached. Within this limited sphere, however, its influence still remained intact. It was in fact the only area of union supremacy remaining in the port, and the trials of recent months had only strengthened the society's determination to defend this stronghold to the uttermost. This defensive mood clearly moulded the union's attitude towards the amalgamation. Had it resisted the encroachments of employers so stubbornly, only to see its influence eventually destroyed by a reckless fusion with other organisations who had nothing to lose by amalgamation, and everything to gain? On 8 July the society had proclaimed its doubts about amalgamation. On 14 July it submitted its terms to the N.T.W.F. The manner in which this was done was characteristic. A copy of the society's rules was forwarded to the Federation:

with the intimation that they were the minimum condition we should be prepared to accept and recommend to our members.[126]

There was to be no compromise, any more than there had been with the shipping companies. Amalgamation must leave the prerogatives of the society intact, or it would be rejected.

In the event, the Stevedores' Society did not have to make a final decision in 1914. The war broke out and the amalgamation scheme was shelved. In 1920–1, however, when Ernest Bevin took up the project once more, the same pattern of events repeated itself. All the waterside unions decided in favour of the amalgamation, except the Stevedores.[127] Thus the war had not altered the pattern of union development on the London waterfront. The crucial years had been 1911–12. In that period unionism in the port had really been in a state of flux. The catastrophe of 1912 finally settled matters and determined the future of London unionism. It was a disastrous arbitrator, for it decided against the best traditions of organisation, and thrust them back into an embittered isolation.

Conclusion

In looking back over four decades of trade union history it is perhaps natural to expect a process of evolution, of constructive development. Yet it is doubtful how far trade unionism in the port of London between 1870 and 1914 can be fitted into any meaningful pattern of growth. E. J. Hobsbawm in his study of waterside unionism sees the period as one of positive development, in which port workers generally moved in the direction of organisation on national, industrial lines.[1] He attributes this development to a number of factors, notably the process of concentration in industry and the increasing tendency of employers to act upon a national scale, as in the case of the Shipping Federation. Furthermore he stresses the role of the socialist leaders after 1889 in weaning the unions away from the local and sectional attachments that were so strong in the port industry. There is much to be said for approaching waterside unionism in the period from this standpoint. The changes in the structure of the Stevedores' and Lightermen's unions between 1900 and 1911, the formation of the N.T.W.F., the attempt at national action in 1912, all these developments fit into a pattern of waterside unionism seen as moving towards organisation on industrial lines. Yet the recent history of unionism on the waterfront suggests that there may be something lacking in such an approach, that it only reveals part of the story.

The formation of the Transport and General Workers' Union in 1922 was the final outcome of the movement away from local and sectional groupings. Although incorporating other groups of workers, it was at the outset primarily an industrial union of port and road transport workers. It made a reality of the aspirations towards effective national action on the waterfront, and this was demonstrated in the 1924 strike. Yet the T. and G.W.U. did not resolve the problems of waterside organisation. The failure to incorporate the Stevedores' Union in the 1922 amalgamation might have seemed relatively unimportant at the time; in the long

[1] E. J. Hobsbawm, 'National Unions on the Waterside' in *Labouring Men*, 1964.

term it was disastrous. Trouble began in 1923, only a year after
fusion, when numbers of London dockers seceded from the T. and
G.W.U. and joined the Stevedores. At this time the lightermen
also seceded from the big union, joining the Stevedores first of all
and later breaking away again to form their own union. The events
of 1923 permanently weakened the influence of the T. and
G.W.U. in Britain's major port, and since that time the edifice of
industrial unionism has crumbled at other points. The Glasgow
dockers broke away from the big union in the 1930s, and the
period since the Second World War has seen revolts against the
T. and G.W.U. in the three northern ports of Liverpool, Manchester and Hull. The trouble in the three northern ports was
especially serious, for it was associated with an attempt by the
Stevedores' Union to obtain a foothold outside London. 1923 was
thus re-enacted on a national scale and the conflict between the
Blue (Stevedores) and White (T. and G.W.U.) tickets made
general. How are we to interpret these continuing divisions within
waterside unionism? What light does our study of the period
1870–1914 in London throw upon these more recent problems?

Unity in the port industry has proved to be an elusive goal. The
amalgamation of 1922 might have seemed to be the framework
through which it could be achieved; events have shown otherwise.
It could be argued that, despite appearances to the contrary, the
essential bias in waterside unionism has continued to be sectional
and local, rather than industrial and national. That the trend
towards larger units of organisation was merely the product of the
weakness of unionism prior to 1914, and that where organisation
was firmly established industrial unionism was bound to break
down. Such an argument would point to the cases of the Lightermen and Stevedores as instances of continued sectionalism, and
to the Glasgow breakaway as showing the continued strength of
local feeling. An alternative explanation would be one which
accepts the trend towards industrial unionism as a positive development, and suggests that the failures since 1922 have been the
result of the shortcomings of the T. and G.W.U., regarded as an
industrial union. It would point to the great expansion of that
union in sectors outside the port industry, and suggest that the
discontent of port workers arose from their diminishing relative
importance within the organisation. Such an argument readily
explains the role of the Stevedores' Union as a focus for discontent

in the industry. The Stevedores' organisation, with its absence of elaborate bureaucratic machinery and its character as a purely waterside union, would obviously appeal to dockers who felt their interests going by default in an enormous institution they were no longer able to control. Of these two arguments the latter is probably much the more accurate, but both appear to omit certain vitally important considerations.

At the outset it was suggested that trade unionism on the London waterfront between 1870 and 1914 hardly conformed to any definite pattern of growth. If these four decades are examined it will be seen that for most of the period the influence of unionism in the port was absolutely minimal. Trade union power was largely confined to three limited spells of intense activity—the early 1870s, 1889–91, and 1911–12. The question arises as to how far these three spells are to be considered as forming part of one continuous development. The movement of 1872 was clearly quite distinct from that of 1889 or 1911, and the loose federal structure of the Labour Protection League was not subsequently revived as an instrument of mass organisation. 1889 saw the foundation of the Dockers' Union, the forerunner of the T. and G.W.U., and it is customary to trace the development of modern waterside unionism from this year. Yet by the beginning of the new century the Dockers' Union was moribund in London, and only subsidies from the provinces enabled it to maintain a presence in the metropolis. When the great revival of 1911 came, the Dockers' Union officials had to begin rebuilding the fabric of organisation almost from scratch. The branch and district structure of 1889 had entirely vanished and a new one had to be re-erected in its place. Furthermore the vastly inflated membership of 1911 consisted in the main of men with little, if any, experience of organisation. For all practical purposes it was 1889 all over again. We know now that the revival of 1911 was not in vain, and that mass organisation was never again to suffer setbacks comparable to those of the mid-1870s or early 1890s. For contemporaries, however, there was no guarantee of survival, and in fact at the close of our period trade union influence was in a process of rapid decline, a decline that was only to be halted by the First World War. In the final analysis, the years 1870–1914 appear less as a period of continuous development than as a time of continuing instability. The long-term consequences of this instability are difficult to measure, but they must have been considerable. Periods of mass organisation were of such short duration that the unions, and the Dockers' Union in particular, never had the chance to strike real roots among the general body of port workers. Communication between union officials and the rank and file was bound to be defective in such an unstable environment, and waterside unions were continuously plagued by problems of discipline and internal dissension. Furthermore the brief periods of union power always precipitated serious industrial conflicts, and these invariably left behind an aftermath of bitterness and disillusionment, as in 1912. It is in this perspective that the events of 1923 must be seen. The fund of loyalty, understanding and discipline upon which the T. and G.W.U. could draw in London was strictly limited, and for the source of this limitation we must look to waterside unionism's acutely unstable past.

The instability of organisation in London between 1870 and 1914 has been stressed, but it may be objected that this instability throws little light upon subsequent difficulties in provincial ports. This objection is easily answered, for the instability that characterised London unionism was present also in other ports, to a greater or lesser degree. Instability was in fact a reflection of the casual system, a system common to all ports, and because the casual system did not end in 1914, neither did the problems of waterfront organisation. The problems presented by the system did, however, vary in emphasis, both from port to port, and over a period of time. In the pre-1914 period, and in London especially, the central problem for the unions was the need to obtain an influence over hiring procedures. It was the intractable nature of this issue which retarded the development of a rational system of industrial relations on the waterfront. By 1920, however, a number of factors—changed employer attitudes, registration schemes, the War, union recognition—had combined to take the sting out of this problem. Henceforward waterside organisations could at least be sure of survival. As Tillett once commented, however, it is 'easier to conquer a city than to control it', and in more recent years the problems posed by the casual system for the unions have tended to be internal rather than external in character.

There was a time when casual employment was a common enough feature of industry in general, but in the present century its importance has greatly declined. Yet the port industry has remained strangely immune from change. The system has been greatly modified, but it remains intact, a well preserved relic of the nineteenth century.[1] The persistence of casual employment has meant the perpetuation of the attitudes and way of life that are inseparable from such a system. It has, furthermore, reinforced the isolation of the waterfront from the rest of industry. In many respects the characteristics of port workers have remained much as Booth described them; a highly volatile body of men, impatient of regulation, distrustful of any authority, fearful of change. Waterside society has retained its attachment to customary methods, its clannishness, and its insularity; a world narrow in horizons but rich in character. In such an atmosphere as this formal trade unionism has never found it easy to function, and the dilemma of the T. and G.W.U. need surprise no one. Spontaneous unofficial movements have always been congenial to the docker, and trade unions far less cumbrous and remote than the T. and G.W.U. have found it difficult to assert their authority. In this perspective the whole history of waterside organisation falls into place. The paradoxical situation of the pre-1914 period, with its massive strikes but weak and unstable unionism, and the problems of more recent years, with continuous organisation but vigorous and disruptive unofficial movements, form part of the same pattern. As a group port workers have developed a great capacity for spontaneous and militant industrial action, yet the extent to which trade unions have been able to harness, direct and control these forces has remained limited. The casual system lies at the root of the institutional weakness of waterside organisation.

[1] This was first written in 1965. Since then of course decasualisation has become a major issue. Any comments on very recent developments would, however, be inappropriate in this study.

Appendix

TRADE UNION STRUCTURE IN LONDON, 1889–91

In the period 1889 to 1891 the port was perhaps more thoroughly organised than at any other time before 1914. Detailed information has survived concerning the branch and district structure of the various unions at this time, and this is set out below:

Dockers' Union

London District No. 1   *List of Branches*

(Uptown Warehouses)

Branch	
Assembly Hall	
Black Bull	
Cutler Street	
Excelsior	
Monarch	Warehouse Workers;
Monument	mainly tea and wool
Oak	
Whitechapel	
Commercial Rd	
Fruit Porters	

London District No. 2   *List of Branches*

(London Docks and Wapping Wharves)

Branch	
Fish Porters	
Paddy's Goose	Dockers
St George's	Dockers
St Mary's	Dockers
Trafalgar No. 1	Dockers
Trafalgar No. 2	Dockers
Trafalgar No. 3	Dockers
Wapping No. 1	River Shipworkers
Wapping No. 2	Wharf Workers
Wapping No. 3	Wharf Workers
Wapping No. 4	Wharf Workers
London Dock	Dockers

London District No. 3   *List of Branches*
(Poplar and Millwall)

Blackwall	Oil Millers
Brewery No. 1	Brewery Workers
Britannia	Grain Workers
East India Dock	Dockers
Export	Export Dockers
Limehouse	Wharf Workers
Millwall	Grain Workers
Poplar	Dockers
South Dock	Dockers
West India Dock	Dockers
Wood Wharf	Dockers

London District No. 4   *List of Branches*
(South Side)

Carlile	River Shipworkers
Brewery No. 3	Brewery Workers
Deal Porters	
Dreadnought	Grain Trimmers
Charrington(?)	
Hope of Rotherhithe(?)	
Horsleydown(?)	
Hydraulic	Crane Drivers
Neptune(?)	
Prince Alfred	Grain and Timber Workers
Thorn	Wharf Workers
Tooley Street	Wharf Workers
Vine	Wharf Workers

London District No. 5   *List of Branches*
(Albert and Victoria docks)

Barking Rd	Dockers
Export	Export Dockers
Hack Rd	Dockers
North Woolwich	Dockers
Plaistow	Dockers
Railway and Engineers	
Stratford	Dockers
Swanscombe Street	Dockers
Tidal Basin	Dockers
Tobacco	Tobacco Storage Workers
Victoria Dock District	Dockers and Meat Storage Workers

London District No. 6   *List of Branches*
(Tilbury)

Gravesend	Dockers
Grays	Dockers
Tilbury Dock	Dockers
Tilbury	Dockers

Northfleet District   *List of Branches*

Coopers	Cement and Paper Industries
Northfleet	Cement and Paper Industries
Swanscombe	Cement and Paper Industries
Greenhithe	Cement and Paper Industries

Stevedores' Union

List of Branches

No. 1 Shadwell	No. 8 Rotherhithe
No. 2 Millwall	No. 9 Canning Town
Nos 3, 4 and 5 Poplar	No. 10 Tidal Basin
No. 6 Deptford	No. 11 Limehouse
No. 7 Wapping	No. 12 Custom House

No. 13 Tilbury

South Side Labour Protection League

List of Branches by Occupation

2 Branches of Shipworkers (at Wapping and Bermondsey)
4 Branches of Granary Corn Porters
1 Branch of Quay Corn Porters (Surrey Docks)
1 Branch of Overside Corn Porters (Surrey Docks)
1 Branch of Warehousemen (Surrey Docks)
6 Branches of General Wharf Labourers
1 Branch of Deal Porters
1 Branch of Arsenal Labourers (Woolwich)
1 Branch of Engineers' Helpers (Deptford)

Non-Freemen's Society

List of Branches

No. 1 Kingston	No. 5 City Rd
No. 2 Brentford	No. 6 Poplar
No. 3 Limehouse	No. 7 Canning Town
No. 4 Paddington	No. 8 Deptford

No. 9 Tilbury

Amalgamated Society of Engine Drivers and Firemen
(Land and Marine)

London Branches   Poplar
                               Battersea
                               Bermondsey

Amalgamated Protective Union of Engine Drivers,
Crane Drivers, Hydraulic and Boiler Attendants

London Branches   Woolwich
                               Lambeth
                               Canning Town

Other organisations: for which branch information not available:
   Amalgamated Society of Watermen and Lightermen
   Thames Steamship Workers' Association (3 branches)
   Ballast Heavers' Society
   Coal Porters Winchmen's Association (2 branches)

Bibliography

A. Manuscript Sources

In the writing of this book I have drawn heavily upon three vital manuscript collections: the Booth Collection and the Webb Trade Union Collection (both at the British Library of Political Science), and the records of the Stevedores' Union, at the headquarters of the National Amalgamated Stevedores' and Dockers' Union. The last-named collection consists mainly of Executive Council minute books, but also includes some branch records. I have also made use of the papers of John Burns at the British Museum.

B. Printed Records

Dock, Wharf, Riverside and General Workers' Union: Annual Reports, Minutes of Annual Delegate Meetings, and Rules.

International Federation of Ship, Dock and River Workers: Report of 1897 Conference.

National Amalgamated Sailors' and Firemen's Union: Annual Reports, Rules, Executive Minutes and Circulars.

National Transport Workers' Federation: Reports of Annual General Council Meetings, and 'Map of unions in British ports' (1913?)

National Transport Workers' Federation and General Labourers' National Council: Special Conference on Amalgamation, July 1914.

National Union of Dock Labourers: Reports of Executive and Rules.

C. Parliamentary Papers

There are three Royal Commissions which provide a mass of information on the port industry before 1914:

Royal Commission on Labour.
Royal Commission on the Port of London.
Royal Commission on the Poor Laws.

Other sources:

Select Committee upon the Improvement of the Port of London (1799).
Select Committee on the Port of London (1836).
Select Committee on the Sweating System (1888).
Joint Select Committee on the Port of London Bill of 1908.
Departmental Committee on the Checking of Piece-Work Wages in Dock Labour (1908)
Annual Report of Chief Inspector of Factories and Workshops for 1899, containing *Special Report* by Maitland and Eraut (1900).
Report on Dock Labour in Relation to Poor Law Relief (1908).

Report on the Relation of Industrial and Sanitary Conditions to Pauperism (1909).

Report upon the Present Disputes affecting Transport Workers in the Port of London and on the Medway (Clarke Enquiry) (1912).

Transport Workers' Strike, Report on Certain Disturbances at Rotherhithe (1912).

Industrial Council, Enquiry into Industrial Agreements (1913).

Report of an Enquiry by the Board of Trade into Working Class Rents and Retail Prices (1913).

Court of Enquiry concerning Transport Workers' Wages and Conditions of Employment of Dock Labour (Shaw Enquiry) (1920).

I have also made use of the following:

Annual Reports of the Commissioners of H.M. Customs.

Annual Statements of the Navigation and Shipping of the United Kingdom.

Annual Reports by the Port of London Authority.

D. Newspapers and Journals

The Bee-Hive, Daily Chronicle, Daily News, Dockers' Record, East End News, East London Observer, Eastern Post, Fairplay, Labour Elector, The People's Press, The Times, The Trade Unionist, The Southwark Annual, The Star, Toynbee Record, Seafaring, Southwark Recorder, Workman's Times.

E. Autobiographies

Collison, W., *The Apostle of Free Labour* (1913).
Gosling, H., *Up and Down Stream* (1927).
Mann, T., *Memoirs* (1923).
Sexton, Sir James, *Sir James Sexton, Agitator* (1936).
Thorne, W., *My Life's Battles* (1925).
Tillett, B., *Memories and Reflections* (1931).
Wilson, J. H., *My Stormy Voyage Through Life* (1925).

F. Books and Pamphlets

Allen, V. L., *Trade Union Leadership* (1957).
Askwith, Lord, *Industrial Problems and Disputes* (1920).
Barnes, C., *The Longshoremen* (New York, 1915).
Beveridge, W., *Unemployment: a Problem of Industry* (1909).
Booth, C., *Life and Labour of the People in London* (1902 ed.).
Broodbank, Sir Joseph, *History of the Port of London* (1921).
Bullock, A., *The Life and Times of Ernest Bevin*, vol. 1 (1960).
Capper, C., *The Port and Trade of London* (1862).

Charity Organisation Society, *Report on Unskilled Labour* (1908).

Clegg, H. A., Fox, A., and Thompson, A. F., *A History of British Trade Unions since 1889*, vol. 1 (Oxford, 1964).

Cole, G. D. H., *The World of Labour* (1913).

Colquhoun, P., *A Treatise on the Police of the Metropolis* (1800).

Course, E., *London Railways* (1962).

Crowley, D. W., 'The Origins of the Revolt of the British Labour Movement from Liberalism 1875–1906', Ph.D thesis (London, 1952).

Cunningham, Brysson, *Cargo Handling at Ports* (1926).

Dangerfield, G., *The Strange Death of Liberal England* (1936).

George, M. Dorothy, *London Life in the Eighteenth Century* (1925).

Hanham, F. G., *Report of enquiry into casual labour in the Merseyside area* (Liverpool, 1930).

Harrison, Royden, *Before the Socialists* (1965).

Hobsbawm, E. J., *Labouring Men* (1964).

Howarth, E. G., and Wilson, M., *West Ham* (1907).

Howell, G., *Trade Unionism – New and Old* (1891).

Humpherus, *History of the Watermen's Company* (1887).

Hyde, F. E., *Blue Funnel* (Liverpool, 1956).

Jones, D. Caradog, *Survey of Merseyside* (1934).

Jones, Rodwell, *The Geography of the London River* (1931).

Knowles, K. G., *Strikes* (1952).

Larrowe, C. P., *Shape-Up and Hiring Hall* (Berkeley, 1955).

Lascelles, E. C. P., and Bullock, S. S., *Dock Labour and Decasualisation* (1924).

Liverpool, *Commission of Inquiry into the Subject of the Unemployed* (Liverpool, 1894).

Liverpool Economic and Statistical Society, *How the Casual Labourer Lives* (no date).

Liverpool University, *The Dock Worker* (Liverpool, 1954).

Mann, T., *The Position of the Dockers and Sailors in 1897* (Clarion Pamphlet No. 18).

Mayhew, H., *London Labour and London Poor* (1861–2).

Mess, H. A., *Casual Labour at the Docks* (1916).

Owen, Sir David, *The Origin and Development of the Ports of the United Kingdom* (1939).

Phelps Brown, E. H., *The Growth of British Industrial Relations* (1960).

Powell, L. H., *The Shipping Federation* (1950).

Rathbone, E. F., *Labour at the Liverpool Docks* (Liverpool, 1904).

Redford, A., *Labour Migration in England 1800–50* (Manchester, 1926).

Rees, H., *British Ports and Shipping* (1958).

Rose, M., *The East End of London* (1951).

Rousiers, P. de, *The Labour Question in Britain* (1896).

Russell, C., and Lewis H., *The Jew in London* (1900).

Saville, J., 'Trade Unions and Free Labour', in A. Briggs and J. Saville (eds) *Essays in Labour History* (1960).

Smith, H. Llewellyn, and Nash, V., *The Story of the Dockers' Strike* (1889).

Smith, R., *Sea Coal for London* (1961).
Stafford, Ann, *A Match to Fire the Thames* (1961).
Stern, W. M., *The Porters of London* (1960).
Thompson, Paul, *Socialists, Liberals and Labour* (1967).
Tillett, B., *A Brief History of the Dockers' Union* (1910).
Tillett, B., *History of the London Transport Workers' Strike 1911* (1912).
Tillett, B., *The Dock Labourers' Bitter Cry* (1889).
Torr, Dona, *Tom Mann and His Times* (1956).
Turner, H. A., *Trade Union Growth Structure and Policy* (1962).
Watney, C., and Little, J., *Industrial Warfare* (1912).
Webb, B., *My Apprenticeship* (1926).
Wheble, C. L., 'The London Lighterage Trade', M.Sc. thesis (London, 1939).
Williams, R., *The Liverpool Docks Problem* (Liverpool, 1912).
Williams, R., *The First Year's Working of the Liverpool Docks Scheme* (Liverpool, 1914).

Notes

Abbreviations

C.O.S. = Charity Organisation Society
R.C.   = *Royal Commission*
R.S.C. = *Report of Select Committee*

CHAPTER I

1. Figures in *British Parliamentary Papers*, LX (1847) 123.
2. *Report of Select Committee on the Port of London* (1836) XIV 3.
3. E. Course, *London Railways* (1962) chs 6 and 7.
4. For a full account of the early history of the London docks see Sir Joseph Broodbank, *History of the Port of London* (1921) I, chs viii–xv.
5. Rodwell Jones, *The Geography of the London River* (1931) p. 30.
6. *Second Report of Select Committee upon Improvement of the Port of London* (1799) XXIII, app. D2, p. 73.
7. P. Colquhoun, *A Treatise on the Police of the Metropolis*, 6th ed. (1800) pp. 218–39.
8. For account of origins of London and West India docks see W. M. Stern, 'The First London Dock Boom', in *Economica*, February 1952.
9. *West India Dock Act, 1799*, 39 Geo. III, c. 69, sect. 138
10. Sir David Owen, *The Origin and Development of the Ports of the United Kingdom* (1939) pp. 67 and 70.
11. Henry Mayhew, *London Labour and London Poor* (1861–2) III 303, 310 and 312.
12. Broodbank, *History of the Port of London*, I 131.
13. Stern, in *Economica*, February 1952, pp. 72–3 and 77.
14. See evidence of Mr Scott, *Royal Commission on the Port of London* (1902), Cd 1152, Evidence Qs 5581–4.
15. Broodbank, *History of the Port of London*, I 197.
16. *Report of Select Committee on the Port of London* (1836) XIV, app. 7, p. 532.
17. Jones, *Geography of London River*, pp. 107–8.
18. *Report of Select Committee on the Port of London* (1836) XIV, 3.
19. Broodbank, *History of the Port of London*, I 183.
20. *Royal Commission on the Port of London* (1902), Cd 1151, Report pp. 76–7.
21. In 1889 the two companies controlled the following docks: London; St Katherine's; East, West and South India; Victoria; Albert; and Tilbury.

22. *R.C. on Port of London* (1902), Cd 1151, Evidence Q 5584.
23. *Royal Commission on the Port of London* (1902), Cd 1151, Report p. 17.
24. Broodbank, *History of the Port of London*, 1 198.
25. *Second Report from the Select Committee on the Sweating System* (1888) XXI, Evidence Q 14343. Also *R.C. on Port of London* (1902), Cd 1152, Evidence Qs 5584 and 5597.
26. *R.C. on Port of London* (1902), Cd 1152, Evidence Q 5588.
27. Ibid. Q 5584.
28. *Annual Report of the Commissioners of H.M. Customs*, XIV (1859) 11.
29. *Annual Report of Customs*, XXI (1867) 41–2.
30. *Annual Report of Customs*, XX (1870) 57.
31. *R.C. on Port of London* (1902), Cd 1152, Evidence Q 5597.
32. Ibid. Report p. 78.
33. *Second Report from the Select Committee on the Sweating System* (1888) XXI, Evidence Q 14429. See also Charles Booth, *Life and Labour of the People in London* (1902 ed.) IV, 1st ser., p. 33.
34. Broodbank, *History of the Port of London*, 1 263–4.
35. Ibid. p. 268.
36. *R.C. on Port of London* (1902), Cd 1151, Report p. 29.
37. For a study of the lighterage trade in London see C. L. Wheble, 'The London Lighterage Trade' (M.Sc. thesis, London, 1939).
38. Jones, *Geography of London River*, pp. 163–7, contains a description of the various categories, but I have relied mainly upon the mass of information contained in the Booth Collection (British Library of Political Science, London School of Economics). In particular Group B, CXLI 97–106 and CXLII 49–59. See also Millicent Rose, *The East End of London* (1951) p. 143.
39. *Annual Report of Customs*, XXI (1867) app. W, pp. 101–7.
40. *R.C. on Port of London* (1902), Cd 1152, Evidence Q 2452.
41. C.O.S., *Report on Unskilled Labour* (1908) p. 29.
42. Broodbank, *History of the Port of London*, 1 193.
43. C. Capper, *The Port and Trade of London* (1862) p. 161.
44. Jones, *Geography of London River*, pp. 113 and 115–16.
45. Broodbank, *History of the Port of London*, 1 225.
46. Ibid. vol. I, chs xix and xxi, for full account of dock development at this time.
47. G. Graham, 'The Ascendancy of the Sailing Ship', in *Economic History Review*, August 1956. See also F. Hyde, *Blue Funnel* (Liverpool, 1956) pp. 15–23.
48. *R.C. on Port of London* (1902), Cd 1151, Report p. 25.
49. Ibid. Report p. 27.
50. For dock construction in Liverpool see H. Rees, *British Ports and Shipping* (1958) p. 36.
51. An account of this rivalry is in Broodbank, *History of the Port of London*, chs xxiv–xxv.
52. Jones, *Geography of London River*, p. 116.
53. Ibid.

54. *R.S.C. on Sweating System* (1888) XXI, Evidence Qs 14335–8 and 15019.
55. *R.C. on Port of London* (1902), Cd 1151, Report pp. 111–12.
56. *R.S.C. on Sweating System* (1888) XXI, Evidence Q 15019.
57. Broodbank, *History of the Port of London*, I, pp. 221 ff.
58. For timber trade see J. Potter, 'The British Timber Duties 1815–1860', in *Economica*, May 1955.
59. *R.C. on Port of London* (1902), Cd 1151, Report p. 112.
60. *R.C. on Labour* (1892), C. 6708, Evidence Group B, vol. 1, Q 6233.
61. *R.C. on Port of London* (1902), Cd 1151, Report p. 67.
62. Broodbank, *History of the Port of London*, I 213.
63. *R.C. on Port of London* (1902), Cd 1151, Report p. 67.
64. Ibid. Report p. 65.
65. C.O.S., *Report on Unskilled Labour* (1908) p. 27.
66. E. G. Howarth and M. Wilson, *West Ham* (1907) p. 186.
67. C.O.S., *Report on Unskilled Labour*, p. 27.
68. Table compiled from ibid.
69. Foreign trade only, and exclusive of Millwall and Surrey systems.
70. W. M. Langdon 'Casual Labour at the Docks', in *Toynbee Record*, February 1912, p. 63.
71. Jones, *Geography of London River*, pp. 129–30 and 155.
72. For development of West Ham see Howarth and Wilson, *West Ham*.
73. Booth, *Life and Labour*, IV, 1st ser., p. 32.
74. S. Pollard, 'The Decline of Shipbuilding on the Thames', in *Economic History Review*, III, 2nd ser. (1950) no. 1.
75. Rose, *The East End*, has some evocative descriptions of Thames-side industries, see especially pp. 142–3 and 148–9.
76. *R.C. on Port of London* (1902), Cd 1152, Evidence Q 5596. See also Brysson Cunningham, *Cargo Handling at Ports* (1926) p. 1.
77. See Hyde, *Blue Funnel*, p. 115.
78. Capper, *Port and Trade*, p. 161.
79. Smith, *Sea Coal for London* (1961) pp. 285–90.
80. Cunningham, *Cargo Handling*, p. 9.
81. Smith, *Sea Coal*, p. 317.
82. *R.C. on Port of London* (1902), Cd 1152, Evidence Q 5665.
83. Smith, *Sea Coal*, p. 289.
84. See evidence of a London stevedore in *R.C. on Labour* (1892), C. 6708, Evidence Group B, vol. 1, Q 4085.
85. Cunningham, *Cargo Handling*, p. 22.
86. *R.C. on Port of London* (1902), Cd 1152, Evidence Qs 5665 and 2259.
87. Charles Barnes, *The Longshoremen* (New York, 1915) ch. iv, especially pp. 34–40.
88. *R.C. on Port of London* (1902), Cd 1152, Evidence Q 6704.
89. Cunningham, *Cargo Handling*, p. 22.
90. For the importance of the luffing motion, see ibid. p. 61. For the tardy development of this motion see *R.C. on Port of London* (1902), Cd 1152, Evidence Qs 4014, 3924, and 11530–42.

91. *Annual Reports by P.L.A. for 1912–13*, pp. 9–10.
92. *Report on Dock Labour in Relation to Poor Law Relief* (1908), Cd 4391, app. D, p. 37.
93. *Annual Report of Chief Inspector of Factories and Workshops for 1899* (1900), Cd 223. Special Report by Maitland and Eraut.
94. *R.C. on Labour* (1892), C. 6708, Evidence Group B, 1, Qs 6080 and 6935.
95. Ibid. Q 6080.
96. Barnes, *Longshoremen*, app. E, p. 212.
97. E. F. Rathbone, *Labour at the Liverpool Docks* (Liverpool, 1904) p. 16.
98. *Annual Report of the Chief Inspector of Factories and Workshops for 1899* (1900), Cd 223, p. 76 of Special Report.
99. Richard Williams, *The Liverpool Docks Problem* (Liverpool, 1912) p. 22.
100. Broodbank, *History of the Port of London*, I 152.

CHAPTER 2

1. Casual employment was a feature of many industries besides the port industry in the nineteenth century – see E. H. Phelps Brown, *The Growth of British Industrial Relations* (1960) pp. 83–4. What made the port industry so distinctive was its localisation, for this circumstance concentrated large masses of casual labourers in clearly defined districts. Thus, in 1908, the six London boroughs where the number of men casually employed bore the largest proportion to the population were all riverside districts. See C.O.S., *Report on Unskilled Labour* (1908) pp. 53–4, which makes this point very well.
2. The causes of these fluctuations are well summarised in Alan Bullock, *The Life and Times of Ernest Bevin* (1960) p. 116.
3. For a full study of the mechanisms of the casual labour market see W. Beveridge, *Unemployment: a Problem of Industry* (1909) ch. v, especially pp. 77–95 for the waterfront.
4. See Ch. 5.
5. Booth Collection Group B, CXLII 55–8.
6. This fact emerges clearly from Booth's investigations in the early 1890s. Booth Collection Group B, CXL–CXLII. The same was as true of Liverpool as of London; see R. Williams, *The Liverpool Docks Problem* (Liverpool, 1912) p. 11.
7. For this attitude see, for example, H. Llewellyn Smith and Vaughan Nash, *The Story of the Dockers' Strike* (1889) p. 24.
8. See Liverpool University, *The Dock Worker* (Liverpool, 1954) pp. 55–6.
9. These men were the Class B of Booth's survey. See Charles Booth, *Life and Labour of the People in London*, I (1902 ed.) 1st ser. 42–4. For a vivid description of this group see Beatrice Webb, *My Apprenticeship* (1926) pp. 231, 256–7 and 376.
10. For an example of this resentment see *Labour Elector*, 21 September 1889, p. 180.

11. An analysis of the sources from which ordinary dockers were recruited appears in Booth, *Life and Labour*, III, 1st ser. 87–95.

12. This process was fully investigated in the *Report on the Relation of Industrial and Sanitary Conditions to Pauperism: Steel-Maitland and Squire* (1909), Cd 4653, especially pp. 37, 79 and 81.

13. For New York see Charles Barnes, *The Longshoremen* (New York, 1915) p. 72; also C. P. Larrowe, *Shape-Up and Hiring Hall* (Berkeley, 1955) p. 50.

14. *R.C. on Labour* (1892), C. 6708, Evidence Group B, I, Qs 903, 629–30, 3101–4.

15. Booth Collection Group B, CXL 59–60.

16. Ibid.

17. See Ch. 1.

18. For this aspect see D. Caradog Jones, *Survey of Merseyside* (1934) II 136.

19. Booth Collection Group B, CXL 1102. The importance to the port worker of being 'known' at a particular centre emerges clearly in *R.C. on Labour* (1892), C. 6708, Evidence Group B, vol. 1, Qs 385 and 560.

20. C.O.S., *Report on Unskilled Labour*, p. 201. In this work see also evidence of another wharfinger, Mr Spurling, pp. 181–3.

21. R. Williams, *The Liverpool Docks Problem* (Liverpool, 1912) p. 6.

22. For example, see case of Hay's Wharf, *R.C. on Labour* (1892), C. 6708, Evidence Group B, vol. 1, Q 6312.

23. Oversupply on the waterfront was, however, part of a wider, national problem that sprang from the mass of unqualified labour existing in Britain at the time. See Phelps Brown, *British Industrial Relations*, pp. 84–5.

24. Booth, *Life and Labour*, VII, 2nd ser. 419. Figures exclusive of Tilbury.

25. In this respect the history of the New York waterfront is strictly comparable with that of London, and both exhibit strikingly similar features. For New York see Larrowe, *Shape-Up*, and Barnes, *Longshoremen*.

26. For Liverpool see E. F. Rathbone, *Labour at the Liverpool Docks* (Liverpool, 1904); R. Williams, *The Liverpool Docks Problem*, and the same author's *The First Year's Working of the Liverpool Docks Scheme* (Liverpool, 1914). For London see W. M. Langdon, 'Casual Labour at the Docks', in *Toynbee Record*, February and March 1912; E. G. Howarth and M. Wilson, *West Ham* (1907) deals largely with the waterfront in London, as does the C.O.S. Report of 1908, *Unskilled Labour*. Two other works deal with the industry generally, but are particularly relevant to London and Liverpool: Hon. G. Walsh, *Dock Labour in Relation to Poor Law Relief* (1908), Cd 4391, and *Report on the Relation of Industrial and Sanitary Conditions to Pauperism: Steel-Maitland and Squire* (1909), Cd 4653. H. A. Mess, *Casual Labour at the Docks* (1916) is also a general study.

27. R. Williams, *The Liverpool Docks Problem* (Liverpool, 1912) p. 11.
28. Williams, *First Year's Working*, p. 85.
29. This aspect is fully treated in W. M. Langdon, 'Casual Labour', pp. 81–2.
30. Ibid. p. 81.
31. Ibid.
32. This stratification is well described in Sir James Sexton, *Sir James Sexton, Agitator* (1936) pp. 109–12.
33. For a description of the scheme and the obstacles that confronted it see Williams, *First Year's Working*.
34. In Ch. 5.
35. *R.C. on Labour* (1892), C. 6708, Evidence Group B, vol. 1, Q 261. For similar sentiments see Qs 2061 and 2462.
36. Williams has well described this independence in his *Liverpool Docks Problem*, pp. 18–20. See also Langdon, 'Casual Labour', pp. 82–4.
37. For London see *R.S.C. on Sweating System*, XXI (1888) Qs 12781–6, 13341 and 15268. For Liverpool E. F. Rathbone, *Labour at the Liverpool Docks*, pp. 7–8. For Manchester see Steel-Maitland and Squire, *Industrial and Sanitary Conditions*, p. 82. For New York and Hamburg see Barnes, *Longshoremen*, p. 31 and appendix E, p. 212.
38. *R.S.C. on Sweating System*, XXI (1888) Q 15276.
39. Sexton, *Agitator*, p. 66.
40. Booth Collection Group B, CXLII 50, CXLIII 3–4.
41. Description in C. Watney and J. Little, *Industrial Warfare* (1912) p. 72.
42. For the best survey of methods of working at this period see *Annual Report of Chief Inspector of Factories and Workshops for 1899* (1900), Cd 223, special report by Maitland and Eraut.
43. Rathbone, *Labour at the Liverpool Docks*, p. 8.
44. Occasionally two or more gangs were worked in one hatchway to secure greater dispatch. For description of gangs see Webb Trade Union Collection (British Library of Political Science, London School of Economics) sect. A, XLII, fo. 214. Also Barnes, *Longshoremen*, pp. 31–3.
45. For skills involved in stowing see Booth, *Life and Labour*, VII, 2nd ser. 428.
46. *R.S.C. on Sweating System*, XXI (1888) Q 14673.
47. *R.C. on Labour* (1892) C. 6708, Evidence Group B, vol. 1, Qs 4085 and 4207.
48. *R.S.C. on Sweating System*, XXI (1888) Q 14097.
49. Ibid. Q 12786.
50. Ibid. Qs 14493–5, 14702 and 15268.
51. Ibid. Qs 14080–3 and 15323.
52. *R.C. on Labour* (1892), C. 6708, Evidence Group B, vol. 1, Q 4085.
53. For description of deck work see Maitland and Eraut, *Factories and Workshops*, p. 76.

54. Webb T.U. Collection, sect. A, vol. xlii, Rules of Stevedores' Union, fo. 224.
55. *R.S.C. on Sweating System*, xxi (1888) Qs 13341 and 14643–6.
56. For the frequency of accidents see Maitland and Eraut, *Factories and Workshops*; also *R.C. on Labour* (1892), C. 6708, Evidence Group B, vol. 1, Qs 396, 893 and 1695.
57. See vivid description in Barnes, *Longshoremen*, p. 33.
58. Caradog Jones treats the two spheres quite separately in his *Survey*, ii 122–3.
59. The description of quay work given below is drawn from the following sources: Brysson Cunningham, *Cargo Handling at Ports* (1926) pp. 11–12 and 43–5; Booth Collection Group A, xxiv 133; *R.S.C. on Sweating System*, xxi (1888) Qs 12784, 13341 and 15268.
60. Langdon, 'Casual Labour', p. 79.
61. *R.S.C. on Sweating System*, xxi (1888) Q 13779.
62. Ibid. Q 14702.
63. *R.C. on Port of London* (1902), Cd 1152, Evidence Qs 2170 and 2259.
64. Booth Collection Group B, cxli 87.
65. The phrase is from Barnes, *Longshoremen*, p. 33.
66. Ibid. pp. 15 and 182.
67. Booth Collection Group B, cxli 42.
68. Rathbone, *Labour at the Liverpool Docks*, p. 7.
69. Booth Collection Group A, xxiv 118.
70. See statement in *Daily Chronicle*, 6 September 1895, p. 6.
71. For Liverpool see Rathbone, *Labour at the Liverpool Docks*, p. 7.
72. W. Stern, 'The First London Dock Boom', in *Economica*, February 1952, pp. 62–72.
73. *R.S.C. on Sweating System*, xxi (1888) Qs 14379 and 14448–9; also *R.C. on Labour* (1892), C. 6708, Evidence Group B, vol. 1, Qs 6980–2.
74. Ibid. Qs 6976–7.
75. Ibid. Q 4120.
76. As in Booth, *Life and Labour*, vii, 2nd ser. 402 and 428.
77. See *R.C. on Labour* (1892), C. 6708, Evidence Group B, vol. 1, Q 3353.
78. See Ch. 3.
79. Booth Collection Group A, xxiv 90.
80. Rathbone, *Labour at the Liverpool Docks*, pp. 8 and 11.
81. *R.C. on Labour* (1892), C. 6708, Evidence Group B, vol. 1, Q 4085.
82. Ibid. Q 4667; see also Howarth and Wilson, *West Ham*, p. 194.
83. See letter in *The People's Press*, 6 December 1890, p. 12.
84. Stevedores' Union Minutes (National Amalgamated Stevedores and Dockers Union, 653 Commercial Rd, London E14), Executive Council Meeting, 16 December 1890.
85. Ibid. Executive Council Meeting, 13 January 1891.
86. These problems will be more fully elaborated in the later chapters of this book, for they are bound up with the history of the waterside unions.
87. The division was very pronounced in American ports. See Barnes,

s.d .—8*

Longshoremen, pp. 15, 101 and 181. For Liverpool see Rathbone, *Labour at the Liverpool Docks*, pp. 9 and 12.

88. Webb T.U. Collection, sect. A, vol. XLII, fo. 218.

89. *R.C. on Labour* (1892), C. 6708, Evidence Group B, vol. 1, Qs 1945–60 and 8525.

90. Booth, *Life and Labour*, VII, 2nd ser. 400–1; also Stevedores' Union Minutes, Executive Council Meeting, 12 March 1895.

91. Booth Collection Group B, CXLII 49–54.

92. Ibid. Group B, CXLI 64–8, 94–5, 103–5.

93. Rathbone, *Labour at the Liverpool Docks*, pp. 7–8, 13 and 21.

94. See *R.S.C. on Sweating System*, XXI (1888) Qs 12781–4 and 15268.

95. Ibid. Qs 13841–2.

96. See Ch. 1.

97. Rathbone, *Labour at Liverpool Docks*.

98. L. Smith and V. Nash, *The Story of the Dockers' Strike* (1889) pp. 50 and 54.

99. For these developments see Booth Collection Group B, CXL 58, and CXLI 76, 79 and 88. Also C.O.S., *Unskilled Labour*, p. 143.

100. Ibid. p. 217.

101. Booth Collection Group B, CXLI 76, and Group A, XXIV 8–9.

102. Ibid. Group B, CXLII 55–9.

103. The following account of warehouse work is drawn from the Booth Collection. For tea and wool trade see Group A, XXIV 104–10; for 'colonial' warehouses Group B, CXLI 97–106 and CXLII 55–9; for cold storage workers Group B, CXLI 80–1. For comparison with Liverpool see Caradog Jones, *Survey*, II 123 ff.

104. *R.S.C. on Sweating System*, XXI (1888) Q 14343.

105. *R.C. on Labour* (1892), C. 6708, Evidence Group B, vol. 1, Qs 144–74.

106. The metaphor is that of a docker – Mr Atkins, ibid. Q 902.

107. Booth Collection Group A, XXIV 107.

108. As Langdon, 'Casual Labour', revealed in 1912.

109. For grain shipwork Booth Collection Group B, CXLII 28–36 and 45.

110. *R.C. on Labour* (1892), C. 6708, Evidence Group B, vol. 1, Qs 6418, 6715 and 6720.

111. *R.S.C. on Sweating System*, XXI (1888) Q. 13341. See also Ch. 1.

112. Webb T.U. Collection, sect. A, vol. XLII, fo. 134.

113. Langdon, 'Casual Labour', p. 82.

114. For shore corn porters see Booth Collection Group B, CXLII 12–28 and 47.

115. For specialisation of Surrey docks in grain and timber see Ch. 1.

116. Henry Mayhew, *London Labour and London Poor*, III (1861–2) 288–92.

117. The work of the deal porters is described in ibid. pp. 297–9; also *R.C. on Labour* (1892), C. 6708, Evidence Group B, vol. 1, Q. 6078.

118. For this group see Raymond Smith, *Sea Coal for London* (1961) pp. 309–18.

119. Webb T.U. Collection, sect. A, vol. XLII, fo. 267.

120. Ibid. folios 267–8.
121. Watney and Little, *Industrial Warfare*, p. 75.
122. The unloading of colliers at the turn of the century is described in Booth, *Life and Labour*, VII, 2nd ser. 435–8.
123. See Booth, *Life and Labour*, III, 1st ser. 96–9, 120 and 146; also M. Dorothy George, *London Life in the 18th Century* (1925) pp. 110–11.
124. Ibid.
125. This fact emerges clearly in *R.C. on Labour* (1892), C. 6708, Evidence Group B, vol. I, Qs 658, 706, 735–6 and 1710–12.
126. M. Dorothy George, 'The London Coal Heavers', in *Economic History*, May 1927, p. 248.
127. Quoted in A. Redford, *Labour Migration in England 1800–50* (Manchester, 1926) p. 130.
128. Booth Collection Group A, XXIV 120.
129. Webb T.U. Collection, sect. A, vol. XLII, folios 220–1.
130. The Irish immigration is fully described in Redford, *Labour Migration*, pp. 115–42.
131. See Mayhew, *London Labour*, pp. 288–93, 297–9 for condition of timber workers, and p. 272 for ballast heavers. For coal trade see article by Dorothy George cited above, note 123.
132. See Millicent Rose, *The East End of London* (1951) pp. 198–202.
133. Caradog Jones, *Survey*, I 322 and II 136–9.
134. See the situation in West Ham for instance, described in Howarth and Wilson, *West Ham*, especially p. 199.
135. See, for instance, Booth's description of south London, *Life and Labour*, I, 1st ser. 277 and 286.

CHAPTER 3

1. See, for example, references in M. Dorothy George, 'The London Coal Heavers', *Economic History*, May 1927.
2. There is a reference to a strike in 1853 in the *Eastern Post*, 4 November 1871.
3. Ibid.
4. See Royden Harrison, *Before the Socialists* (1965), especially ch. i.
5. *Eastern Post*, 4 November 1871.
6. See Harrison, *Before the Socialists*, pp. 220–1.
7. *Eastern Post*, 26 November 1871.
8. Ibid. 16 December 1871.
9. Harrison, *Before the Socialists*, p. 240.
10. *Eastern Post*, 27 January 1872.
11. Ibid. In contrast to later leaders of waterside unionism, who mostly wrote autobiographies, little is known about the League's leading personalities—Venner and Ellwood especially. If rather more is known about Keen and Hennessey this is chiefly because of their connections with outside organisations.
12. Booth Collection Group B, CXLI 105.
13. *Eastern Post*, 27 January 1872.
14. Ibid. 27 April 1872.

15. *Eastern Post*, 30 March 1872.
16. See weekly reports of Executive Council meetings in *Eastern Post*, during August and September 1872.
17. Ibid. 4 May 1872.
18. Ibid. 1 June 1872.
19. Webb T.U. Collection, sect. A, vol. XLII, fo. 210.
20. The supply of labour on the waterfront tended to be greater in winter than summer because of the influx of seasonally unemployed workers—e.g. from the building trades.
21. *Eastern Post*, 11 May 1872.
22. Ibid. 30 June 1872.
23. Ibid. 7 July 1872.
24. Ibid. 19 October 1872.
25. Ibid. 7 July 1872.
26. Ibid. 1 June and 27 July 1872.
27. *The Bee-Hive*, 6 and 13 July 1872.
28. Evidence of Mr Falvy, a granary corn porter, in *R.C. on Labour* (1892), C. 6708, Evidence Group B, vol. 1, Q 2649.
29. See sect. 2 of this chapter.
30. *Eastern Post*, 16 June 1872, and *East End News*, 14 June 1872.
31. *Eastern Post*, 30 June 1872, report of Branch meeting.
32. Ibid. 30 June 1872.
33. *East End News*, 14 June 1872.
34. *Eastern Post*, 30 June 1872; see also Venner's speech reported on 7 July.
35. Ibid. 7 July 1872, report of Executive Council meeting.
36. Ibid. 23 June 1872.
37. Sir Joseph Broodbank, *History of the Port of London*, II (1921) ch. xxxv, 440; also *East End News*, 5 July 1872.
38. *The Bee-Hive*, 6 July 1872.
39. Broodbank, *Port of London*, p. 440.
40. *East End News*, 23 August 1872, report of Millwall Dock Company shareholders' meeting.
41. *East London Observer*, 6 July 1872.
42. Ibid.
43. *East End News*, 2 August 1872.
44. Broodbank, *Port of London*, p. 441.
45. *Eastern Post*, 7 July 1872.
46. *The Bee-Hive*, 24 February 1872.
47. *Eastern Post*, 7 July 1872, letter by Charles Keen.
48. Ibid.
49. Ibid. 4 May 1872.
50. Ibid. 16 June 1872.
51. Ibid.; also *The Bee-Hive*, 11 May 1872.
52. *Eastern Post*, 8 June 1872.
53. Ibid. 14 July 1872.
54. Ibid. report of Executive Council meeting.
55. Ibid. 7 July 1872, letter from League member.

56. Ibid. 14 September 1872, report of Executive Council meeting.
57. Booth Collection Group A, xxiv 87.
58. For the lightermen see sect. 2 of this chapter; for coal whippers see Webb T.U. Collection, sect. A, vol. XLII, folios 266–7.
59. Webb T.U. Collection, sect. A, vol. XLII, folios 135–6.
60. For the experience of New York see Charles Barnes, *The Longshoremen*, p. 127.
61. Sir James Sexton (1856–1938). General Secretary of the Liverpool dockers' organisation—the National Union of Dock Labourers (founded 1889)—from 1893 to 1921. Until the rise of Bevin, Sexton was perhaps the most competent union leader on the waterfront. Before becoming a full-time union official he had worked as a sailor and a docker.
62. Sir James Sexton, *Sir James Sexton, Agitator* (1936) p. 109.
63. *Eastern Post*, 3 August 1872.
64. Sir James Sexton, *Agitator*.
65. *Eastern Post*, 3 August 1872, report of Executive Council meeting.
66. For the Rules of the League see Booth Collection Group A, xxiv 147–53. This contains both the original and revised (1874) editions.
67. *Eastern Post*, 22 September 1872, report of Executive Council meeting.
68. See E. J. Hobsbawm, 'National Unions on the Waterside', in *Labouring Men* (1964). Hobsbawm records the existence of the League, but sees the movement of 1889 as being the really significant landmark in waterside unionism. In this connection see the Conclusion, where further reference is made to the above work.
69. For the 1880s we do, however, have the records of the stevedores' branches of the League, and these will be fully drawn upon in sect. 2 of this chapter.
70. The analogy between the early 1870s and late 1880s has of course been emphasised by Royden Harrison in *Before the Socialists*. See especially pp. 244–5.
71. For the Dockers' Union see Chs 4 and 5.
72. See general account in H. A. Clegg, Alan Fox and A. F. Thompson, *A History of British Trade Unions* (Oxford, 1964) 1 i.
73. *R.C. on Labour* (1892), C. 6708 Evidence Group B, vol. 1, Q 130.
74. *Eastern Post*, 22 December 1872.
75. Webb T.U. Collection, sect. A, vol. XLII, folios 137 and 143; also *R.C. on Labour* (1892), C. 6708, Evidence Group B, vol. 1, Qs 7159–60.
76. See chapter by Beatrice Potter on 'The Docks' in Charles Booth, *Life and Labour of the People in London*, IV, 1st ser.
77. Broodbank, *Port of London*, II 441.
78. Stevedores' Union Minutes, Committee Meetings, 11 January and 22 February 1881.
79. Stevedores' Union Minutes, reports of Council delegates 1881–3.
80. Booth Collection Group A, xxiv 87–8; also Webb T.U. Collection, sect. A, XLII, fo. 219.
81. See Ch. 4.

82. The following description is based mainly upon the Stevedores' Union Minutes. The society is, however, fully described in the Booth Collection Group B, CXLIII.
83. McCarthy is an important figure in the history of waterside unionism; see Ch. 4.
84. Webb T.U. Collection, sect. A, vol. XLII, fo. 214.
85. Ibid. fo. 213.
86. Ibid. fo. 210. See also *R.C. on Labour* (1892), C. 6708, Evidence Group B, vol. 1, Qs 4088–92.
87. See interesting statement by a master stevedore in *Report upon the Present Disputes affecting Transport Workers in the Port of London and on the Medway* (1912), Cd 6229, p. 36.
88. Until 1891 the master stevedores had no trade association. In that year the London Master Stevedores' Association was formed, which the Stevedores' Union at first refused to recognise (Stevedores' Union Minutes, Executive Council Meeting, 31 March 1891). The 1890s, however, saw a gradual transition from a system of unilateral union regulation to one of collective bargaining.
89. In Glasgow there grew up in the 1850s a society remarkably like that of the London stevedores. It, too, was based on recognition accorded to it by master stevedores. For information on this 'Glasgow Harbour Labourers' Union', see Webb T.U. Collection, sect. A, vol. XLII, folios 169–73.
90. Booth Collection Group A, XXIV 102.
91. See description in Ben Tillett, *Memories and Reflections* (1931) p. 76.
92. Webb T.U. Collection, sect. A, vol. XLII, fo. 215.
93. See *Rules of the Amalgamated Stevedores' Labour Protection League*, in ibid. fo. 223. The Glasgow society had the same rule, fo. 172.
94. See description in *R.C. on Labour* (1892), C. 6708, Evidence Group B, vol. 1, Qs 4165 and 4197. The same practices prevailed in Glasgow.
95. *R.S.C. on Sweating System* (1888) vol. XXI, Q 14106.
96. Stephen Sims (union secretary in 1890) told an observer: 'The growth of business is irregular, and not so great as to compensate for the quicker handling of the goods caused by the use of labour saving machinery.' He instanced the steam winch. Webb T.U. Collection, sect. A, vol. XLII, fo. 213.
97. Ibid. fo. 210.
98. Booth, *Life and Labour*, VII, 2nd ser. 429.
99. See Ch. 2, sect. 6.
100. *R.C. on Labour* (1892), C. 6708, Evidence Group B, vol. 1, Qs 3202–4.
101. *R.S.C. on Sweating System* (1888) XXI, Q 14752.
102. Stevedores' Union Minutes, Committee Meeting, 9 August 1881.
103. *R.C. on Labour* (1892), C. 6708, Evidence Group B, vol. 1, Qs 3481–9 and 4371.
104. Booth Collection Group B, CXLIII 3.
105. Tillett, *Memories*, p. 74.
106. Stevedores' Union Minutes, Executive Council Meeting, 19 September 1892.

107. E. G. Howarth and M. Wilson, *West Ham* (1907) p. 214.
108. In this port the dockers' organisation failed to obtain recognition at North End, where the large steamship lines were the employers, but stabilised itself at the South End where the small firms were situated.
109. Webb T.U. Collection, sect. A, vol. XLII, folios 169–77.
110. Barnes, *Longshoremen*, pp. 96–9.
111. Webb T.U. Collection, sect. A, vol. XLII, fo. 219.
112. *R.S.C. on Sweating System* (1888) XXI, Qs 13853–4.
113. Stevedores' Union Minutes, Branch 4 Meeting, 27 March 1882.
114. Ibid. Branch 4 Meeting, 7 March 1881. Council delegates' report.
115. Ibid. Committee Meeting, 4 April 1882.
116. Webb T.U. Collection, sect. A, vol. XLII, fo. 220.
117. *R.S.C. on Sweating System* (1888) XXI, Q 14036.
118. Webb T.U. Collection, sect. A, vol. XLII, fo. 215. Stephen Sims, who succeeded McCarthy as Secretary in 1889, was the first full-time official employed by the society.
119. See Ch. 2.
120. Stevedores' Union Minutes, Branch 4 meeting, 27 February 1882.
121. On 25 September 1882, for example, when the overside corn-porters' branch promised Branch 4 financial assistance for an action under the Employers' Liability Act (Stevedores' Union Minutes).
122. Stevedores' Union Minutes, Executive Council Meeting, 14 July 1891.
123. Ibid. Executive Council Meeting, 9 July 1895.
124. See Harry Gosling, *Up and Down Stream* (1927) p. 145.
125. There is a thorough survey of the lightermen's history and organisation in C. L. Wheble, 'The London Lighterage Trade' (M.Sc. thesis, London, 1939).
126. These societies were known as Turnway societies; they grew up at all the riverside 'stairs' for the purpose of regulating the distribution of work. See Gosling, *Up and Down Stream*, pp. 51–3.
127. Webb T.U. Collection, sect. A, vol. XLI, fo. 77.
128. An account of conditions in the lighterage trade is to be found in Booth, *Life and Labour*, VII, 2nd ser., ch. 5, p. 358.
129. Webb T.U. Collection, sect. A., vol. XLI, fo. 73.
130. Ibid. fo. 71.
131. Ibid. fo. 77.
132. Booth, *Life and Labour*, VII, 2nd ser. 373.
133. Gosling, *Up and Down Stream*, p. 42.
134. These men are fully described in the Webb T.U. Collection, sect. A, vol. XLI, folios 95–101.
135. Gosling, *Up and Down Stream*, p. 144.
136. In Sydney, Australia, the waterside union had a £5 entrance fee prior to its defeat in the strike of 1890. See *The People's Press*, 17 January 1891, p. 8.

CHAPTER 4

1. There is a good account of the great strike and its origins, written by two men who were closely involved in the course of events, and

I have drawn heavily on this work in the narrative that follows: see H. L. Smith and V. Nash, *The Story of the Dockers' Strike* (1889). There is also a popular modern account of the strike in Ann Stafford, *A Match to Fire the Thames* (1961).

2. Webb T.U. Collection, sect. A, vol. XLII, folios 137 and 140; also *R.C. on Labour* (1892), C. 6708, Evidence Group B, vol. 1, Qs 2638–9.

3. *R.S.C. on Sweating System* (1888) vol. XXI, Qs 13774–88.

4. Ibid. Q 15012, also 13403–4.

5. Ibid. Qs 13678–80. For a general description of the contract system see Smith and Nash, *Dockers' Strike*, pp. 52–4.

6. See especially the evidence of Messrs Tillett, Gray, Driscoll and Welsh.

7. Smith and Nash, *Dockers' Strike*, pp. 48–9; also Broodbank, *History of the Port of London*, II xxxv.

8. See accounts in Ben Tillett, *Memories and Reflections* (1931) pp. 94–7, and *The Dockers' Record*, May 1890, pp. 1–2.

9. Frank Brien for example: see *R.C. on Labour* (1892), C. 6708, Evidence Group B, vol. 1, Q 130.

10. For Tillett's early life see his autobiography, cited above.

11. *The Trade Unionist*, 8 August 1891, p. 8.

12. Much of Tillett's personality can be recaptured in his writing. Apart from his autobiography, see *A Brief History of the Dockers' Union* (1910) and *History of the London Transport Workers' Strike 1911* (1912).

13. Orbell later became (together with McCarthy) Organiser in the dockers' union formed after the great strike. Born in 1858, of a poor family, he became a skilled writing-desk maker, but was eventually forced by unemployment to seek work at the waterside. In 1887 he was working at the tea warehouses, as a repairer of tea chests. He was a devoutly religious man, and universally respected for his integrity. He remained Organiser of the Dockers' Union until his death in 1914, at which date he was also on the Executive of the Labour Party and a member of the P.L.A. His funeral was an extraordinary occasion, attended by all the leading figures in the labour movement, and conducted with the most elaborate ceremony. (See *Dockers' Record*, April 1914, pp. 8–10.)

14. Tillett, *Memories*, p. 87.

15. Tillett, *A Brief History of the Dockers' Union*.

16. See his autobiography, pp. 98–114; also George Howell, *Trade Unionism – New and Old* (1891) pp. 152–4.

17. Tillett, *Memories*, p. 105.

18. McCarthy remained a crucial figure in the Dockers' Union until his death in 1899. For details of his life see *Dockers' Record*, August 1890 and April 1914. See also his views expressed in evidence before *R.S.C. on Sweating System* (1888) XXI. See also reference in Tillett, *Memories*, pp. 113–14.

19. J. H. Wilson, *My Stormy Voyage Through Life* (1925) p. 159.

20. Webb T.U. Collection, sect. A, vol. XLII, folios 205 and 258.

21. Tillett, *Memories*, p. 113; Howell, *Trade Unionism*, p. 153.
22. Howell, *Trade Unionism*, p. 153.
23. Webb T.U. Collection, sect. A, vol. XLII, fo. 108.
24. The following account is drawn from Howell, *Trade Unionism*, pp. 152–4, and J. Saville, 'Trade Unions and Free Labour: the background to the Taff Vale Decision', in *Essays in Labour History* (1960), ed. by Asa Briggs and J. Saville.
25. Tillett, *Memories*, p. 106.
26. For the activity of the Social Democratic Federation in London see Dona Torr, *Tom Mann and His Times* (1956); also Paul Thompson, *Socialists, Liberals and Labour: the Struggle for London 1885–1914* (1967).
27. Will Thorne, *My Life's Battles* (1925) pp. 67–73.
28. See especially E. J. Hobsbawm, 'British Gas-Workers 1873–1914', in *Labouring Men* (1964).
29. Smith and Nash, *Dockers' Strike*, p. 33.
30. Thorne, *My Life's Battles*, p. 83.
31. Ibid. p. 83.
32. *Labour Elector*, 10 August 1889.
33. Thorne, *My Life's Battles*, pp. 83–4.
34. *The Star*, 27 September 1889.
35. For Tillett's account see *Memories*, pp. 118–20.
36. *The Star*, 17 August 1889.
37. For Mann's early life see Dona Torr, *Tom Mann*, and his own *Memoirs* (1923). See also Tillett, *Memories*, pp. 114–15 and 120–1.
38. Smith and Nash, *Dockers' Strike*, pp. 45–54.
39. Ibid. pp. 38, 63–4 and 103.
40. *The Star*, 17 August 1889.
41. Tillett, *Memories*, p. 121.
42. Smith and Nash, *Dockers' Strike*, pp. 39–40.
43. Ibid. p. 61.
44. Ibid. p. 64.
45. Ibid.
46. Ibid. p. 62.
47. *The Star*, 22 August 1889.
48. Smith and Nash, *Dockers' Strike*, pp. 63, 89 and 96.
49. Ibid. pp. 95–6.
50. Booth Collection Group B, CXLI 19.
51. This policy caused much conflict in the immediate aftermath of the strike, see *The Star*, 16, 17, 18, 19 and 27 September 1889.
52. *The Star*, 16 September 1889.
53. *The Star*, 31 August and 16 September 1889.
54. Tillett, *Memories*, pp. 125–8.
55. Smith and Nash, *Dockers' Strike*, p. 106.
56. *The Star*, 21 August 1889.
57. *The Star*, 31 August 1889.
58. Webb T.U. Collection, sect. A, vol. XLII, fo. 143. Statement by Harry Quelch.

59. Smith and Nash, *Dockers' Strike*, p. 131.
60. Ibid.
61. *The Star*, 11 September 1889.
62. *The Star*, 26 August 1889.
63. *The Star*, 30 August 1889.
64. *The Star*, 30 and 31 August 1889.
65. *The Star*, 30 August and 2 September 1889. See also account in Tillett, *Memories*, pp. 141–5.
66. Smith and Nash, *Dockers' Strike*, pp. 125–7.
67. *The Star*, 2 and 3 September, 1889.
68. Smith and Nash, *Dockers' Strike*, pp. 127–8.
69. *The Star*, 4 and 5 September 1889.
70. The negotiations are described in Smith and Nash, *Dockers' Strike*. See also Tillett, *Memories*, p. 152 especially, where he describes the meeting at the Catholic School in Poplar when Cardinal Manning persuaded the Strike Committee to accept a compromise arrangement. It was Tillett who, almost alone among the strike leaders, opposed the compromise. It seems that he wished to step up the men's demands, in order that the docker might achieve parity of status with the stevedore. This was an issue that was to recur again and again in the future, most notably in 1911. It also foreshadowed a prolonged period of bitter controversy between the stevedores' and dockers' unions, a controversy that wrecked the fruitful partnership of 1889.
71. The October agreement, and its significance (much greater than that of Mansion House) are fully dealt with in Ch. 5.
72. *The Star*, 27 and 28 August 1889.
    Southwark Recorder, 31 August 1889.
73. See Ch. 3.
74. *The Star*, 27 August 1889.
75. *The Star*, 26 September, 3 October, 10 October, 1889.
76. For a description of the emergence of the S.S.L.P.L. see Webb T.U. Collection, sect. A, vol. XLII, folios 143–4.
77. *Labour Elector*, 26 October, p. 269, 16 November, p. 318, 23 November, p. 334, 1889.
78. *Labour Elector*, 30 November 1889, p. 351.
79. See Ben Tillett, *Memories and Reflections* (1931), p. 157.
80. See letter of Mr Brett, the S.S.L.P.L. chairman, in *The People's Press*, 17 May 1890, p. 14.
81. There is a complete survey of the S.S.L.P.L. in the Booth Collection Group B, CXLII.
82. Harry Quelch was the first General Secretary of the S.S.L.P.L., a post he held until 1892, when he became editor of *Justice*. A Berkshire man, he drifted in early life through a number of trades, from cattle-dealing to paper-hanging. He was never a port worker, although he had sought for employment at the waterside when out of work. By 1887, however, he had become well known in the waterside districts of South London as a result of his attack upon the

corrupt Bermondsey Select Vestry. Quelch was an active member of the S.D.F., and his house, in Southwark Park Rd, was a focal-point for local left-wing political activity in the later 1880s. (Dona Torr, *Tom Mann and His Times* (1956) I 230 and 350*n*.)

83. *Labour Elector*, 28 September 1889, p. 206.
84. See Dockers' Union: Minutes of Annual Delegate Meeting, Swansea, 1892, p. 31.
85. See his statement in Dockers' Union: Minutes of A.D.M., Hull, 1891, p. 21.
86. The Burns Papers (at the British Museum), v 48.
87. See Dockers' Union: Minutes of A.D.M., Swansea, 1892, pp. 30–1.
88. In Liverpool the National Union of Dock Labourers permitted its branches to retain wide powers of local self-government. See N.U.D.L.: Rules 1890 and 1894. For the decentralised structure of waterside unionism in New York see Barnes, *Longshoremen*, pp. 96, 99 and 114.
89. *Labour Elector*, 21 September 1889, p. 184.
90. *Labour Elector*, 14 December 1889, p. 383.
91. *Dockers' Record*, August 1890, p. 4.
92. See the criticisms of Burns, in Burns Papers, v 121.
93. Dockers' Union: Rules 1891, p. 40.
94. See statement by McCarthy, Dockers' Union: Minutes of A.D.M., Grimsby, 1894, p. 7.
95. D. W. Crowley, 'The Origins of the Revolt of the British Labour Movement from Liberalism, 1875–1906' (Ph.D. thesis, London, 1952), ch. xi.
96. In particular J. Havelock Wilson, *My Stormy Voyage Through Life* (1925) I. Also Sir James Sexton, *Sir James Sexton, Agitator* (1936).
97. Booth Collection Group B, CXL–CXLI.
98. Ibid. Group B, CXL 2.
99. *Labour Elector*, 19 October 1889, p. 252.
100. Booth, *Life and Labour*, VII, 2nd ser. 406–7.
101. For the movement at the wharves see *R.C. on Labour* (1892), C. 6708, Evidence Group B, I, app. 38; also letter in *Dockers' Record*, December 1890, p. 15.
102. Burns Papers, v 86–7.
103. For the stress on centralisation see, for example, the article in the *Labour Elector*, 19 October 1889, pp. 252–3.
104. Webb T.U. Collection, sect. A, vol. XLII, fo. 144.
105. See Costello's interesting letter in Burns Papers, VI 96.
106. See his article in *Labour Elector*, 4 January 1890, p. 10.
107. See description by the society's secretary (Mr Webb) in *R.C. on Labour* (1892), C. 6708, Evidence Group B, vol. II.
108. Webb T.U. Collection, sect. A, vol. XLI, folios 48–52.
109. For the proliferation of unions in the ship-repairing trades see S. Pollard, 'The Decline of Shipbuilding on the Thames', *Econ. Hist. Review*, 2nd ser. III (1950) no. 1, p. 75. For the coal workers see Webb T.U. Collection, sect. A, vol. XLII, folios 259–70.

110. See Ch. 3.
111. Webb T.U. Collection, sect. A, vol. XLII, fo. 209.
112. *Labour Elector*, 26 October 1889, p. 267.
113. *The Star*, 31 August 1889.
114. Harry Gosling, *Up and Down Stream* (1927) pp. 53–4.
115. Gosling came from an old family of Thames rivermen, but, unlike most of his fellows in the trade, he quickly developed an interest in the affairs of the wider labour movement. He became General Secretary of the Lightermen's Union in 1893. He was active in local labour politics and became a member of the L.C.C. in 1898. Between 1910 and 1914 he was, apart from Tillett, the most influential union leader on the London waterfront. A gentle, tactful man, he was, as Bullock has said, the perfect chairman (Alan Bullock, *The Life and Times of Ernest Bevin* (1960) p. 62).
116. *Dockers' Record*, July 1890.
117. The Dockers' Union adopted an extremely aggressive policy towards smaller unions, both in London and in provincial ports. Stevedores' Union Minutes, Executive Council Meeting, 14 October 1890. Webb T.U. Collection, sect. A, vol. XLII, folios 193, 205, 258.
118. See Booth Collection Group B, CXLII.

CHAPTER 5

1. Booth Collection Group A, XXIV 14.
2. *R.C. on Labour* (1892), C. 6708, Evidence Group B, vol. 1, Q 4856.
3. *Labour Elector*, 30 November 1889, pp. 344–5.
4. Dockers' Union: Annual Reports 1890–1900.
5. Clement Edwards, 'The Hull Shipping Dispute', *The Economic Journal*, III (1893) 345–51.
6. E. F. Rathbone, *Labour at the Liverpool Docks* (Liverpool, 1904) pp. 9 and 14–15. See also Sexton, *Agitator*, pp. 102–7.
7. See Ch. 3.
8. *Fairplay*, 17 July 1891, pp. 123–4.
9. Stevedores' Union Minutes, Executive Council Meetings 1890–1, and 1911–12, at which periods the big lines recognised the society. See also *R.C. on Labour* (1892), C. 6708, Evidence Group B, vol. 1, Qs 6474–5.
10. The official history of this body is L. H. Powell, *The Shipping Federation* (1950).
11. Powell, *Shipping Federation*, p. 5. An excellent description of the activities of the Federation is to be found in John Saville, 'Trade Unions and Free Labour: The Background to the Taff Vale Decision', in *Essays in Labour History in Memory of G. D. H. Cole* (1960) pp. 323–40.
12. See sect. 2 of this chapter.
13. *Daily Chronicle*, 14 June, 16 June and 22 June 1900.
14. The vital importance of the closed shop to waterside unions is fully treated in C. P. Larrowe, *Shape-Up and Hiring Hall* (Berkeley, 1955), especially p. 54.

15. *The Star*, 3 October 1889, p. 2.
16. See Ch. 3.
17. *Labour Elector*, 4 January 1890, p. 13.
18. *Dockers' Record*, September 1890, pp. 2–3 and 16.
19. See Ch. 3.
20. *Dockers' Record*, September 1890, p. 16.
21. See Ch. 1.
22. See *R.C. on Labour* (1892), C. 6708, Evidence Group B, vol. 1, Qs 4699, 4856, 6458–60; also *Dockers' Record*, October 1890, pp. 5–7.
23. *Labour Elector*, 30 November p. 350, 7 December p. 365, 1889.
24. *Dockers' Record*, August 1890, pp. 2–3. For the attempt to establish 'co-operative' working see *R.C. on Labour* (1892), C. 6708, Evidence Group B, vol. 1, Qs 4784–4800.
25. *R.C. on Labour*, Qs 6480, 6500, 6626–51, 6738, 6744.
26. Ibid. Q 6469.
27. Ibid. Qs 6961–2.
28. Dockers' Union: Annual Report for 1900, p. 6.
29. Bullock, *Ernest Bevin*, p. 192.
30. See Ch. 3.
31. Stevedores' Union Minutes, Executive Council Meeting, 31 March 1891.
32. See Ch. 4, sect. 3.
33. See Ch. 3.
34. Stevedores' Union Minutes, Finance Committee Proceedings, 8 November 1889.
35. See Ch. 3.
36. *R.C. on Labour* (1892), C. 6708, Evidence Group B, vol. 1, Q 7168.
37. For the formation of the joint committee see Ch. 1.
38. *Dockers' Record*, December 1890, p. 8.
39. For Norwood see Ch. 4.
40. Smith and Nash, *Dockers' Strike*, p. 160.
41. The agreement is reprinted in the *Labour Elector*, 2 November 1889, p. 286.
42. See Ch. 4.
43. *R.C. on Labour* (1892), C. 6708, Evidence Group B, vol. 1, Q 4608.
44. Smith and Nash, *Dockers' Strike*, p. 163.
45. Booth Collection Group B, CXLII 62.
46. Webb T.U. Collection, sect. A, vol. XLII, fo. 149. The Dockers' Union refused from the outset to recognise the Permanent Labourers' Union, and regarded it as a company union. See *Labour Elector*, 4 January 1890, pp. 12 and 15.
47. The best description of the peculiar place occupied by the permanent labourer in waterside society is to be found in Beatrice Potter's chapter 'The Docks' in Booth, *Life and Labour*, Poverty ser. IV.
48. *R.C. on Labour* (1892), C. 6708, Evidence Group B, vol. 1, Q 1498.
49. *The Trade Unionist*, 18 April 1891, p. 14.
50. See sect. 3 of this chapter.
51. Burns Papers, V 45.

52. *Labour Elector*, 18 January 1890, p. 47.

53. *Dockers' Record*, August 1890, p. 5.

54. For the foundation of this union see Wilson, *My Stormy Voyage Through Life*, pp. 103–10.

55. See Webb T.U. Collection, sect. A, vol. XLI, fo. 33.

56. *R.C. on Labour* (1892), C. 6708, Evidence Group B, I, Qs 9229 and 9694.

57. See Wilson, *My Stormy Voyage*, pp. 76–7, also *R.C. on Labour* (1892), C. 6708, Evidence Group B, vol. I, Q 9348.

58. Joseph H. Wilson was, of course, the General Secretary of the N.A.S. and F.U. A man of remarkable energy, he was at this time probably the most dynamic union leader in the country.

59. See Wilson, *My Stormy Voyage*, pp. 190–1.

60. Ibid. p. 191.

61. *R.C. on Labour* (1892), C. 6708, Evidence Group B, vol. I, Qs 4925–33 and 9446–8.

62. Ibid. Qs 9272, 9291, 9293–5. Wilson, *My Stormy Voyage*, pp. 180, 189, 190.

63. See Ch. 3.

64. As represented by the Watermen's Court, see Ch. 3.

65. For these developments see C. L. Wheble, 'The London Lighterage Trade' (M.Sc. thesis, London 1939), especially pp. 122, 133, 162, 188–9.

66. See Gosling, *Up and Down Stream*, pp. 38 and 60–1.

67. See Booth, *Life and Labour*, 2nd ser. ch. 5 (p. 358), where these problems are considered in detail.

68. See *Report upon the Present Disputes* (1912), Cd 6229, p. 25.

69. At the docks at any rate. See *R.C. on Labour* (1892), C. 6708, Evidence Group B, vol. I, Q 4856.

70. See ibid. Qs 1710, 3594. The winter of 1890–1 was particularly bad. See *The People's Press*, 27 December 1890, pp. 7–9.

71. The crisis of early November is fully described in the *Dockers' Record*, December 1890, pp. 8–9 and 14. See also Dockers' Union: Annual Report for 1890, p. 6.

72. Quoted in *Seafaring*, 8 November 1890, p. 3.

73. *Seafaring*, 8 November 1890, pp. 2–3.

74. *Dockers' Record*, December 1890, p. 8.

75. See Booth Collection Group B, CXL–CXLI, where numerous union officials testify to the adverse results of the Committee's action.

76. Booth Collection Group A, XXIV 8–10; also *Dockers' Record*, January 1891, p. 11. *R.C. on Labour* (1892), C. 6708, Evidence Group B, vol. I, Q 905.

77. For these developments see *R.C. on Labour*, Qs 4612, 4667, 4856 and 6644.

78. Ibid. Qs 4633 f.

79. See sect. 2 of this chapter.

80. For a full description of the scheme see W. Beveridge, *Unemployment: a Problem of Industry* (1909) ch. v.

81. The deeply felt prejudice against the Joint Committee's scheme emerges clearly in two articles in *The Trade Unionist*, 4 April, p. 14, and 18 April, p. 14, 1891.
82. Dockers' Union: Annual Report for 1890, p. 6.
83. Booth Collection Group B CXL–CXLI.
84. *R.C. on Labour* (1892), C. 6708, Evidence Group B, vol. 1, Qs 957, 1000–6, 1164, 1315, 1324–6.
85. Ibid. Qs 3180 –.
86. Ibid. Qs. 1326, 1331.
87. See, for example, the analysis given in H. A. Clegg, A. Fox and A. F. Thompson, *A History of British Trade Unions since 1889*, vol. 1 (Oxford, 1964) p. 71.
88. *R.C. on Labour* (1892), C. 6708, Evidence Group B, vol. 1, Q 7168.
89. Ibid. Q 9468.
90. For the formation of the U.L.C. see *Labour Elector*, 4 January, pp. 12–13, 11 January, pp. 28–9, and 18 January, p. 46, 1890.
91. *Seafaring*, 29 November 1890, p. 2.
92. *R.C. on Labour* (1892), C. 6708, Evidence Group B, vol. 1, Q 4954.
93. Ibid.; also *Seafaring*, 13 December 1890, p. 11.
94. See *R.C. on Labour*, Qs 4252–3.
95. Stevedores' Union Minutes, Executive Council Meeting, 7 December 1890.
96. *R.C. on Labour*, Q 4954.
97. Stevedores' Union Minutes, Executive Council Meeting, 10 February 1891.
98. Booth Collection Group B, CXLI, 86, 90.
99. *R.C. on Labour*, Q 5486.
100. Stevedores' Union Minutes, Executive Council Meetings, 15 and 16 January 1891. On this line the stevedores had struck in defiance of union instructions to remain at work.
101. *R.C. on Labour*, Q 4956.
102. For attempts at negotiations see *R.C. on Labour*, Qs 8631–2.
103. Ibid. Qs 8861–3 and 8877–84.
104. Ibid. Qs 5486–8.
105. See Ch. 3.
106. Ibid. Qs 6860–6.
107. Stevedores' Union Minutes, Executive Council Meeting, 12 January 1892.
108. Stevedores' Union Minutes, Executive Council Meetings, July 1891–May 1892. This period marks the transition from unilateral union regulation to a new system of collective bargaining with the L.M.S.A.
109. The following description is based upon the Stevedores' Union Minutes, E.C. and Branch 4 Meetings, 1890–2.
110. *R.C. on Labour* (1892), C. 6708, Evidence Group B, vol. 1, Qs 7208, 7329 and 7331.
111. Stevedores' Union Minutes, Executive Council Meetings, 3 and 7 July 1891.

112. Booth Collection Group B, CXL 59 and CXLI 37 f.
113. See Ch. 3.
114. Thus Mr Gearing of Branch 9 was chairman of the U.L.C. in 1890. *Seafaring,* 29 November 1890, p. 2.
115. Stevedores' Union Minutes, Executive Council Meetings, October 1890.
116. This issue dominated the proceedings of the union in November and December 1890.
117. See *Dockers' Record,* March 1891, p. 11.
118. See *Labour Elector,* 4 January, pp. 12–13, 11 January, pp. 28–9, 18 January, p. 46, 1890.
119. See Clem Edwards, 'Labour Federations', in *The Economic Journal,* III (1893) 419.
120. The position of the Dockers' Union in 1891 is fully analysed in the Booth Collection Group B, CXL–CXLI.
121. Ibid. Group B, CXL 11, CXLI 61.
122. For the background to this merger see *The Trade Unionist,* 2 May, p. 11, 30 May, p. 15, 13 June, p. 13, 11 July, p. 7, 1 August, p. 10, 1891.
123. Burns Papers, V 86–7. For this dispute see also *R.C. on Labour* (1892), C. 6708, Evidence Group B, vol. 1, Qs 8597–8, 9115–16, 9153.
124. Stevedores' Union Minutes, Executive Council Meeting, 6 October 1891.
125. Executive Council Meeting, 20 October 1891.
126. Executive Council Meeting, 8 December 1891.
127. Executive Council Meetings, 24 November and 1 December 1891.
128. Executive Council Meeting, 27 August 1895.
129. See Ch. 1.
130. Booth Collection Group B, CXL 53–61, and CXLI 17, 37 and 76.
131. The annual income of the Vict. and Albert District was £2880 in 1890; £1349 in 1893; £1056 in 1895; and £976 in 1898. (Dockers' Union: Annual Reports.)
132. Dockers' Union: Annual Reports for 1893–1900.
133. The following account of this strike is drawn from the *Daily Chronicle,* 7–23 June 1900.
134. Stevedores' Union Minutes, E.C. Meeting, 19 June 1900. The society justified its refusal to take sympathetic action on the grounds that it had recently negotiated an agreement with the L.M.S.A.
135. Dockers' Union: Annual Reports for 1900 and 1906.
136. Annual Report for 1908.
137. Stevedores' Union Minutes, E.C. Meeting, 12 April 1904. See Ch. 3.
138. See Ch. 1.
139. Stevedores' Union Minutes, E.C. Meetings, 27 April and 15 July 1909.
140. Executive Council Meetings, 16 November 1909 and 8 March 1910.
141. Executive Council Meeting, 17 January 1911.
142. Executive Council Meetings, 13 December 1910, 21 March 1911.

143. See Ch. 4.
144. *Daily Chronicle*, 6 September, p. 6, 13 September, p. 8, 14 September, p. 6, 1895.
145. Dockers' Union: Annual Reports for 1895, p. 11, for 1896, p. 5, for 1897, p. 6.
146. See Ch. 6.
147. Stevedores' Union Minutes, Executive Council Meetings, 15 April, 13 May, 27 May, 1902.
148. Anderson succeeded Sims as General Secretary in the early 1890s. Very little is known of his background or personality. It is clear, however, that he was an exceedingly competent Secretary and appears to have shared Gosling's progressive outlook.
149. Stevedores' Union Minutes, Executive Council Meeting, 16 June 1903.
150. Executive Council Meeting, 6 November 1902.
151. Executive Council Meeting, 29 March 1904.
152. In 1897–8.
153. Executive Council Meetings, 12 and 19 January 1904.
154. The Stevedores demanded a full enquiry by the T.U.C. in order that the charge could be publicly refuted. The enquiry was held and the verdict given in favour of the Stevedores. (Executive Council Meetings, 3 July, 31 July, and 11 September 1900, 19 February 1901.)

CHAPTER 6

1. For the initiative of the Dockers' Union in this respect see Harry Gosling, *Up and Down Stream* (1927) p. 147.
2. See *Report upon the Present Disputes* (1912), Cd 6229, p. 33.
3. Gosling, *Up and Down Stream*, pp. 145–6.
4. Ibid. p. 146.
5. See Ch. 4, sect. 3.
6. *Report upon the Present Disputes* (1912), Cd 6229, p. 29.
7. See Ch. 5.
8. Departmental Committee on *The Checking of Piece-work Wages in Dock Labour* (1908), Cd 4380.
9. Stevedores' Union Minutes, Executive Council Meeting, 9 March 1909. (Gosling was also appointed.)
10. See Ch. 5. The Stevedores' and Dockers' unions had also fought a long battle in 1891 for a controlling influence in discharging work at the Millwall Docks; a battle from which the Stevedores eventually emerged triumphant. (Stevedores' Union Minutes, Executive Council Meetings, 1891.)
11. See Ch. 2.
12. Tillett's behaviour in 1900 was not quickly forgotten (Ch. 5).
13. *Annual Statement of the Navigation and Shipping of the U.K. for 1910* (1911), Cd 5840, p. 346.
14. Stevedores' Union Minutes, Executive Council Meeting, 29 July 1909.

15. Ch. 5.
16. Stevedores' Union Minutes, Executive Council Meeting, 7 September 1909.
17. Executive Council Meeting, 25 August 1910.
18. Executive Council Meeting, 28 March 1911.
19. For the formation of the N.T.W.F. see *Dockers' Record*, September 1910, p. 5, December 1910, p. 10, March 1911, p. 14. The creation of the Federation must have owed much to the inspiration of Tom Mann, whose return to England was hailed in the columns of the *Dockers' Record*, June 1910.
20. *Dockers' Record*, June 1911, p. 2. Also Gosling, *Up and Down Stream*, p. 147.
21. Dockers' Union. Annual Report for 1911.
22. Annual Reports for 1900–10.
23. *Dockers' Record*, March 1911, p. 14.
24. Gosling, *Up and Down Stream*, p. 148.
25. See Ch. 4.
26. Ben Tillett, *History of the London Transport Workers' Strike 1911* (1912) p. 1.
27. Stevedores' Union Minutes, Executive Council Meeting, 28 March 1911.
28. Tillett, *London Transport Workers' Strike*, p. 2.
29. Stevedores' Union Minutes, Executive Council Meeting, 2 May 1911.
30. See sect. 1 of this chapter.
31. J. H. Clapham, *An Economic History of Modern Britain* (Cambridge, 1938) book IV, pp. 60–1.
32. *Daily News*, 8 July 1911, p. 5.
33. *Report of an enquiry by the Board of Trade into Working-Class Rents and Retail Prices* (1913), Cd. 6955, p. xliii.
34. Basic hourly wage rates were the same in 1911 as they had been in 1891, in all spheres of port employment. However, the proportion of work paid for by the piece increased markedly in this period. (See Howarth and Wilson, *West Ham* (1907) p. 195.) It is impossible to say to what extent this development compensated for the stagnation of time rates.
35. *Dockers' Record*, June 1910, p. 4.
36. *Dockers' Record*, Sept. 1910, pp. 4 and 5.
37. See especially his views in Dockers' Union: Annual Report for 1912, pp. 5–9.
38. *Daily News*, 3 August 1911, p. 1.
39. *Dockers' Record*, June 1910, p. 6.
40. E. H. Phelps Brown, *The Growth of British Industrial Relations* (1960) pp. 320–1.
41. For a summary of the 1911 movement see G. D. H. Cole, *A Short History of the British Working-Class Movement 1789–1947* (1948 ed.) pp. 328–33. For detailed descriptions of the early strikes of 1911 see Lord (G. R.) Askwith, *Industrial Problems and Disputes* (1920).

42. N.T.W.F.: Report of 1st Annual General Council Meeting, Liverpool, 1911, p. 4.
43. *Daily News*, 29 June 1911, p. 1.
44. *Daily News*, 3 July 1911, p. 7.
45. See Tillett, *London Transport Workers' Strike*, p. 2. See also C. Watney and J. Little, *Industrial Warfare* (1912) pp. 78–80.
46. *Report upon the Present Disputes* (1912), Cd 6229, p. 29.
47. Stevedores' Union Minutes, Executive Council Meeting, 3 July 1911.
48. E.C. Meetings, 29 June, 1 July, 3 July, 4 July, 1911. See also Tillett, *London Transport Workers' Strike*, pp. 6 and 14.
49. Stevedores' Union Minutes, Executive Council Meetings, 30 June and 4 July 1911.
50. The *Daily News* wrote on 29 July (p. 4) of the 'troubles now finished at the ports'.
51. Only the Mansion House Agreement of 1889 offered any sort of precedent for a port-wide settlement.
52. Stevedores' Union Minutes, E.C. Meeting, 11 July 1911. See also Tillett, *London Transport Workers' Strike*, p. 4.
53. The P.L.A. had, in 1908, taken over the labour departments of the Joint Committee and the Surrey and Millwall dock companies. It was thus the largest single employer of port labour in London. It had maintained intact the 'classified' system of employment inaugurated by the Joint Committee in 1890 (see Ch. 5).
54. Tillett, *London Transport Workers' Strike*, p. 4.
55. Ibid.
56. See Ch. 2.
57. See Tom Mann, 'The Position of Dockers and Sailors in 1897', *Clarion Pamphlet*, No. 18, p. 10.
58. *Report upon the Present Disputes* (1912), Cd. 6229, p. 18.
59. See Ch. 2.
60. For these difficulties see, however, Ch. 7.
61. Not to be confused with the Shipping Federation ticket, a document obliging its holder to work with non-unionists.
62. Booth Collection Group B, CXLIII 8.
63. *Report upon the Present Disputes* (1912), Cd 6229, p. 18.
64. See Ch. 2.
65. Stevedores' Union Minutes, Executive Council Meeting, 11 July 1911.
66. For a description of the conferences see Tillett, *London Transport Workers' Strike*, pp. 7–11.
67. Ibid. p. 10.
68. Ibid. p. 11. Gosling, *Up and Down Stream*, p. 149.
69. *Report upon the Present Disputes* (1912), Cd 6229, pp. 5 and 34–5.
70. The terms of the agreement are reprinted in full in Tillett, *London Transport Workers' Strike*, pp. 11–12.
71. *Report upon the Present Disputes* (1912), Cd 6229, p. 29.
72. See Ch. 5.
73. *Report upon the Present Disputes* (1912), Cd 6229, p. 34.

74. Tillett, *London Transport Workers' Strike*, p. 13.
75. See sect. 1 of this chapter.
76. Stevedores' Union Minutes, Executive Council Meetings, 1 and 3 July 1911.
77. Executive Council Meeting, 1 July 1911.
78. Executive Council Meeting, 13 July 1911. The entrance fee had previously been at least £1.
79. See Ch. 5.
80. Executive Council Meetings, July 1911. The earlier plans for joint consultation were thrown aside.
81. Executive Council Meeting, 4 July 1911.
82. The Thames Steamship Workers' Association. (See Ch. 4.)
83. Executive Council Meeting, 5 July 1911.
84. Executive Council Meeting, 8 July 1911.
85. See Ch. 5.
86. Executive Council Meetings, 7 and 10 July 1911.
87. Executive Council Meeting, 13 July 1911.
88. Executive Council Meeting, 7 July 1911.
89. Dockers' Union: Annual Report for 1890.
90. The conflicting union jurisdictions in these spheres are considered below in Ch. 7.
91. See sect. 3 of this chapter.
92. See Tillett, *London Transport Workers' Strike*, pp. 13–14, and Gosling, *Up and Down Stream*, p. 150.
93. *Report upon the Present Disputes* (1912), Cd. 6229, p. 29.
94. Watney and Little, *Industrial Warfare*, p. 81.
95. *Daily News*, 1 August 1911, p. 5.
96. *Daily News*, 2 and 3 August 1911.
97. See Ch. 5.
98. See interview in *Daily News*, 2 August 1911, p. 1.
99. *Daily News*, 3 August 1911, p. 1.
100. *Daily News*, 3 August 1911, p. 2.
101. *Report upon the Present Disputes* (1912), Cd 6229, p. 33.
102. See Sir Joseph Broodbank, *History of the Port of London* (1921) II 449–51.
103. *Report upon the Present Disputes* (1912), Cd 6229, p. 29.
104. Gosling, *Up and Down Stream*, p. 150.
105. *Daily News*, 4 August 1911, p. 1.
106. Gosling, *Up and Down Stream*, p. 151.
107. *Daily News*, 7 August 1911, p. 1.
108. Tillett, *London Transport Workers' Strike*, pp. 19–23.
109. Stevedores' Union Minutes, Executive Council Meeting, 7 August 1911.
110. Executive Council Meetings, 1, 5 and 9 August 1911.
111. Executive Council Meetings, 7 and 8 August 1911.
112. See Ch. 7.
113. Executive Council Meeting, 9 August 1911.
114. Gosling, *Up and Down Stream*, p. 153.

115. These negotiations are well described in ibid. pp. 153–4.
116. *Report upon the Present Disputes* (1912), Cd 6229, p. 33.
117. The agreements are reprinted in Tillett, *London Transport Workers' Strike*, app., pp. 63–71.
118. Ibid. p. 26.
119. Ibid. p. 31.
120. Gosling, *Up and Down Stream*, pp. 154–5.
121. Ibid. p. 155.
122. See manifestoes reprinted in Tillett, *London Transport Workers' Strike*, pp. 31–4.
123. Ibid. p. 25.
124. Watney and Little, *Industrial Warfare*, pp. 84–5.
125. Dockers' Union: Annual Report for 1911.
126. Stevedores' Union Minutes, Executive Council Meetings, July and August 1911.
127. See sect. 2 of this chapter.
128. The resolution was reported in the Stevedores' Union Minutes, Executive Council Meeting, 17 August 1911.
129. Executive Council Meetings, 14 and 15 August 1911.
130. *Report upon the Present Disputes* (1912), Cd 6229, p. 30.
131. For the formation of this union see Ch. 5.
132. *Report upon the Present Disputes* (1912), Cd 6229, pp. 25–6.
133. Ibid. p. 30.
134. Stevedores' Union Minutes, Executive Council Meeting, 19 August 1911.
135. This agreement is reprinted in Tillett, *London Transport Workers' Strike*, pp. 37–8.
136. *Report upon the Present Disputes* (1912), Cd 6229, p. 35.
137. Ibid. p. 30.
138. The following account is based upon evidence given in ibid. pp. 37–41.
139. See Ch. 1.
140. See sect. 2 of this chapter.
141. For evidence of this see ibid. p. 43; also N.T.W.F. manifesto reprinted in Tillett, *London Transport Workers' Strike*, p. 39.
142. Stevedores' Union Minutes, Executive Council Meeting, 18 August 1911.
143. *Report upon the Present Disputes* (1912), Cd 6229, p. 43.
144. See above, this chapter.
145. Stevedores' Union Minutes, Executive Council Meeting, 21 August 1911.
146. See manifesto in Tillett, *London Transport Workers' Strike*, p. 39.
147. Stevedores' Union Minutes, Executive Council Meeting, 22 August 1911.
148. *Report upon the Present Disputes* (1912), Cd 6229, p. 5; also Stevedores' Union Minutes, Executive Council Meeting, 22 August 1911.
149. Executive Council Meeting, 31 August 1911.
150. The award is reprinted in Tillett, *London Transport Workers' Strike*, app., p. 71.

CHAPTER 7

1. Stevedores' Union Minutes, Executive Council Meetings, 26 September, 10 and 26 October, 2, 14, 28 November, 22 December 1911.
2. *Report upon the Present Disputes* (1912), Cd 6229, p. 36.
3. Stevedores' Union Minutes, Executive Council Meeting, 1 August 1911, also Branch 1 Meetings, 23 July and 4 August 1911.
4. Executive Council Meeting, 9 August 1911.
5. Executive Council Meeting, 21 August 1911.
6. Executive Council Meetings, 29 August and 7 September 1911.
7. See Ch. 6.
8. Executive Council Meeting, 5 October 1911.
9. See Gosling's description of the incident in *Report upon the Present Disputes* (1912), Cd 6229, pp. 18–19. For Leach's own version of the affair see ibid. pp. 42–3.
10. Executive Council Meetings, 24 and 26 October 1911.
11. Executive Council Meetings, 2 and 8 November 1911.
12. *Report upon the Present Disputes* (1912), Cd 6229, p. 43.
13. Ibid.
14. See Ch. 6.
15. *Report upon the Present Disputes* (1912), Cd 6229, pp. 19, 38 and 41.
16. Stevedores' Union Minutes, Executive Council Meeting, 3 January 1912.
17. *Report upon the Present Disputes* (1912), Cd 6229, p. 19.
18. Executive Council Meeting, 26 October 1911.
19. Executive Council Meeting, 16 November 1911.
20. Executive Council Meeting, 8 November 1911.
21. Executive Council Meetings, 11 and 18 January 1912.
22. *Report upon the Present Disputes* (1912), Cd 6229, p. 36; also see Ch. 3.
23. See above, this chapter.
24. Executive Council Meeting, 14 November 1911.
25. Executive Council Meeting, 14 December 1911.
26. Executive Council Meeting, 27 February 1912.
27. Now known simply as the 'Labour Protection League', for it had dropped the words 'South Side' from its title.
28. N.T.W.F.: Report of Special General Council Meeting, Salford, 1912, pp. 4–5.
29. N.T.W.F.: Report of 2nd Annual General Council Meeting, Westminster, 1912, pp. 16–17.
30. Stevedores' Union Minutes, Executive Council Meeting, 3 May 1912.
31. Executive Council Meeting, 29 March 1912.
32. Executive Council Meeting, 3 May 1912.
33. Executive Council Meeting, 14 May 1912.
34. See sect. 2 of this chapter.
35. See Ch. 5.

36. See Ch. 6.
37. Executive Council Meetings, December 1911 and January 1912.
38. Executive Council Meetings, 3 and 14 May 1912.
39. Executive Council Meeting, 5 October 1911.
40. Executive Council Meeting, 14 May 1912.
41. See Ch. 5.
42. Executive Council Meeting, 31 August 1911.
43. Executive Council Meetings, 7 and 12 September 1911.
44. Executive Council Meeting, 5 October 1911.
45. Executive Council Meeting, 14 May 1912.
46. Executive Council Meeting, 21 May 1912.
47. See Ch. 6.
48. For the tensions in this sphere see *Report upon the Present Disputes* (1912), Cd 6229, pp. 6 and 17.
49. Ibid. p. 17.
50. For developments in this sector see ibid. pp. 5–6 and 32.
51. Partly as a result of the multiplicity of unions operating in this sphere. See Ch. 4.
52. See below, this chapter.
53. See Ch. 6.
54. *Report upon the Present Disputes* (1912), Cd 6229, p. 33.
55. Ibid. p. 31.
56. The Thomas incident is fully described in ibid. pp. 4–5.
57. See above, this chapter.
58. The letter is quoted in full in ibid. p. 33.
59. See Ch. 6.
60. For this development see ibid. pp. 4–5 and 36; also Stevedores' Union Minutes, Executive Council Meetings, 21 and 24 May 1912.
61. The decision to establish district committees at important transport centres had been taken at the conference in February 1912. See N.T.W.F.: Report of Special General Council Meeting, Salford, 1912, p. 5.
62. C. Watney and J. Little, *Industrial Warfare* (1912) p. 90.
63. See below, this chapter.
64. For Gosling's evidence at the enquiry see *Report upon the Present Disputes* (1912), Cd 6229, pp. 9–22 and 27.
65. For a full discussion of this issue see Ch. 5.
66. *Report upon the Present Disputes* (1912), Cd 6229, p. 13.
67. See ibid. p. 28.
68. Ibid. pp. 14 and 35.
69. Ibid. pp. 6–7.
70. For the relationship of the Dockers' Union with the P.L.A. see evidence of Harry Orbell in *Industrial Council – Enquiry into Industrial Agreements* (1913), Cd 6953, Evidence, Qs 366–487.
71. *Daily News*, 7 August 1911.
72. See Ch. 5.
73. *Dockers' Record*, August 1911, pp. 2 and 8.
74. *Report upon the Present Disputes* (1912), Cd 6229, p. 28.

75. Stevedores' Union Minutes, Executive Council Meeting, 24 May 1912.
76. Lord (G. R.) Askwith, *Industrial Problems and Disputes* (1920). For a description of the strike see also Watney and Little, *Industrial Warfare*, pp. 90–6. Another account of the stoppage is to be found in Harry Gosling, *Up and Down Stream* (1927) pp. 158–66.
77. Stevedores' Union Minutes, Executive Council Meetings, 18 and 19 July 1912.
78. Executive Council Meeting, 23 July 1912.
79. Executive Council Meeting, 27 July 1912.
80. Executive Council Meeting, 31 July 1912.
81. See N.T.W.F.: Report of 3rd Annual General Council Meeting, Newport, 1913, p. 14.
82. Dockers' Union: Annual Reports for 1912–16.
83. Stevedores' Union Minutes, Executive Council Meeting, 25 August 1914.
84. Executive Council Meetings, 27, 29, 30 and 31 July 1912.
85. See Ch. 5.
86. Executive Council Meeting, 21 June 1912.
87. Executive Council Meeting, 29 July 1912.
88. Executive Council Meeting, 1 August 1912.
89. See sect. 1 of this chapter.
90. Executive Council Meeting, 25 June 1912.
91. Executive Council Meeting, 11 August 1912.
92. Executive Council Meetings, 3, 6, 13 and 20 August 1912.
93. Executive Council Meeting, 5 September 1912.
94. Executive Council Meeting, 15 July 1913.
95. See report of that Committee in N.T.W.F.: Report of 4th Annual General Council Meeting, Hull, 1914, app. p. 60.
96. Executive Council Meeting, 20 May 1913.
97. Executive Council Meeting, 29 July 1912.
98. Executive Council Meetings, 6 and 11 August 1912.
99. Executive Council Meeting, 3 August 1912.
100. Executive Council Meeting, 11 August 1912.
101. Executive Council Meetings, 13 and 27 August 1912.
102. Executive Council Meeting, 11 August 1912.
103. Executive Council Meetings, 11 and 13 August 1912.
104. Executive Council Meeting, 5 September 1912.
105. Executive Council Meeting, 17 September 1912.
106. Executive Council Meeting, 3 December 1912.
107. See Ch. 3.
108. Executive Council Meetings, 4 June and 7 October 1913.
109. Executive Council Meetings, 5 and 7 May 1914.
110. N.T.W.F.: Report of 3rd Annual General Council Meeting, Newport, 1913, pp. 55–6.
111. See report of the Committee in N.T.W.F.: Report of 4th Annual General Council Meeting, Hull, 1914, app. p. 60.
112. Stevedores' Union Minutes, Executive Council Meeting, 14 October 1913.

113. Executive Council Meeting, 7 May 1914.

114. For an excellent study of the British waterfront in the early post-war years see E. C. P. Lascelles and S. S. Bullock, *Dock Labour and Decasualisation* (1924).

115. See *Dockers' Record*, December 1910, p. 10.

116. See Gosling's statement in N.T.W.F.: Report of 3rd Annual General Council Meeting, Newport, 1913, p. 8.

117. Stevedores' Union Minutes, Executive Council Meeting, 15 October 1912.

118. See *Dockers' Record*, December 1912, p. 12.

119. N.T.W.F.: Report of 3rd Annual General Council Meeting, Newport, 1913, p. 40. For the ensuing debate see pp. 41–5.

120. N.T.W.F.: Report of 4th Annual General Council Meeting, Hull, 1914, p. 9.

121. A loose federal organisation formed in 1908. See H. A. Clegg, A. Fox and A. F. Thompson, *A History of British Trade Unions since 1889*, vol. 1 (Oxford, 1964) p. 450.

122. *Dockers' Record*, April 1914, p. 14.

123. N.T.W.F.: Report of 4th Annual General Council Meeting, Hull, 1914, p. 9.

124. These proposals are set out in the *Dockers' Record*, April 1914, p. 14.

125. G.L.N.C. and N.T.W.F.: Special Conference on Amalgamation, Caxton Hall, Westminster, 8 July 1914.

126. Stevedores' Union Minutes, Executive Council Meeting, 14 July 1914.

127. Alan Bullock, *The Life and Times of Ernest Bevin* (1960) p. 190.

Index

accidents, compensation for, 87–8

Admiralty, jurisdiction over Thames, 15

Albert Dock, 26, 45, 142, 203; opened, 23, 83; dominates port's foreign commerce, 24–5; tonnage entering (1899 and 1904), 25; under-employment in, 32; 'gearers' at, 37; company control of labour, 43, 137; wage-rates, 49, 160; transfer of ocean shipping to, 83; Tea Operatives and, 99, 101; contract system, 102–3; and 1889 strike, 103, 104; unofficial corn-gang stoppages, 126; and 'free' labour, 139, 140, 141; and 1900 unofficial strike, 146; Stevedores' recruiting (1911), 164; and 1911 strike, 167–8; attempt to prevent shipowners taking on men inside gates, 168, 173, 205, 206; Dockers' monopoly, 188

Alverstone, Lord, 185

'Amalgamated Labour Union', 74

Amalgamated Protective Union of Engine Drivers, Crane Drivers, Hydraulic and Boiler Attendants, 118

Amalgamated Society of Engine Drivers and Firemen (Land and Marine), 118

Amalgamated Society of Foremen Lightermen, 134, 174, 195

Amalgamated Society of Watermen and Lightermen, see Lightermen's Union

Amalgamated Stevedores Labour Protection League, 76

Amalgamated Stevedores' Union, see Stevedores' Union

amalgamation, 209–13, 214, 215

'Amalgamation, Special Conference on' (July 1913), 211–12

Anderson, James, 171; Gen. Sec. of Stevedores' Union, 149, 151; attempt to open union to shipworkers, 152; Gen. Sec. of N.T.W.F., 154, 186

Askwith, Lord, 172, 196, 200

Associated Portland Cement Manufacturers, 147, 191

Association of Foremen and Clerks of the Docks, Wharves and Warehouses, 130–1

Association of Master Lightermen and Bargeowners, 157, 159, 165, 169, 193–4, 198

ballast heavers, 118, 166

Baltic Dock Company, 13

barge workers, 91; in Lightermen's Union, 150, 193, 194

Beckton gas works, East Ham, 99

Bermondsey, 19, 20, 54, 58

Bethnal Green, 68, 69

Bevin, Ernest, 127, 210

Birt, Colonel (of Millwall Dock Company), 126

blackleg labour, 103–4, 107–8, 111, 123, 139, 200, 201

44, 45–6; distinct from short-sea
workers, 46; wage-rates, 49, 60,
66, 93, 130, 154, 161; transformed status, 49–50; warehouse
workers superior to, 51–2; and
formation of Labour Protection
League, 60–2

Dockers' Record, 200

Dockers' Union, 97, 101, 122, 180,
198; compared with Labour
Protection League, 73, 74; successor to Tea Operatives' Association, 114; Tillett as Gen.
Sec., 114, 115–16, 118, 124, 135;
centralised constitution, 115,
116–18, 120; branch organisation, 115–16, 119; Wapping
wharf workers' independence of,
116–17; regarded by Mann as
educational as well as industrial
institution, 118, 126; fails to
carry south-side sector, 117–18;
gulf between smaller unions and,
118, 120; dominates scene but
strategically weak, 119, 148;
virtually extinct in London by
1906, 122, 127, 146, 148; aim to
force monopoly, 124–7, 129, 130,
131–2; influence over hiring
procedures, 124, 126, 129–30,
135; entrance restrictions, 124–5;
and 'ca'canny' practices, 125–6;
and struggle for power with
other unions, 127–32, 134–8,
140, 142–8; relations with London and East and West India
joint committee, 129–32, 134–7,
140, 144; piece-work agreement
(1889), 129–30; organisation of
casual north-bank docker, 130;
failure to extend monopoly to
permanent grades, 130, 136–7;
Cutler Street strike over non-
unionists (1890), 131; termination of 1889 agreement by joint
committee, 134–5, 144; north-
bank monopoly shattered, 135,
144; influence in upstream docks

destroyed by permanent labour,
135–7, 140, 146; maintains influence in Tilbury, Victoria and
Albert docks, 137, 146, 188; and
'free' labour, 140, 142; hope to
absorb smaller unions, 143;
instability and decreased membership, 144; hopes for comprehensive waterside federation,
144, 148; federates with Sailors
and S.S.L.P.L., 144; merges
with U.L.C., 144; effect of
growth of Tilbury, 146–7, 164;
1900 defeat, 146, 167; drift
towards extinction, 148, 151;
schemes for federation, 148;
disputes with Stevedores, 149,
152, 154–5, 160, 166, 190, 192,
205–7; and revival of unionism,
153–4, 156, 158, 163–4, 166–7,
173, 194, 216–17; 1911 campaign
for wage increase, 154, 157, 168;
and syndicalism, 156; and 1911
strike, 168; 1912 strike, 197, 199,
201, 202; decline in membership,
202; favours amalgamation, 209,
210, 212

Docks and Riverside Labourers'
Council, 98

Du Plat Taylor, Colonel, 60, 67

East and West India Dock Company, 13; decline in fortunes of,
15, 17, 60, 93; rivalry with London Dock Company, 23; builds
Tilbury Dock, 23; amalgamates
with London company, 23–4;
control of labour, 43, 48, 49;
demarcation lines, 43, 49; stevedores, 44; unrest due to wage
reductions (1871), 60–3, 67;
bankruptcy, 93; wage-rates, 93;
and plus system, 93, 99, 100, 102;
wage reduction for tea workers,
94; and 1889 strike, 101–2,
103–4; Dockers' Union monopoly, 129

East Country Dock, 13